Notes from the Underground

Notes from the Underground

The Whittaker Chambers -
Ralph de Toledano
Letters: 1949-1960

Edited and Annotated by
Ralph de Toledano
Introduction by Terry Teachout

REGNERY PUBLISHING, INC.
Washington, D.C.

Library of Congress Cataloging-in-Publication Data

Chambers, Whittaker
        Notes from the underground : the Whittaker Chambers - Ralph de Toledano
    letters, 1949-1960 / edited by Ralph de Toledano ; introduction by Terry
    Teachout.
            p.   cm
        Includes index.
        ISBN 0-89526-425-0 (alk. paper)
        1. Chambers, Whittaker—Correspondence. 2. Toledano, Ralph de,
    1916- —Correspondence. 3. Spies—United States—Correspondence.
    4. Journalists United States—Correspondence. 5. United States—
    Politics and government—1945-1953—Sources. 6. United States—
    Politics and government—1953-1961—Sources. 7. Subversive
    activities—United States—History—20th century—Sources. 8. Anti-
    communist movements—United States—History—20th century—Sources.
    9. Hiss, Alger. I. Toledano, Ralph de, 1916- . II. Title.
    E743.5.C45 1997   97-27563
    973.918'092'2—dc21   CIP

Published in the United States by
Regnery Publishing, Inc.
An Eagle Publishing Company
422 First Street, SE, Suite 300
Washington, DC 20003

Distributed to the trade by
National Book Network
4720-A Boston Way
Lanham, MD 20706

Printed on acid-free paper.
Manufactured in the United States of America

10 9 8 7 6 5 4 3 2 1

Books are available in quantity for promotional or premium use. Write to Director of Special Sales, Regnery Publishing, Inc., 422 First Street, SE, Suite 300, Washington, DC 20003, for information on discounts and terms or call (202) 546-5005.

For Edwin J. Feulner, Jr.

Heilande muss man in den Bergen schürfen
wo man das Harte aus dem Harten bricht

Contents

Introduction

THE LETTERS COLLECTED in this volume, long known to historians of the Cold War but here made available to the reading public for the first time, tell the story of a friendship forged under the most trying of circumstances. In 1948 Whittaker Chambers, a senior editor of *Time*, testified before the House Un-American Activities Committee (HUAC) about his career as a Soviet spy, identifying Alger Hiss, president of the Carnegie Endowment for World Peace and a senior State Department official under Franklin Roosevelt and Harry Truman, as one of his accomplices. Hiss, who denied Chambers's accusations under oath, was indicted for perjury, tried twice, convicted the second time, and sent to prison. Ralph de Toledano, a prominent anti-Communist journalist, covered the Hiss case for *Newsweek*, in the process becoming one of Chambers's closest friends; the two men began exchanging letters in 1949, and wrote to each other for the rest of Chambers's life. It was Chambers's wish that their correspondence be published in its entirety. Now, nearly forty years after he sent his last letter to Toledano, his intentions have at last been carried out.

Among the not-so-minor consolations of history is the fact that Alger Hiss lived long enough to witness the protracted suicide of the

evil empire he served so faithfully, and to see its archives thrown open
to the searching scrutiny of Western eyes. Today, a decade after the
collapse of the Soviet Union, we now know that Whittaker Chambers
will be remembered not for having slandered a prominent New
Dealer, but for having told the truth about Communism at a time
when few wanted to hear it, both in the courtroom and in the pages
of *Witness*, a book which is both a classic of modern American autobiography and one of the founding documents of postwar American
conservatism.

But Hiss's guilt was long seen by the liberal establishment as an
open question at best, and throughout the period covered by these letters, his accuser wandered in the wilderness of public disrepute.
Chambers's decision to testify before HUAC had brought to an end his
distinguished career as a magazine journalist. Henry Luce asked for his
resignation from *Time*, for which he had written since 1939, and even
after a jury convicted Hiss of perjury, thereby confirming the truth of
Chambers's congressional testimony, no reputable magazine would
consider hiring him as a writer or editor. It was not merely that as an
admitted ex-Communist, he was by definition "controversial."
Chambers had also committed what many liberals, uneasily aware of
the extent to which their own movement was tainted by Stalinism,
saw as the ultimate act of heresy: he revealed that the administration of
Franklin Roosevelt, the patron saint of American liberalism, had been
infiltrated by Communists whose first loyalty was to the Soviet Union.
For this, he could not be forgiven.

Chambers then compounded his sin by writing *Witness*, in which he
expounded at length his belief that "the crisis of the Western world
exists to the degree in which it is indifferent to God." His indictment
of secularism drew much of its force from the fact that he was repudi-
ating his own birthright: he had been taught from earliest childhood
that there is no truth, and spent the rest of his life searching for it.
His father was a bisexual magazine illustrator, his mother an arty,

shabby-genteel agnostic. As an undergraduate at Columbia University, he dazzled such teachers as Mark Van Doren (and such students as Lionel Trilling) with his literary gifts, but soon discovered that words alone could not fill the empty places in his soul. Tormented by inchoate homosexual longings, painfully aware of the squalor and misery in which the "other half" of America in the '20s lived, Chambers sought deliverance in the secular religion that was Marxism, abandoning a promising career as a poet and translator to become a Communist journalist and, later, a spy. Idealism drove him into the arms of mass murderers, and idealism forced him in time to confront the enormity of what he and his Communist brethren had done: Chambers embraced Christianity, chose to testify against Alger Hiss, and, in Arthur Koestler's memorable phrase, "knowingly committed moral suicide to atone for the guilt of our generation."

Though Chambers was not the first person to interpret the Cold War—and, by implication, modernity itself—as a struggle between faith in God and faith in man, it was his searing account of the struggle that reached the largest audience. *Witness* was serialized in the *Saturday Evening Post* and chosen as a main selection of the Book-of-the-Month Club; the trade edition was one of the ten best-selling books of 1952. That such a book should have found so vast a readership was even more disturbing to the thoroughly secularized liberal establishment, already shaken by the revelation that Alger Hiss, who seemed the very personification of the fervent left-liberal idealism of the '30s, had been a Soviet agent. Therein lay Chambers's immediate significance: for the first time since Roosevelt entered the White House in 1933, secular liberalism had a thoughtful, articulate opponent whom ordinary Americans took seriously.

It was for this reason that many liberals (though by no means all) chose to "respond" to *Witness* by smearing its author. "It can't be treated simply as a book," Mary McCarthy wrote to Hannah Arendt in 1952. "The great effort of this new Right is to get itself accepted as *normal*, and its publications as a *normal* part of publishing… and this, it seems to me, must be scotched, if it's not already too late." Arendt's response was to publish a savage review of *Witness* in the liberal Catholic magazine *Commonweal*, in which she declared that Chambers belonged "in a police state where people have been organized and split into two ever-changing categories: those who have the privilege to be informers and those who are dominated by the fear of being informed upon."

Such criticisms were all too typical of the liberal response to *Witness*, which served to isolate Chambers still further. While the popular success of *Witness* made it possible for him to publish occasionally in such mass-market magazines as *Life*, *Look*, and the *Saturday Evening Post*, he nevertheless remained a pariah both in the tight little world of New York journalism and among the vast majority of American intellectuals. In the nine years between the publication of *Witness* and his death in 1961, he produced only a handful of signed articles, most of them written for *National Review*, which in the '50s was widely seen as a house organ of McCarthyism. His most important writing was done not for publication, but privately: Chambers corresponded regularly with a small, devoted band of politically sympathetic friends, including Ralph de Toledano and William F. Buckley, Jr. Three years after his death, some of his letters appeared in *Cold Friday*, a collection of unpublished writings, and in 1969, Buckley brought out *Odyssey of a Friend*, a volume of the letters he received from Chambers between 1954 and 1961.

Buckley published *Odyssey of a Friend* in response to the continuing efforts of Hiss and his supporters to brand Chambers as a psychopathic liar in the court of public opinion. He saw the book as a character witness, writing in the introduction that its contents would "help the reader to judge the plausibility of the attacks on Whittaker Chambers's character…. [I]t was I who opened the envelopes that brought these communications, finding in them a sublimity which I most frankly acknowledge as having been as much influential as the goddamn Woodstock typewriter in convincing me of the credentials of Whittaker Chambers." At the time, comparatively few reviewers agreed with Buckley, but in retrospect, *Odyssey of a Friend* can be seen as an early step in the eventual rehabilitation of Chambers, who proved in his letters to be a figure of greater intellectual breadth and subtlety than had been generally acknowledged.

Nine years later, Allen Weinstein published *Perjury: The Hiss-Chambers Case*, an exhaustively researched study which confirmed beyond reasonable doubt that Chambers had testified truthfully about his association with Alger Hiss. After *Perjury*, it was possible for respectable liberals to openly acknowledge Hiss's guilt, and some began to do so. Still, many others refused, even when confronted with such devastating revelations as the release by the National Security Agency of intercepted Soviet cable traffic which revealed that in 1945, Hiss flew directly from Yalta to Moscow, where Andrei Vyshinsky personally thanked him for his long years of service to the Soviet Union. The liberal habit of defending Hiss lasted to the bitter end: when he died in 1996, few obituary writers were willing flatly to declare him guilty of espionage, and two network TV anchormen went so far as to suggest in their evening newscasts that he had been framed.

Yet Hiss's death turned out to be the next-to-last step in the long-delayed rehabilitation of Chambers. Sam Tanenhaus's *Whittaker Chambers: A Biography*, the first full-scale biography, was published just three months later, and, despite the fact that its treatment of Chambers was frankly sympathetic, the book was welcomed by critics of all political persuasions, and reviewed favorably in venues ranging from *National Review* and *Commentary* to the *New York Times Book Review* and the *New Republic*; even the *Nation*, the last redoubt of unreconstructed Hiss worship, gave Tanenhaus's book a surprisingly balanced review. It was as if the death of the ninety-two-year-old Hiss had broken the spell which for so long had held American liberals captive, making it possible to write about Chambers not as a monster, but as an emblematic figure of America in the twentieth century. The witness had emerged at last from the wilderness.

It is thus singularly appropriate that Chambers's correspondence with Ralph de Toledano should be seeing the light of day at this particular moment in American history. To read their letters is to deepen immeasurably one's understanding of Chambers's life and personality, and to confront anew the profound pessimism with which he viewed the struggle against Communism. "I know that I am leaving the winning side for the losing side," he famously declared in 1948, "but it is better to die on the losing side than to live under Communism." This pessimism, which disturbed many of his contemporaries, has come to seem all but inexplicable to those conservatives who fail to realize that when Chambers called the West "the losing side," he was speaking as much of the enemy within as the enemy without: "History," he wrote in *Witness*, "is cluttered with the wreckage of nations that became indifferent to God, and died."

To be sure, the high seriousness of these letters is not infrequently matched by the high spirits of the men who exchanged them. Those who knew Chambers only from reading *Witness* were invariably surprised on meeting him to discover that he was, in the words of William Rusher, "this great corpulent ho-ho sort of guy." Indeed, he not only had a sense of humor, but was even capable, as his letters reveal, of joking about his own forbidding reputation:

> Obviously this is the point to say that I should like to write another book. It's the book nobody wants. It's called *The Spanish Civil War*. It's never been written, or am I presuming? And what a story! Poor Cerf [Bennett Cerf, the publisher of *Witness*], found there in his office with the smoking revolver in his hand and the first few chapters on the Spanish Civil War scattered around his chair. We must talk about it some time.

But Chambers's historical pessimism was the dark sun around which his consciousness continually orbited. His great fear was that his witness would prove vain, that America would in time be overwhelmed by the secular materialism it had uncomprehendingly embraced almost as completely as had the Soviet Union. "Add to this," he wrote to Toledano in 1950, five days after Alger Hiss was convicted of perjury, "the feeling that it was all for nothing, that nothing has been gained except the misery of others, that it was the tale of the end and not the beginning of something.... You cannot save what cannot save itself. These things happened in the first place because our sector of the world could not understand what was happening to it."

This fear never abated. If anything, it grew more intense as Chambers grew older and recognized ever more clearly that his quarrel was less with Communism in particular than modernity in general. It was this larger perspective that separated Chambers and Toledano from the anti-Communist politicians of the '50s (most notably Joseph McCarthy, whom both men initially supported for tactical reasons but ultimately came to feel had done grave, perhaps irreversible damage to the anti-Communist cause). On the many occasions when Chambers found himself reflecting on the Hiss case, he invariably framed its significance in the broadest possible philosophical terms:

The horror of the age isn't that H-bombs may vaporize us all: the horror of the age is that people think they want to reach the moon. The first is an effect, however vast. The second is on the main line of dementia; it tells us what the matter is. So does Alger's guilt: that is why he has to be innocent, why he has to be believed innocent, the more fiercely, the more incontrovertibly, [when] in terms of proof he is manifestly guilty. With Alger the justification of the entire age stands or falls—technology, votes for women, UN, noble experiment, food made from plastics; it's all of a piece, and Alger is one with it; gives it, in fact, precisely the physiognomic form such a one-way trip to Hell must have. That is all Alger's "innocence" means. If he is guilty, not the New Deal, but the whole Age of Reason is guilty.

In Ralph de Toledano, Chambers found the ideal recipient of his anguished philosophical reflections. Born in 1916, Toledano attended Columbia University in the '30s, a decade after Chambers (one of his fellow undergraduates was Thomas Merton, author of *The Seven Storey Mountain*, with whom Chambers would correspond briefly in the '50s). Like Chambers, Toledano started out as a man of the left, but disillusion set in early, and he became one of the first American journalists to attack Communism in print; the subsequent experience of covering the Hiss case caused him to turn his back on liberalism as well. As he was later to write in *Lament for a Generation* (1960), a political memoir which ranks with *Witness* as one of the most powerful and illuminating books of its genre, "In the context of morals, politics, and economics, liberalism was corrupt. And its corruption stemmed from one corrupting influence: the doctrine that all absolutes are evil with the exception of the absolute State."

In 1950 Toledano wrote the first important book about the Hiss case, the best-selling *Seeds of Treason*, while he was still a member of the staff of *Newsweek*. But his close relationships with Chambers and Richard Nixon made it difficult for him to function effectively in the world of mainstream journalism. It was, he recalls, a time of "bad politics and worse reporting" (among other things, his letters to Chambers provide an unprecedentedly close look at the gradual hardening of the "anti-anti-Communist" position among liberal journalists of the '50s), and as Toledano's own politics came into sharper focus, he became increasingly identified with the group of writers and thinkers who would form the nucleus of the postwar conservative intellectual movement. During this time he wrote frequently to Chambers, whose own political positions were considerably more ambivalent and nuanced than is commonly understood, and their correspondence sheds invaluable light on the origins of modern American conservatism.

Chambers's own place in the history of conservative thought is indisputable: more than anyone else, he persuaded his contemporaries that religious belief was central to the tradition they proposed to defend. "Political freedom, as the Western world has known it, is only a political reading of the Bible," he wrote in *Witness*. "Religion and freedom are indivisible.... Economics is not the central problem of this century. It is a relative problem which can be solved in relative ways. Faith is the central problem of this age." His words were anathema to laissez-faire individualists, who were far more concerned with the rise of centralized government in America than the overall spiritual condition of the West (and who for the same reason were in turn anathema to Chambers, as the present volume makes surpassingly clear). But while classical economic analysis would remain central to conservative dogmatics, it was in large part because of Chambers that the movement which crystallized around William F. Buckley, Jr., and *National Review* was from the outset committed to the proposition that, in Chambers's words, "God alone is the inciter and guarantor of freedom."

Whether or not conservatives of the twenty-first century will continue to share this certainty remains to be seen. One doubts, though, that Whittaker Chambers would have been greatly surprised to learn that the movement at whose creation he was present had begun at century's end to doubt the central meaning of his witness. One day late in 1952, as he lay in a hospital bed recovering from a heart attack, Chambers was visited by a Passionist monk. "Father," he asked, "what am I to answer those people who keep writing me that I was wrong to write in *Witness* that I had left the winning side for the losing side? They say that by calling the West the losing side, I have implied that evil can ultimately overcome good." The monk replied, "Who says that the West deserves to be saved?" That question echoes continually through the pages of this troubling book.

Terry Teachout

A Few Words of Explanation

WHITTAKER CHAMBERS WAS not given to false modesty—and he
knew the impact he had made on the intellectual and spiritual reactions
of many Americans. But he also knew that to many of his supporters
and disciples, he was basically a figure on the stage of history who spoke
ex cathedra to those who held on, perhaps by only a hair, to his vision of
God and man. Few knew Whittaker Chambers as I did, for we had
suffered and anguished through bitter controversy and the two trials
that brought not only Alger Hiss but also the great conspiracy against
our Judeo-Christian civilization temporarily to its knees.

In the 1990s, when all that once gave America dignity and meaning has fallen hiccuping at the foot of a toppling cross, these words may
seem meaningless. But in the late 1950s, we had not quite yet, as Paul
of Tarsus would have it, "fallen asleep." It was then that I said to
Chambers: "You are struggling to write a book that will be a kind of
explication de texte of the history of our time's plague. But it will say little about you. The world knows you almost as an abstraction, and
abstractions don't live on. Israel's greatest king was David, but we
remember his greatness not only for his deeds but also because he
danced before the Ark of the Covenant. These letters show you not

only taking the Ark into battle, but also in supplication. Nothing you've written since *Witness* tells us what you are as well as the letters you've written me. They should be published." Whittaker thought for a moment.

"Perhaps they say too much," he answered, "just as I said too little in *Witness*." He paused for another moment and said, "I always wanted to work with you, and we were collaborating when we wrote to each other. So, if my letters to you are to be published, they must be published with yours to me." That was one of his conditions, but there were others. There should be no publication until after his death, and the correspondence should be, for copyright purposes, solely mine. After I had given the originals to the Hoover Institution, I attempted to by-pass the condition that the letters be a "collaboration." But it was generally argued that Whittaker's letters alone left large gaps and should be filled by mine.

Chambers must have been aware of this, because having agreed to my suggestion, he smiled his ambiguous and puckish smile. "You are," he said *"la pared."* He was referring to a conversation I had mentioned between the great Catholic poet and philosopher, Miguel de Unamuno, and my aunt, Zarita Nahon. Unamuno had said that ideas must be tossed against *la pared*, the wall of discussion and argument, to develop their meaning—and I was his *pared*.

The letters began as a routine exchange of comment and information in the early days of the Hiss case. They rapidly became much more than that as the friendship grew between Whittaker Chambers and one who became both a friend and a disciple. They can be read for what they tell of the man Whittaker Chambers—both in his words and mine—much as today we read the letters of other great men. They can also be read in the context of what was happening to *la pared* in a society that judged men mostly by the devices on their neckties, particularly by those who did not live through the events they chronicled, as commentary on a period obscured by bad politics and worse reporting. They can be read as the record of a friendship which transcended the usual bounds of friendship—a friendship which changed my life and my understanding of life as I walked the pitted road to my own Damascus. In these randipole times, it is painful and dangerous to raise one's flag—and then to discover that no one has been watching—and this may be the fate of my contribution to this collaboration.

There were times when I could say to Whittaker Chambers that he was *mon ami, mon semblable, mon frère*—and after his death, that he was my father, my brother, and my son. These letters may explain. And they should be more than an adumbration as to why hardly a day has passed in the more than three decades since his death that I have not thought of him, have not mourned him, and have not rejoiced that I knew him. Were he alive today, in his ninety-sixth year, he would be patiently explaining that the "cold war" of the past was still continuing, not across oceans but here within a once-great country which had broken its compact with God and with itself, and sold its soul for a mess of pottage. He believed, as I do, that one could not believe in God without acknowledging the existence of the Devil—and today he would point to the Devil's spoor that is all about us.

Whittaker Chambers walked into my house and my life in 1949, when I was writing *Seeds of Treason*, my account of what the press was calling the "Hiss-Chambers case." He was showing the exhaustion of a day with an FBI which was dredging from his memory what for a decade he had been attempting to forget. He did not really know whether I meant him ill or good, but when I said to him, *"Está en su casa"* ["You are in your own house"], he relaxed, and by the end of the evening we were on the way to being friends.

I was then an editor of *Newsweek*, covering what was the most sensational news story of the time, as well as the two trials, and these brought me together with the prosecutor, Thomas F. Murphy, and with the FBI agents assigned to the case (they always referred to Chambers as "Uncle Whit"), though never with the Hiss defense which, while claiming that Hiss was a "conservative," said that it would not expose him to a "red-baiter" and refused to have anything to do with me. My *Newsweek* stories were, I have been told, notable for their accuracy and objectivity. But simultaneous with this, I was growing closer to Whittaker Chambers, to his wife Esther, and to his family. He and I had also begun to communicate in letters that, on both our parts, were self-revelatory.

Weep not for Adonais. Life's sole barrier is death, and Whittaker Chambers has crossed it. In his lifetime, we would play intellectual games with that nonsensical quotation of Sophocles, "Not to be born is best." Whether death came upon Whittaker or he enticed it is a matter for vain conjecture—although there are hints in the letters of his response to the pain, physical and emotional, and the burden of living. He had, as he reminded me, made his God and his life, in the words of Rilke, *"das Harte aus dem Harten"* ["the hard from the hard"]. How he died is of little consequence when we should be concerned with how he lived.

In moments of deep emotion, I think in Spanish—the language which, with French, English, and Arabic, I lived the first years of my life. And so of him and of myself I could recall the words of John of the Cross, which we had quoted to each other, when I learned that Whittaker was dead:

Que muerte habrá	What death can equal
que se iguale	my sorry life
a mi vivir lastimero,	since the more I live
pués si más vivo más muero.	the more I die.

To which in my mourning I added my own:

Caen las lágrimas	Tears fall
de tus ojos	from your eyes
y son estrellas.	and they are stars.
Caen las mías	Tears fall from mine
y son cenizas.	and they are ashes.

These letters are not ashes, nor are they tears. They are instead a *stele* giving us an insight into a great man and a great heart. And they should give a clue as to what his answer might have been to the question I am repeatedly asked since the "collapse" of the Soviet Union: "What would Whittaker Chambers say now about being on the 'losing' side?" He still would repeat it, for that "collapse" has not meant the redemption of the West. The Nechaevists and Marxists and Leninists may have lost a staging area. But their concept of Man as opposed to God, and their war on faith and the human spirit, continue to govern the West. Man has yet to reach the vision of Golgotha about which he wrote in *Witness*—and the evidence is in every day's newspaper and newscast. Whatever the virtue of these letters, they are a record of two men facing cataclysm. History has already illumined the words of Whittaker Chambers, and mine are but an *obbligato*.

Ralph de Toledano

The Letters

1949–50

[THE FRIENDSHIP BETWEEN Whittaker Chambers and me began on a winter night early in 1949, in the period when the government was preparing the first trial of Alger Hiss. I was not only covering the case for *Newsweek*, but also working on a book, later to be titled *Seeds of Treason*, and I had been denied interviews by the two protagonists—by Hiss's lawyer because, as he put it, he did not want to expose his client to a "red-baiter"; by Chambers because he wanted no contact with the press. But at the strong urging of Benjamin Stolberg, a writer of note and a trusted friend of both Chambers and me, an interview was arranged.

The first meeting, begun at my New York apartment, lasted well past 1 AM. The talk between us covered Chambers's early life, his Columbia experience—I was Columbia, Class of '38; his years in the open Communist Party; details of his work for the Soviet *apparat*; and his relationship and underground work with Alger Hiss of the State Department, Assistant Secretary of the Treasury Harry Dexter White, and others in the U.S. government. But what came through for me, far more than Chambers's account of his life—some of the details would be part of trial testimony—was his deep historical

1

perceptions, his intellectual depth, and the greatness of his spirit and character.

There were times when Chambers looked at me quizzically. He had been describing the house in Greenwich Village where, early on, microfilm had been processed. "That was at 17 Gay Street?" I asked. Later, Chambers spoke of a well-known literary agent who had been in the *apparat*. "You mean Maxim Lieber?" Repeatedly I would fill in blanks which, Chambers explained, were about those not directly involved in the case. Months afterward, when we had become friends, Chambers asked me when I had been in the Communist underground. "Never," I said. "In the Party, then," Chambers pressed.

"Not in the Party, either. But I've spent many years learning about the *apparat*."

That winter night—what John Donne might have called a "fatal interview"—was the beginning of the deepest friendship in the lives of the two of us, and is reflected in the correspondence that follows. At first, however, there were only telephone calls to the Chambers farm in Westminster, Maryland; visits by Chambers when he was in New York undergoing the probing questions of the FBI and of the prosecutor, Assistant U.S. Attorney Thomas F. Murphy; and a few routine letters. From this small beginning grew a correspondence of hundreds of letters which became a far-ranging discussion of our lives and our views on what I always referred to as "the time's plague"—a phrase from *King Lear*.

When, after the conviction of Alger Hiss there were crises in New York affecting Chambers—publication of Lord Jowitt's "account" of the case or a threatened libel action, which required active rebuttal—my wife Nora and I stepped in as agents and surrogates. On other occasions, too, Chambers called on me, as when he was stricken by a heart attack at the time when preparation for the British edition of *Witness* called for drastic cuts and important editing, and said of me that I was "the only man he could trust" to do the job. It is indicative of our friendship that Chambers tried to give me the royalties for the British edition and I flatly refused. The bounds of our friendship were demonstrated when I agreed that should the need arise, I would stand *in loco parentis* to Whittaker's son John, taking over the financial obligation of putting him through college—and at Whittaker Chambers's later request, of giving him a start in radio and TV journalism.

But there was much more to the relationship than this. William F. Buckley once remarked that there was "no experience in life like a friendship with Whittaker Chambers." For me, it influenced my thinking, my view of life, and the way I perceived God and the world. The great humanity of Whittaker Chambers also encompassed humor and wit and laughter—though it does not become apparent in the early letters. But it lived on in the friendship and the sharing of the ordeal that was the fate of Whittaker Chambers.

In 1959 I felt strongly that the Chambers letters should be published since they showed an important but unknown side of Whittaker Chambers. At first he demurred; he then agreed. His conditions were (1) that there be no publication until after his death; (2) that any references to people still alive which might do them hurt be deleted; (3) that they be published along with mine, as a collaboration; and (4) that all royalties go to me to compensate for my labors in editing the British edition, for my many services to the Chambers family, and in recompense for what I had done for his son, John.]

22 January 1949
Dear Whittaker:

Is this information of any value? Ralph de Sola called me last night and told me that he met Alger Hiss in 1937. It was at the [Maryland] home of two Communist women [celebrating their "wedding anniversary"]. Everyone there was a Communist Party member. Ralph and Hiss were introduced as people who had similar interests in ornithology—Hiss and his wife had been bird-watching along the Potomac—and the revolution.

Ralph

[?] *January 1949*
Dear Whittaker:

This is the score on R. He's holding down a job which is controlled by people who would have his head if he testified before a grand jury. Because he is the sole support of five people, he cannot afford to be courageous. So the following is passed on to you strictly on the understanding that he will not be brought publicly into the case.

Ralph

[Ralph de Sola, listed in *Men of Science*, had been a member of a pow-erful Communist cell in the WPA Writers Project. When he broke with the Party, he was denounced and persecuted. My letter continued with specific information: the names of the two women, details of the meet-ing, and so on. The FBI located the women, but they refused either to corroborate or deny Ralph de Sola's account. In discussing the episode with me, Ralph de Sola remarked that he would have forgot-ten the meeting but for his reaction at the time that "Hiss" was a strange Party name.]

11 *July 1949*
Dear Whittaker:

We were tempted to call you the minute we heard of the jury dead-lock. Just because we knew that your phone would be humming, we decided to hold off. I think the 8-4 breakdown was a victory. With the cards stacked by [Judge Samuel] Kaufman, [defense counsel Lloyd

Paul] Stryker, and the one dishonest juror, the truth made out very well. How do you feel about it?

I know, of course, what the new trial will mean to you and Esther. It was that thought which prevented me from letting out a big whoop when the verdict was announced. But without sounding pompous about it, I know that both of you have the inner resources to withstand the second ordeal.

If you had seen Alger and Priscilla Hiss in court and watched the trial marking their faces, you would be convinced that the only thing that bolsters them up is the magnitude of their lies. I have some pity for Mrs. Hiss. She has been on the verge of hysteria for weeks and was heavily sedated when she testified. I don't know how she will be able to take the stand for a second time. I feel no pity for Alger; he harbors pity for no man.

Ralph

[It was discovered early in the first trial that the foreman of the jury had stated to his mother, before the proceedings had even begun, that as long as he served on the jury, Alger Hiss would not be convicted. The discovery came about by one of those happenstances that marked much of the trial. The foreman's mother was in a nursing home. One of her fellow patients, to whom she had quoted her son, was the mother of Tom Donegan, assistant prosecutor in the case. Throughout the trial, however, Judge Kaufman, who had shown a strong pro-Hiss bias, even to leaving the bench to shake hands with two of Hiss's character witnesses, flatly refused to remove the offending foreman, offering only to declare a mistrial, which he knew would be impolitic for the government to request.]

7 October 1949
Dear Whittaker:

As you probably have read, Alger is being smart again. But his plea for a change of venue may boomerang if it is not granted. People here are a little annoyed by his attitude that the trial is somehow a private thing and for his own convenience which the newspapers had no right reporting in detail.

If the trial does stay in New York and does begin at the scheduled time, and if the government does not object to your appearance on the *Newsweek* program, would you still be willing to go on? I'll be the only one to interview you. The show will be handled by Cornelius Ryan, who worked for you at *Time* and whose admiration for you is unlimited.

I don't like to pressure you. As a matter of fact, I debated it seriously before I broached the subject. I'm sure [a television appearance] will do no harm and may do quite a bit of good. [In the early days of television, *Newsweek* had its own program for the now-departed Dumont network. Cornelius Ryan, producer of the show—and later to write *The Longest Journey*, the book and movie about D-Day—had pressed me to get Chambers to appear on the show. There was a question of the reaction of the prosecution, but I cleared it with Tom Murphy. In those days, the ubiquity of television was not taken as a matter of course. Chambers appeared on 17 October 1949.]

Ralph

Dec. 31, 1949
Dear Ralph,

I am enclosing an anonymous letter that came this morning. It touched a nerve because it seems to come from someone who senses that in New York all is not going quite right [in the second trial]. I too have sensed this. Even when I was there, I felt what I thought was too great a complacency, too much feeling: "Anybody can see he is guilty, therefore the 12 must see it too."

I also felt that one defense tactic was to key everything low so that the drama inherent in the conflict would sift down into boredom and sordid detail. I am not sure how conscious the defense was in this tactic, but it seemed to me that it had an instinctive sense that that was what to do.

I suppose what disturbs me most is something that to you will seem rather foolish. I have a great faith in my sixth sense—a peculiar instinct I have had from childhood when something is not quite right in a situation. It is below the rational level and I should guess is something that makes animals sense instantly when you have a special intention toward them—giving medicine, for example. Now what disturbs me is this: I had almost no concern about the trial after I left the stand—or Esther did. But I do have this peculiar concern about the past week of trial II. I know, of course, that my feelings can be explained in quite different ways.

In any case, what if anything is *Newsweek* doing about the lie detector? Would using the lie detector give grounds for a mistrial? If not, why not use it?

Whittaker

[In the first trial, Lloyd Paul Stryker, a shrewd and flamboyant trial lawyer, had gotten wide press coverage by making wild charges in court—one of them being that Chambers had once cohabited with a prostitute known as "One-Eyed Annie"—which the press had picked up although the charges had been demolished in court. It was Hiss's belief that this sensationalism had hurt his case, and after refusing to pay Stryker and firing him, he had retained a dull-mannered corporation lawyer to defend him. Since much of the evidence adduced had already seen print during the first trial, press coverage reflected the

droning tone of the Hiss defense. In court, however, the jury had listened as carefully as it had during the first trial.

Before the start of the second trial, *Newsweek* had proposed to give
both Chambers and Hiss polygraph tests on TV. Chambers had agreed;
Hiss had refused. When I discussed the possibility of testing
Chambers, Tom Murphy and the government emphatically vetoed
the plan, and *Newsweek* dropped it. What had prompted it in the first
place was the echoing question, going back to the congressional hearings: "Who is lying, Hiss or Chambers?"]

VIA Western Union: After the jury had brought in its verdict of guilty:
QUOTE BEHOLD IT IS COME AND IT IS DONE, SAITH THE LORD.
THIS IS THE DAY WHEREOF I HAVE SPOKEN UNQUOTE. THIS IN ALL
JOY AND HUMILITY. TOLEDANO

Jan. 26, 1950
Dear Ralph,

The first of my "must" letters goes to you and Nora. Words can no
more suggest what Esther and I owe to you both—your prompt and
deep understanding, your patience, tact, faith, and your great practical assistance. You have greatly earned our gratitude and won our
affection—for what so poor a thing is worth. Without doubt, I should
stop here, but I am weak enough to touch on my present mood. The
days that will diminish the echoes of the trial already reveal to us that
I have an almost incurable wound. My good, intuitive friend,
Marjorie Kinnan Rawlings, wrote during the first trial: "When it is
over, I believe that you are planning to kill yourself." In a literal
sense, this was not true, but it was so close to my feeling from the
beginning that I have never trusted myself to answer her. At the end
of that day of turmoil in which I decided to put the Baltimore papers
[documentary proof of Hiss's guilt] in evidence, I thought: "Because
of Esther and the children, I cannot pray to God to let me die, but I

cannot keep hoping that He will." Now, that feeling dogs me through these beautiful unseasonable days and in the hours of night when I wake. There keep running through my head two epitaphs that Byron saw in an Italian graveyard: "*X—implora eterna pace*," ["Pleads for eternal peace"] and "*X—implora eterna quietà*" ["pleads for eternal rest"]. "All they ask for is peace," he noted, "and that they implore."

Add to this the feeling that it was all for nothing, that nothing has been gained except the misery of others, that it was the tale of the end and not the beginning of something. The editorials in the [*New York*] *Herald Tribune*, the *Baltimore Sun*, and the *Washington Post* seem to confirm this. You cannot save what cannot save itself. These things happened in the first place because our sector of the world could not understand what was happening to it. It does not understand yet, nor does it understand this case. I am taking advantage of your kindness in writing about these things—which are unanswerable.

Whittaker

[This letter was written after the conviction of Alger Hiss in the second trial, on January 20, 1955. Following this, Representative Richard Nixon had delivered a speech on the floor of the House of Representatives outlining the facts of the Hiss case and disclosing the efforts of the Truman Justice Department to kill it or to indict Chambers. Nixon had been instrumental not only in pressing the case but also in lighting a fire under the administration to proceed with the prosecution of Hiss for committing perjury in denying espionage for the Soviet Union. The speech, Nixon's finest, shook Congress and placed him in the center of the national political stage. The Baltimore papers referred to were the stack of highly classified documents copied on Hiss's Woodstock typewriter, several memos in Hiss's handwriting, and rolls of microfilm. These had been left in the house of his wife's nephew when Chambers broke with the Soviet *apparat*—and they were presented to Hiss's lawyers when they asked, during depositions

taken in Hiss's libel action against Chambers, for proof that Hiss had
been an underground Communist in the State Department.]

Jan. 27, 1950
Dear Ralph,

Hearing from you was a life-saver, for this was the morning when
Nixon's House speech started a fragmentation bombing by the press.
I have been pretty cranky and very undiplomatic in insisting that the
newsmen read what Nixon said instead of what AP said that he said.
Your letter [lost] underlines what I have more and more felt: the
people who were with us in the beginning were with us at the end.
Only they know what it is all about. And their roster can be told on
one hand.

   I have had a letter from [Henry] Luce at last. He said *inter alia*
that he could appreciate my ordeal because he, too, had, "in however
small a measure," been facing an ordeal: trying to decide whether to
run for the Senate. "When ignorant armies clash by night...."

Whittaker

[My answer to the news about Henry Luce is also lost. As I recall, it
would have reduced him to ashes.]

Jan. 28, 1950
Dear Ralph,

...Secret & Not For Dissemination in any form: Very quietly &
poker-faced, I have been asked to return to the Luce Corporation
(Arch. Forum). It is good strategy. I will give you the details when I
see you. I do not especially like the offer, but I may take it for the
usual reasons. You realize that if you mention this before I am actually back at work, it may lose me the chance. So please be careful.

I am telling you now because I want your advice. The job I really want is the foreign news editorship of *Newsweek*. My instinct tells me that there is not a chance. That *Newsweek* would be just as frightened of me at this point as *Time*. Will you take some quick soundings and let me know…. I had another offer, just before Christmas, managing editor of a magazine [Toronto *Saturday Night*] with a circulation of 500,000. I am turning it down….

I have pulled myself above the mood of my last letter. But I am like a man who has grasped a little bush to keep from falling into a 100-foot well….

Whittaker

[From a 30 January 1950 letter from Nora de Toledano. "Mr. Luce, I'm now convinced, is unsatisfiable. Perhaps there's an 8th circle just for him."]

Feb. 1, 1950
Dear Ralph & Nora,

Esther has fixed me up a very good writing room in the basement of our middle farm—Medfield. It is about a quarter of a mile from the home place & out of sight & sound of almost anything. Once in two or three hours a car or truck goes past on the country road. Here I come on days of discipline, light our old reliable oil heater and write—so far to my great dissatisfaction. This morning I walked over on hills covered with thin sleet—very bracing, and from the ridge I could see the house and barns of Medfield with the Angus standing alert and black against the sleet. This is the farm where we keep the beef cattle and a few dairy mavericks. It is a fair domain, this Pipe Creek, that fans out from the ridge. But I do not visit every part of it as I used to do, for it has been alienated by the last year's experiences.

Nora's letter arrived this morning, Ralph's yesterday. I shall not apologize for writing as I did. My letter was purgative and you were the doctors—how competent your letters prove. When I wrote, it seemed to me that my wretchedness would be lasting. It has already washed down and will no doubt be a kind of permanent water-table under my life, from which intermittent springs and seepages may be expected. I think I wrote out of battle nerves, plus *mal de victoire*— the nausea of victory—the knowledge that when someone wins, someone loses. A news photo had much to do with it—the one of Hiss at bay (never a nice sight) and Priscilla a figure of impending collapse. What of their child, I thought. What if the special filthiness of their fighting was inspired by a desperate hope to save something for the child they had longed for (as they used to tell me) and had had only after I ceased to know them. True, they would have sacrificed my children for that child and have thought it a good idea. But who, being desperate, would not kill for his children, if there were no choice? I should hate to admit that I would not. I am not sure the world would understand this—in fact I begin to have the odd feeling that I do not live among men and women but among Lord & Taylor manikins, Prince Albert smokers and the 30-year-old grandmothers who open lush canned goods and breeze along in lush Buicks in the *Ladies Home Journal* ads. "I did not know death had undone so many."

Now let me firmly close my clinical report. I think that I am equal to my needs again. I wish that in ten months or so, it were possible to go abroad for a while—not too long. I feel I need to be among people who have never quite lost touch with the older altars, and those whose wisdom, gentle and sad, is also forever strong, like Ralph's father's "Life is pain."

Whittaker

[The two letters mentioned by Chambers have been lost, so it is impossible to gauge the virtue of the Toledanos as doctors. At the time, I was busy working on proofs of *Seeds of Treason*, an account of the Hiss-Chambers case and its ramifications, which was being published by Funk & Wagnalls in its *Newsweek* Bookshelf series and being considered for condensation by *Reader's Digest*.]

9 February 1950
Dear Whittaker:

A long time back, Vic Lasky told Bill White [son of the *Emporia Gazette's* William Allen White] that the *Reader's Digest* had an option on *Seeds of Treason*. White expressed much pleasure and asked if he could speak to [*Digest* editor and publisher] DeWitt Wallace to put in a good word for us. Tonight I find that White went to Pleasantville all right, but to sell the *Digest* a book-length piece on you and the trial—by Bill White. Because the people he spoke to knew nothing about the *Digest's* interest in *Seeds*, they gave him an assignment. Of course, Bill never breathed a word of this to us and continued to promise that "good word"....

My first impulse was to put on my coat, grab a cab, and find White. I was so furious that my intention was to smash his face. This kind of gratuitous betrayal is new to me.... Because the final decision has not been made by the *Digest*, I am trying hard to hold off. But I have few hopes that the decision will fall with us. White has lots of friends in high places up there and I am an unknown.... God spare us our "friends."

Ralph

[Victor Lasky was then on night rewrite for the *New York World-Telegram*. He had signed as coauthor with me to write a book on the Hiss-Chambers case, but had more or less disappeared until the book, totally written by me, had been set up in type. Since controversy with him would have delayed publication—the book set publishing records by moving from manuscript to bound books in twenty-three days—I allowed Lasky's name to go on the book and shared with him all royalties on what became a runaway best-seller. The *Reader's Digest* did publish a condensation—and I forgot my anger and resumed what had been a good friendship with Bill White.]

Feb. 11, 1950
Dear Ralph,

No, no—you will do no good punching people in the nose. At the risk of offending you, I will say that I doubt White is as rascally as you suppose. But maybe (for argument's sake) he is. I will contribute this for the record: during the second trial, he asked me if I would fill him in on the meaning of the Berle notes. This I did one afternoon. White told me that he was planning to write a piece for NANA [North American Newspaper Alliance] on the subject. I beg that you will not tangle with him publicly or privately. You are too big for such things. What you have done counts—your book. It alone will speak for you—it and a few who understand you. A man's special truth is in the end what is all there is to him. And with that he must be content though life give him no more, though men give him nothing. Must be content, that is, unless it come upon him that wisdom itself is the ultimate folly, the ultimate presumption. I am myself so much in the sunset that all things cast their shadow eastward from me. I will not belabor this, but I hope it may excuse a remoteness in me.

I should rather not tell you this, but I have no choice: *Time*, having summoned me to New York and worked out in detail the nature of my new employment [with *Architectural Forum*], suddenly, amid crashing embarrassment, found that it must welch on its word. Luce's heart was in the right place, but he outran the pack. He should have polled them first, but he failed to do so, out of fear or wishing to present them with an accomplished fact. When he tossed them the fact, they tore it to bits. Poor man. It hit me hard, the more so because *I* was asked—I would never have put myself in a position where they could do this to me. All this must be kept secret, though too many people know about it so that something, I am afraid, will ooze out.

The man who would save you has disarmed himself, so that it is easy to strike! The man who would betray you has his armor on, so do not turn your back on him. With a bare bodkin....

Do not then be disturbed about White. If he is what you think, he will pass though he fouls your life for a while. I think what you are will not pass.

Whittaker

[In 1939, after the Hitler-Stalin Pact had been signed and war was clearly imminent, Chambers met with Assistant Secretary of State A.A. Berle, to give him the facts about the espionage ring, organized by Hitler's ally, in the government that he had led until the year before. Berle labeled his notes "Underground Espionage Agent" and eventually turned them over to the FBI. Before the House Un-American Activities Committee and at the first trial, Berle testified that Chambers told him only of a "Marxist study group." To Berle's embarrassment, the notes were used as evidence.

As to Luce, Chambers was being charitable. Luce could have overruled the opposition against Chambers—as he had subdued occasional rebellion in the *Time-Life* ranks. In this case, it suited him to surrender to a left-wing cabal in his organization.]

15 February 1950
Dear Whittaker:

"*La vida es pena*" [life is pain], my father would, as I have told you, say. And my mother, a strong woman, would answer, "*Maldita sea la pena!"* [pain be damned!].... That's how I felt when I got your news about Henry Luce. I also felt ashamed because I had burdened you with my own petty troubles at a time when the besetting evil of the world surrounds you. My outburst was partly in anger and partly in warning. Forgive the anger and take the warning for what it's worth.

How this last twist of fortune hit you I can only guess. There were only hints in your letter, perhaps because so much of it was devoted to quieting me. I hope that you too are angry—furious at the *Time* people. This is the moment for cold and premeditated anger, something our side lacks. And if your bridges are burnt—are they?—this last bit of double-dealing should get wide publicity before a garbled version is spread. If you agree with me, just say the word.

In the meanwhile, I will continue my campaign at *Newsweek* [to bring you onto the staff]. The problem there, as I told you, is a delicate and complex one because of our set-up. I know that [Kenneth Crawford, the National Affairs editor] will do his best, but he is contending with ambitious people who know that their hold would be weakened by someone of your calibre. Crawford's attitude is like mine when you and I first met in the dim past of 1959. He liked and respected you immediately [when I brought the two together at my house]. And *Newsweek*'s involvement in *Seeds of Treason* will work in our favor. There is no way of knowing whether or not it will succeed.

Ralph

[I was shutting my eyes to the facts, and in my explanation softening them. It was clear that only the intervention of Vincent Astor, the magazine's dominant stockholder, or Raymond Moley, his surrogate, could move Malcolm Muir, the publisher, to bring Chambers—repugnant to Muir, his Social Register wife, and their pro-Hiss Park Avenue and Wall Street friends—into the fold.]

Mar. 3, 1950
Dear Ralph,

Here is a little bill for *Newsweek* [covering travel and other expenses
for the Chambers appearance on the magazine's TV program]. If
they object, throw it on the floor, thank them for me and walk away.
That's how we feel down here these days....

   This morning, at 7 o'clock, died the friend who knew most about
me, a man on whom I built an absolute trust, and to whose wisdom,
patience, courage and humility I constantly repaired—Calvin Fixx.
He came to religion largely as a result of my own conversion (he
broke with the Communist Party largely as a result of my own break)
and was with one exception, the man of most implicit faith whom I
knew in my generation. To speak selfishly, there will be left no one
who so intensely shared with me both experiences—the new and the
old, or better knew how much of each other was implied in either.
Before I go myself, there will be times when I will say: "If only
Calvin were here"—and know the touch of final sadness.

Whittaker

[Calvin Fixx, the gentlest of men, was one of a small group—
Chambers, John Chamberlain, and one or two others, who were close
to Henry Luce. But one day, having had too much of Harry's shenanigans, Fixx opened the window of his office in the old *Time-Life* building, threw out his typewriter, put on hat and coat, and disappeared.
Luce found him, and after a period in a sanatorium, Fixx returned to
work. Chambers, who kept his friendships compartmentalized, never
discussed what role Fixx played in the Communist Party—and
whether he too was in the underground or simply a secret Party member. It is possible that Fixx was one of those responsible for getting
Chambers his job on *Time*.]

April 5, 1950
Dear Ralph,

That spire you see from our front porch, a couple of miles down the valley, is the spire of Jerusalem Church. You will be happy to learn that the chief topic of talk [this Sunday] at the Jerusalem Church was not the sermon, but *Seeds of Treason*. It was the consensus of the reverent congregation that I had written it myself. They approved.

Thanks for the copy and the inscription—which I cherish. It's nice to think that there are two people in the world who really mean it when the say it. I read the preface, which I like very much—*very good*, as Tom Spencer says with an emphatic drawl. My stopping with the preface is unkind, and must be exasperating, but if I once put myself in the position where I must answer questions on the contents, there will be no peace. Yet in a little while, when the fury and the shouting dies, I shall read it all with pleasure. In the meanwhile, I feel that it is a big gun in the struggle. I also think the fury and the shouting will mount. The enemy isn't routed for a minute. Those Carthaginians are planning a Cannae, probably over [Senator Joseph R.] McCarthy's corpse. But I think they will also go after your book.

I thought Vic Lasky's broadcast with Bert Andrews [Washington Bureau chief of the *New York Herald-Tribune*] did very well—and while he had no business to drop the ONI remark, it certainly raised the dust.

Whittaker

[Tom Spencer was one of the two FBI agents assigned to the Hiss case. In conversation with me, he always referred to Chambers as "Uncle Whit." Chambers was correct about *Seeds*. Though the book was No. 3 on the *New York Times* best-seller list for five months, syndicated by United Features, and condensed by *Reader's Digest*, it was turned down by every paperback house in New York. As to Lasky, Chambers had told him in great confidence that he had worked with

the Office of Naval Intelligence (ONI) during World War II, and Lasky
violated the confidence, to Chambers's distress.]

April 11, 1950
Dear Ralph & Nora,

Catholics are impressive people. The day before Easter, I received a
card from the Convent of Our Lady of the Cenacle in New York. It
said that a crusade of prayers is being offered for me there, that my
name will be placed on the altar and nine masses will be said for me.
Just trying to catch up with the Religious Society of Friends.

I hope that… one of these spring days… you'll all be coming down
here to see us.

Whittaker

[The reference to the Society of Friends was ironic. Though he himself
was a Quaker, the activist American Friends Service Committee, controlled by the Left, gave its open support to Alger Hiss and the back
of its hand to Chambers—a triumph of politics over religion.]

12 April 1950
Dear Whittaker:

…One of the more pleasant results of the publicity which the book
has gotten has been the opportunity it gives me to speak forthrightly
about you on radio and TV. I was very much moved when Godfrey
Schmidt [a New York attorney and prominent Catholic layman, the
defending critic] on *Author Meets the Critics* [then a popular television book discussion program] made an impassioned defense of your
motives and spoke of your "courage" and "nobility" in speaking up. In
a sense, *Seeds of Treason* has carried the battle to the enemy.…

Reviewers and editorial writers outside of New York take the view, by and large, that the book is a defense of Chambers, and as one of them put it, "It's about time, too."

I was much touched by the masses for you. These lines in some masses should bring you comfort: *Judica me, Deus, et discerne causam meam de gente non sancta: ab homine iniquo et doloso erue me* [Sustain my cause, O God; give me redress against a race that knows no piety; save me from a treacherous and cruel foe]. How many of us the Catholics could hold, if....

Ralph

April 20, 1950
Dear Ralph,

Have you ever seen lions at full length in their cages looking straight ahead in an unseeing stare? They are not staring in vacancy at all. They are just not looking at the world, the unendurable world which they do not even wish to see.

Thank goodness lions don't write letters, you may well say. For this is, indeed, a most unfair way to write to you. But there come days when, if man did not turn to what understanding there is, he would walk straight on until he walked off the edge of the world. Self-pity is odious and should be burnt out with a hot iron. But to keep the strength for that, one must relax a little, and so I turn to you.

What I should rather write is that the success of the book is wonderful. All of you should do a war dance. And the good the book is doing is beyond gauging. I come across it on all sides. People do not seem to put the book down once they begin reading it. They finish with a great sigh and say: "So that was it, now I understand." That is a tremendous achievement on your part—a service to history and the nation, not to be underestimated. But forgive me, it is just this which saddens me.... How is it possible that the mass of the country under-

stood my purpose was an illusion? In part, I thought I had the majority of the plain people and now I seem to have had far less than half.
What heroic figures that makes of the jurors and, in this sense, my
feeling about the common man was no illusion. I do not regret it, for
it was one of those illusions that make reality bearable and the right
course able to survive. All the more credit to you for giving this illusion a foothold in reality and the force of fact.

Whittaker

Louis Budenz seems to have done a real job. I hope a lot of people
will write and tell him so. He seems to have walked up much more
calmly than usual, and dropped the hand grenade right inside the
pillbox—at least that's the impression I get here.

[Louis Budenz, former managing editor of the Communist *Daily
Worker* and a man who had been of considerable importance in the
Party, had been writing forthrightly about the perversion of U.S. foreign policy by Communists and fellow travelers in the State
Department. He had been shamefully attacked by the press in general and by columnists such as Joseph Alsop, whose sense of personal
sin made him look for it in others.]

May 10, 1950
Dear Ralph,

I talked before the Maryland Society in N.Y. last Tuesday. Again I
caught the full impact of the effect *Seeds of Treason* is having in the
nation.... When you set aside the annoyances—the unfair hostile
reviews, the tepid or two-headed reviews, the snubs of the top-lofty,
the *trahison des clercs* and all the rest of it—you have nevertheless
struck a telling blow in the great fight. For which we may all be
humbly grateful—not the least I. It is a grand thing for you to know

that you could look back and [see] the slow-footed army through the
pass. But here they come, brought forward another stage by you.
I do not think that they will give ground again. I think this bloody
angle—this particular one—has been won. Let there be sung *Te
Deum* and *Ora pro nobis*....

I wish you could have heard the singing of the *Star-Spangled
Banner*. The anthem has a special meaning for Marylanders anyway.
But I do not think I am reading anything into the experience when I
say that they sang it with a special fierceness that I never remember
having heard. And this was due to the historical moment, the particular episode with which they are intimately in touch and the sense that
in this way, completely unforeseeable, we are somehow coming
through. Your hand is in this too.

John Chambers has just buzzed by, a little bug on a big tractor....
He is off for his third straight day in the fields—no mean job for age
13. He's taking my place since I am out of farming this year, at least
until I finish writing. Yesterday he and Mr. Pennington [a neighbor
farmer who worked for and with the Chamberses at planting and
harvesting time] planted eleven acres of oats. Now, in a fortnight, the
field will turn from dusty brown to green. For the first time, John will
be able to stand at the ridge, look off at the springing field and say,
My work. Thus boys become men.

I reached New York before the Maryland meeting, saw Brandt &
Brandt the next morning and got home that evening in time to clean
the gutters and bed down the cattle. I was very tempted to call you,
but fought it off. And I was right, for I have very little time. We hope
you are planning to be here with us soon. It's an erratic spring, but
the flowering trees, especially the apple orchards, have never been so
beautiful in all the years we've been here....

Whittaker

[Chambers had begun work on his book. Brandt & Brandt were
his agents.]

May 16, 1950
Dear Ralph,

Thanks for D.T.'s [Diana Trilling's] piece. There, she can well say,
brushing the silk threads and snippets from her apron, and carefully
replacing the pinking shears in the top drawer of the sewing table:
A good job. And so it is. So it is. I especially commend the last section to her ilk as outstanding in its realistic fairness.

But two points. (1) I am a conservative, not first for political reasons—the political position follows logically. (2) Repentance! What's
repentance got to do with it? If Alger repented tomorrow, it would
change little or nothing except the FBI files, which would be
updated. No, that's not the key. The key is under a door mat on
which is written: A. Hiss can only be a hero insofar as he does not
repent. This could be shortened to read: faith. For she's right that the
key fits both locks—Hiss and Chambers. The different rooms it
unlocks have something to do with it too. Chambers's refusal to pass
moral judgments on Hiss does not spring from a sense of common
guilt at all. Let us get us to a nunnery. Alger, *mon semblable, mon
frère.* Hogwash! The Chambers attitude, as he has said, is based on
respect for a common power to hold convictions and to act on
them—and the power to hold a faith, of an intensity and with a force
that the D.T.'s do not know or admit. Is it nice? Is dirt nice? Is death
nice? Above all, is dying nice? And in the end, we must ask: is God
nice? I doubt it. *Der Gott der eisen Wachsen liess Er Wollte Keine
Knechte.* And since you refuse to know German, I translate:

"The God who made iron grow—He wanted no slaves."

The world in which you and I exist and bow our heads before the
God who made it, is the world also of the atom bomb and the virus.
The mystery lies beyond the lady's cerebration or yours or mine. But
if the most efficient competent brain denies or by-passes the mystery? That is the point whose blade's edge divides men into breeds
between which mind may be an extenuation of a compromise, but
cannot change or assimilate the breeds. And the breed of Hiss will

always be nearer to the breed of Chambers than either can ever be to the breed of Trilling. Because the first two contain the power to hold faith. The second admits only the ability to entertain reason and a reasoned viewpoint. Admirable—but not in a lightning flash, which is destruction, or the orgasm, which is creation. Reason me not these, sweet reasoner, or your slip is showing.

Such language—and from a Quaker too. It is recorded that at certain meetings of George Fox, the spiritual intensity was such that the walls of the meeting vibrated. Now we have Clarence Pickett.

Whittaker

Later on.

I should always keep my replies a day or so—they make me laugh so much later. It is funny to see yourself fizz out like a bottle of warm pop. So I send my instant reaction to Mrs. Trilling in part in the comic spirit. That rather high moral tone the lady takes also struck me later on as more funny than affected. It suddenly occurred to me that, before the Purge, the Trillings were happy fellow travelers, and the place to find them was around the edges of the C.P. After the Purge, or perhaps a little earlier, they switched to Trotsky. Herbert Solow [a former Communist theoretician who after his break landed on Luce's *Fortune* magazine] also a gifted, if subjective, *poputchik* in his day, takes the same high tone among the teacups that D.T. takes. It never fails to annoy me. He has been barraging me with letters and thoughts on the unsavoryness and unsapience of Jumping Joe Mc. At first I tried explaining that: 1) there is a real situation being acted on; 2) there are all kinds of warfare and ways to wage it. At last, I dropped three letters in the stove unanswered.

[Diana Trilling, wife of Lionel Trilling who had been one of my teachers at Columbia, was at the time establishing herself as a "social critic" in such publications as *Commentary*, where the piece on Hiss and

Chambers had been published. Like many liberals who could not deny Hiss's guilt, she felt called upon to balance that sin by attempting to rend Chambers with armchair analysis. What she wrote seemed to have a certain authority, for Lionel Trilling, who had known Chambers over the years, had written a *roman à clef* which was alleged to deal with Chambers. It was not until years later that Trilling cleared the record in an interesting essay on Chambers and the case.

Clarence Pickett was head of the American Friends Service Committee, and a Hiss defender.]

23 May 1950
Dear Whittaker:

I think you do an unkindness to the good Diana chaste and fair. She too has faith—in Reason, Sigmund Freud, and the Ultimate Good. And because these things mean nothing at all, perhaps hers is the greater faith.

There was an impulse to ask permission to show your letter to her. But perhaps that would be too cruel. It would be interesting to note her reaction. Would it be a blast of indignation or a worried "*Il senso lor m'e duro*" ["The meaning for me is painful"]—if she has ever read the *Inferno*. In all probability neither, but a second effusion of liberal analysis.

As I grow older—each day is a wedding, each day is a death—I tend to subscribe, with vast reservations, to the Manichaean heresy. To that and to the brave belief that I am my own exequatur. So whatever my breed and whatever the unopened door, I may eventually fry in the same saucepan as Alger. Or, the Catholics notwithstanding since so much of their sin is carnal which is the least important, be bound eternally to him like Paolo and Francesca. So much for Diana. The Leopard in the Wood has changed her spots. But Leopard she is.

In another time would it have been batik or Coueism? At any rate, her piece will infuriate the other liberals and may set them to thinking....

I feel too much these days—and I quote one of my "intuitive" verses of my Army days—like the

soldado sin arma	soldier without weapon
en la batalla fría	in the cold battle
que corre del león	who runs from the lion
y llora el tigre.	and mourns the tiger.

Ralph

July 6, 1950
Dear Ralph,

Just as we finished milking this morning, I tried to break my left shoulder in one of the many possible ways we have here. I do not think I succeeded. (I have given it a good wrench. But in any case, I can't do very much but lie around and write letters.)

No sooner had I left you in Baltimore the other day, than I felt with conviction, how poor the visit here had been for you. So long a trip for so primitive a pasture and such harassed people. We are not company for anybody. We are too tired. We have gone right on like this through the case for two years. We need a complete change (the last thing we are likely to get). We are dulled by our soil and our routines become an infatuation. For those not used to enter into them, or the logic of this life, they are stultifying, or seem so.

You must remember I am country-bred [on a Long Island which was far different from the suburbia of today]. I did not just spend a year or two in the country. I was 18 years old before I left the country at all, and even seven years older before I could sever myself from the particular land in which I grew up. In my mother's house, we used oil lamps until after World War I. As late as 1930, I used to look across the inlet [from Great South Bay] and watch them light up the oil lamps in the big house opposite—a house a block from the main street [of Lynbrook], 20 miles from New York. I used to watch it with nostalgia because I shall always prefer oil lamps to electric light. I mention this because this spirit and its manifestations must have seemed strange to you, churlish and uncomfortable for you here. I do not apologize for it, but I am sorry that you should have felt its impact at a time when we were too tired and busy to dissemble it somewhat. I am really saying: I hope it was not so bad that you will never want to come again for, as you once wrote of me, we cherish the Toledanos.

Whittaker

[Whittaker Chambers seemed obsessed with the idea that I was strictly a city boy who could not stand the vicissitudes of farm life and needed the nervous activity of cities to be happy. But I had lived the first five years of my life in Tangier, the International Zone cut out of a primitive Morocco which at the time could not have boasted a half-dozen hotels. In Hasnona, an outlying area of the Zone, there was electricity, but water had to be drawn from a well, and the sunning child Rafaelito had once been rescued from a snake, climbing up the side of his baby carriage, by his mother who crushed its head with a stone. When my mother took me into town, to wander about the *soukhs*, it was on donkey-back. And in the early 1920s, the Long Island on which my family summered boasted of only the Sunrise Highway, a two-lane road in an area now criss-crossed by superhighways.

On the visit that Chambers deplores, I woke early one morning, but remained in my room waiting for the sounds that Whittaker and Esther were up and about. I heard the door of the house opening and looked out the window. A skunk had ventured close in, and as Chambers approached it, I thought, "There it goes. The skunk's tail will rise up and Whittaker will be drenched in the animal's odors." Instead, Chambers walked quietly up to the skunk, speaking softly.

And as quietly the skunk turned and trotted off into the bushes. At milking time, Chambers would stand by the door of the barn, patting each cow on the rump and calling it by name.]

November 14, 1950
Dear Ralph,

No time, no time. We think and speak about you often—but the wires are down for the duration. I'm awaiting what I'm told is a "wonderful piece" by you in the forthcoming *Freeman*. Such a quiet fellow to be having so many impacts on affairs. For they must be quite well aware in Washington that *Seeds of Treason* was the unseen presence in the polling booths.

Whittaker

[The hiatus in communication—from May to November—was a result of my assignments in covering the pivotal 1950 elections, which took me to California for the senatorial contest between Richard Nixon and Helen Gahagan Douglas—a campaign generally misreported—and elsewhere around the country. Chambers was intensely at work on *Witness.*]

17 November 1950
Dear Whittaker:

We had about decided to call you to find out whether all was well, when your letter arrived. It brought, as usual, that sense of presence which is the gift of your pastoral communiques. But the sense is fleeting.... Must we move down to Maryland?

The "no time" urgency I take to mean that you are in the home-stretch with the book. If this is so, the news is welcome. We all of us wait impatiently. By the time it appears, it should have a clear field. The [Alistair] Cooke effort [*A Generation On Trial*] made little dent and even got panned by professional liberals like [Arthur] Schlesinger.

As to the unseen presence in the polling booths, I'm certain it was not *Seeds of Treason* but one Whittaker Chambers. Only in California did it have the impact you mention, and even there it was helped along by my "non-political" speaking at the Commonwealth Club [of San Francisco] and the efforts of Dick Nixon. As I move away from the actual writing of the book, I become more and more convinced that it was not the creation of my typewriter but a kind of spirit writing. So I can be almost impersonal about its effect. I doubt that I shall ever equal the performance. A passion of this dimension comes but once in any man's life.

I was rather pleased by what I take to be John Chamberlain's praise of my piece, *Lament for a Generation.* (Incidentally, it was originally titled *Lament for an Ill-Hatched Generation*—with the Spanish phrase, *un pollo mal sudado*, in the back of my mind—but this was too long to fit a 2-column head.) Much of its thinking comes from your influence, as did the thinking in *The Liberal Disintegration* which the *Freeman* also published. I hope you like them both, or at least feel that I did no violence to the only honorable political viewpoint left to us.

There is little to say of the elections. Since the defeat of [Senator Millard] Tydings and the election of Nixon, my cup brimmeth over. In the 82nd Congress, Dick can assume [Republican] foreign policy leadership, leaving the domestic to [Robert A.] Taft. [Arthur] Vandenburg is out, [Henry Cabot] Lodge is a fool, and there's nobody to claim this role by right of inheritance. I have written this to Dick and I hope his advisers second the motion.

The only news from me is negative. I am at the moment fed up with *Newsweek*, mostly because Hal Lavine [with me the top writers on the magazine] is back from Korea and getting most of the important assignments. I have embarked on a novel, but the going is

rough… and only Nora's misguided belief in it keeps me at work.
That and pride, which in me is no little thing.

Ralph

[Senator Tydings, who had survived the purge efforts of FDR in the
1930s, had headed the committee which "investigated" Senator Joe
McCarthy's early charges. His report, a thorough whitewash on the
issue of Communist infiltration of the government, had gratuitously
smeared me, accusing me of being a "professional anti-Communist"
whose "livelihood" depended on stoking fears of Communism, and to
the great amusement of my friends thought to demolish me by dis-
missing me as a "Puerto Rican."

I was one of those close to Senator Nixon who urged him to relinquish his preeminence in the anti-Communist field and to establish
himself as the Republican spokesman on foreign policy.

The *Freeman* piece which Chambers had mentioned was not
Lament but *The Liberal Disintegration*.]

December 2, 1950
Dear Ralph,

You put me constantly in your debt. *The Liberal Disintegration* is
very good; no one that I have talked to has this understanding of the
depth of the Case and of my purposes. You put your finger on something when you wrote that not what I did, but what I am infuriated
the Liberals. That was what they could give no quarter to. And they
had been long aware of it, for I was known, personally or by name, to
a mass of them with whom my feud has gone on for years. The Hiss
case merely gave them their chance to get at me….

My guess, subject to instant revision, is that the Chinese Communists hope to drive the U.S. to the 38th parallel—at which point the Soviet war bloc can beat the drums for peace which, in the eyes of the unthinking... it will then be the great patron of.

I am sorry you could not get here when you were in Washington... because the book is coming along to the point where I should like to show you a small section of it. I want you to be able to say to the cats of the intelligentsia when they ask: "Didn't you see the MS [manuscript]?" Naturally, a weightier point is your comment. But there will be time and to spare.

Christmas is at our throats again. Somehow it should be a good one.... For the first time, we have a quarter-page ad in the *Sheepman* [one of the bovine journals of opinion]. John was glowing over it and I asked him why. "For the first time," he said, "our farm is going to the whole nation (no less) and we're greeting all sheepmen for Christmas." So the 20th century child says to certain poor shepherds: "Noel! Noel!"

Whittaker

[It should be noted with a small degree of irony, that when Chambers went to work for *Time*, the large Communist cell there rejoiced because they knew of him only that he had written stories for the *New Masses*, a Party publication, which had echoed around the world—one being dramatized by the WPA Theater. When the cell was warned that Chambers had not only broken with the Party, almost a hanging offense, but had also deserted the *apparat*, an Ice Age descended around his desk. Research for the stories he was working on would disappear and he became the target of rumors and vilification. To make matters worse, he joined the American Newspaper Guild and was one of a group which fought Communist control and eventually ended it.]

6 December 1950
Dear Whittaker:

Jim McGuinness died Monday morning. Perhaps the name means
something to you, perhaps not; he was one of the toughest and most
effective fighters on our side in Hollywood. He was buried today, and
we stood or sat or kneeled in St. Patrick's at one of the most solemn of
solemn High Masses, with the Cardinal officiating. But there was no
sense of God in the great, cold Cathedral. Perhaps God doesn't visit in
so vast a place.

I did not know him very well—in the sense of long or intimately—
but I knew him deeply, in the quick outgoing to a man of courage and
strength and soul. He died quickly and mercifully in one of the dark
moments of our country's history, and those who mourned today
mourned more for themselves than for him.

But the feeling of God and the soul's continuance came tonight as I
sat here in a quiet room and looked at the chair in which he had sat
just a few days before. A premonition touched me delicately of the
dark interior night which comes before the unburdening of a faith
which I can only approximate. Perhaps it was only fatigue or nerves; or
perhaps the premonition was real and a glimmer of the harsh God we
must accept without comprehension.

I thought of you, because you know and I do not, because you have
made the acceptance and I have not. I am writing you because even at
this long remove, there can be a laying on of comfort in a proxy
contact.

The Black International was out in force for Jim's funeral, most of
them awed by the majesty of the Church and groping for the first time
with the realization that the ritual is man's attempt to clothe himself in the
dignity of God. Many of them saw for the first time the skeleton lurking
beneath the flesh, and the contemplation gave them no elation....

John Chamberlain tells me that the piece which he referred to as
"wonderful" was the one on the liberals. He tells me that he asked you to

write in answer or in amplification. I should like to see a piece on the same subject by you—but after a decent interval so that the inadequacies of mine may be forgotten. I'm not given to false modesty; the cultured pearl has its pride. But if you write for the *Freeman* on the same subject, there will be too many who see how the real pearl glows.

Ralph

[James Kevin McGuinness, an executive producer at MGM, had been fired for testifying against the Hollywood Communists in the 1947 "Hollywood Hearings." He was part of that purge which included Morrie Ryskind (Pulitzer Prize winner for the musical *Of Thee I Sing* and writer of the great Marx Brothers movies) and Adolphe Menjou, both of whom were also forced out because of their testimony against the Hollywood Ten. In the group also were Irene Dunne, John Wayne, Ward Bond, and Ronald Reagan.]

December 8, 1950
Dear Whittaker:

We just received this letter, by airmail from France, and Ralph asked me to send it to you.

Dear Mr. Toledano:

Last night I finished reading your book, Seeds of Treason, *and I want to thank you for writing it. You have done a great service to our country. Many Americans have been aware that something was wrong. Your lucid book has made it very clear. I wish your book could be read by everyone in our country. I expect all the Communists have so there will be no more slips on typewriters, Ford cars, etc. but it is the others who should.*

Mr. Whittaker Chambers I should like to write to but I fear to rush in where angels fear to tread. Could you tell him for me that like his

*wife I feel he is a great man, a very great man, and that I wish to
thank him with all my heart for the sacrifice he has made for all of us.*

Sincerely yours,

*Mona Williams
(Mrs. Harrison Williams)*

The excerpts of the decision [by the U.S. Court of Appeals, sustaining the conviction of Alger Hiss] are magnificent. We have good reason to believe that the Supreme Court will sustain the conviction by not hearing argument....

Nora

*December 9, 1950
Dear Ralph and Nora:*

Your letters came, together, this morning. I was grateful for them. I should like to have a long talk with you. I have no agenda, just a desire to communicate and swap views. As plans now stand, I plan to drive to New York on the 19, 20, or 21 Dec. to fetch my mother home for Christmas. I want to take Tonia Krivitsky something on my way to [Long Island]. She lives not far from you on Central Park West, and I thought I might drop down, after seeing her, to spend an evening with you. In question is the date, the weather, unforeseen complications. Will you please keep my presence in N.Y. a complete secret? There are so many people to whom I owe visits that, if it is discovered that I have been in town and neglected even one, there will be hurt and hard feelings.

Whittaker

That business about pearls, my cultured pearl, is a lot of crap.

[Tonia Krivitsky was the widow of General Walter Krivitsky, head of Soviet military intelligence in Western Europe who defected in the late 1930s. In *Witness*, Chambers wrote about his meetings with Krivitsky but did not mention that after his murder in a Washington hotel room by the KGB (then NKVD) the night before he was to testify before a congressional committee, he had looked after Mrs. Krivitsky.

On other visits to New York by Chambers, I had been beset by friends for invitations to meet him. Chambers had always been reluctant, but he sometimes deferred to me that these meetings were important to him, Chambers. At one such occasion, the novelist James T. Farrell sat uncharacteristically quiet on the floor in my apartment— "sat at your feet," I remarked to Chambers afterward—"fascinatedly listening."]

10 December 1950
Dear Whittaker:

To repeat—and repeat—you will never be in my debt half so much as I am in yours. Before me are the American and the natty British editions of *Seeds* as the "immutable evidence." But for my sake… let's have no more of this debt business. We are all storm-tossed people….

As to my seeing the manuscript of your book—if my comments can be of value, fine. I needn't mention the greatness of my interest. But there's no need to show it to me just so I can prove to the "intelligentsia" that I am an insider. Being complex of reaction, I have been in a way flattered that you have never let me read the book as it progresses. This is Toledano conceit *in excelsis*….

The military situation seems not so bad and the groundwork for new appeasement is being laid in Washington. The talk is that

[Secretary of State Dean] Acheson will be forced out next week....
So far we have been spared all-out war only by the incredible stupidity of the Soviets. If they knew how weak and divided and confused
we are, they would have been in Paris long ago. The president
[Truman] saps his strength with letters to music critics threatening to
kick them in the family jewels for criticizing his daughter's singing,
and attacking columnists [such as Drew Pearson]. Military prepara-
tions lag. And the answer is always so clear....

You write of Christmas. I hope that in Westminster, as the old
plainsong has it, "There shall sound happy voice."...

Ralph

1951

Jan 20, 1951
Dear Ralph,

The pictures of the little boys [playing with Christmas toys sent by the Chambers family] were wonderful. So, I am told, was your Christmas package. I say "I am told" because I took to my bed briefly around Christmas time, and when I got downstairs again, there wasn't any more package from the Toledanos. I slashed off some of the last scraps from the Edam—the first real Edam I have had since the last war. Among cheeses, Edam is one of my three preferreds.

The shadow you see over my shoulder is [Bennett] Cerf [owner of Random House, which published *Witness*] and [Ben] Hibbs [editor of the *Saturday Evening Post*, which serialized it]. I have sent in a whack of copy amidst great enthusiasm from Brandt & Brandt. The publishers will soon get it and that is the pivot. But I also have been in one of my gloomier moods and, having inflicted one or two lowering letters on others, I thought I should spare you. Esther and I share this mood which makes us impatient of the world, and restless. We had better curb it.

Whittaker

April 19, 1951
Dear Ralph,

After you had left with the copy (and not until then), it suddenly
occurred to me: "Suppose he does not like it. Suppose it is completely
different from what he had hoped for (and I began to tot up its inadequacies). What an embarrassment for both of us." Your letter came as
so much relief that at first I felt only that and did not grasp its deeper
understandings and generosity. From you, it means a great deal to me.
I do not know that I want to say any more about it. I am just deeply
grateful to you and for the fact that here and there are in the world
people with whom I can speak in a natural voice without the help of a
dragoman.

[I had visited Chambers in Westminster, and as we stood waiting for the
train at the Baltimore station, Chambers thrust a large manilla envelope
into my hands. "These are the first chapters of the book," Chambers said.
"Would you please deliver them to Bernice Baumgarten [with whom he
worked at Brandt & Brandt]? You can read them if you wish." On the
train, I was afraid to open the envelope. "Suppose," I thought, "I do not
like it." And then I began reading what was the opening chapter, the
"Letter to My Children." As I later wrote, tears came to my eyes. The letter I wrote Chambers has been lost, but it expressed my emotion at a great
piece of writing and what it conveyed.]

All my life I have felt weighed down by the burden of communication: the feeling that in speaking to most people what I said, though it
seemed perfectly simple to me, had to be filtered through three feet
of *papier mâché* to reach someone else. Everything had to be translated. I rarely have that difficulty with Europeans (we speak within
the same frame of reference), and with Europeans I never feel as I do
with Americans, or seldom. Now, I have hope that I may dissolve that
barrier—but let us not hope too much. (Without getting in too deep, I
suspect that the origins of the uncommunication are religious. No one
has ever tried to speak to Americans religiously, in the simplest sense.)

I was also deeply grateful for the tact with which you convey your belief that some excisions are in order. I agree. Some will result naturally from the fact that Part II must be scaled down for length. Do not tell me what they are. But if you will, tell me later, when we have reached the stage of post-editing. I imagine that I can guess most of them, anyway. But there is always something that we miss, that is different to us than to others.

There was a house for sale for an asking price of $4,500. Sixty acres of land and a small barn to go with it. It lies just beyond our wood and it marches with our line along more than half of the northern border. I should have had little hesitation in urging you to buy it because I should (with any kind of break) always have been willing to buy it back from you, if you tired of it. Dozens of people have been looking at it in the last month, but since that great traffic has been stanched, I am afraid it has been sold. I can ask if you are interested. It was offered to me and I would have bought it out of hand, but our financial condition is not very different from what it used to be when we were on St. Paul Street [in Baltimore, where the Chamberses lived after his break with the Soviet *apparat.*]

In some ways it is worse, for we have the delusion of solvency; but the operating costs eat up the income in a hemorrhage that must end for lack of something to bleed with. This is not a plaint. There are several things we can do (one of them is to sell Pipe Creek Farm); but, above all, I feel the challenge of making it work in its own terms. Only, I can't get free to do it. It can only work if I take over and manage. The problem is not solved by selling the book. It can only be solved by making a profit here on the farm. Otherwise it is only a question of a short time until the farm will swallow any capital we have. To me it is an interesting problem.

I suspect that any satisfaction that may be left to me in life will come from solving it. Now I am holding it off with one hand and looking doggedly away. But I have made a negative start. I have

brought the spring planting to a full stop. It is like holding back a
locomotive with one hand (you will scarcely understand this without
feeling the momentum of planting, the mania to tear up the earth
and seed it that consumes farmers in the spring). My hope is that in
the fall, I can jump in and plan the winter crops without a backlog of
lime and fertilizer bills on my neck....

But I think you should bear in mind two points [if you consider
buying the house]: How Nora will handle the inconveniences of the
countryside and its loneliness (we are not only very busy, but not
innately sociable people); how much both of you would miss a kind
of nervous life or stimulation that just isn't here. Forgive me if I
seem pedantic and do not suppose that I am being condescending,
but if you do not feel at one with the countryside so that everywhere
your eyes rest, they meet with an experience more arresting than
anything you can read or hear about, the countryside is likely to be
or become a geographic bore. Do not misunderstand: there are
thousands of country people who feel as deeply as Marx "the idiocy
of village life," The movies and the radio are dispelling that idiocy for
them. So are the Farm Bureau and the Grange which sponsor weekend trips to New York and other unidiotic human agglomerations.
The last 4H county fair had a fashion show.

But listen to my friend Paul Morelock speaking to me yesterday:
"Just so I can see the flowers the first thing when I wake up in the
morning; just so I can see them the first thing. That makes all the day
right." Last fall he walked up to two young foxes and picked them up
by the scruff of their necks, brought them home and tamed them. He
lays his hand on a stallion and it quiets. He is himself the good earth.
I cannot say more clearly now what I mean. In a later section of
Witness you will find more about him and how great a charge of
strength flowed from him and his family to me during the case.

Whittaker

I read the piece on conductors [*The Cult of the Conductor*, from the *American Mercury*, which I had written in 1949] with great pleasure and complete agreement. I have never been able to bear Toscanini's conducting of Mozart. I have always thought that Stokowski (his forte is Rimsky-Korsakoff) and Koussevitsky were musical shaving cream: "Comes out like a ribbon; lies flat on the brush."

May 23, 1951
Dear Ralph,

...These are grey days, in part for reasons that will presently appear—reasons that I forecast to you. I think we have reached that moment in *The Possessed* when Piotr Stepanovitch sneaks into the dark room to see why Kirilov has not killed himself and is suddenly terrified to find him drawn up rigid between the chests with the revolver in his hand. An instructive book.

  Best to all.

Whittaker

[Those were grey days because Chambers, having finished the long and grueling job of writing *Witness*, was suffering from a disease endemic among creative people, a kind of *post partum* blues. They always vanished when there was pressure on him to get back to his typewriter.]

June 4, 1951
Dear Whittaker:

This letter is to serve a double function—for myself and for Ralph as well. He has been troubled by the need to write to you and by the inability to sit down and do it. Your last letter—for that matter, so much of the communication between us and you this winter of discontent—upset him very much. But with the distress on your part always comes a kind of helplessness. At this late date it seems pointless to do anything more than hope that the difficulty, whatever it may be, is on its way to resolution....

Which leads by a curious association... to the question of Ellen.... [Did I ever tell you that] last spring, when I met Nixon for the first time, we spoke of the children? And he told me that when he took the first trip out to the farm to question you, he was still very troubled about questions of your good faith and such. But, said he, "When I met the children I knew that anyone who had brought them up had to be a good man."...

You may know that Ralph has signed a contract to do a book on Sorge. [Richard Sorge, one of the Kremlin's most effective spies, set up a far-reaching spy espionage *apparat* in wartime China and Japan. He informed Stalin of the imminent attack on Pearl Harbor—information which Stalin failed to pass on to President Roosevelt. Sorge was caught and executed. He left a long confession which was later translated by U.S. intelligence and was quoted extensively in *Spies, Dupes & Diplomats*.] He is shockingly debonair about this one, finding the prospect of having to produce that many words unintimidating.... Aside from that he is still pretty restless, pretty dissatisfied, and very much unresigned to so feeling....

Nora

June 12, 1951
Dear Nora,

Delighted to hear from you, sorry if I caused you all any concern. I am just about convinced now that the whole struggle, the West's struggle, the nation's struggle, everybody's struggle, is foredoomed, that the best thing is to try not to talk about it at all. Somebody must always fight on the losing side in history, and should, but it is discouraging to know too clearly which side you're on. So let us skip it. I've revived the old *Spoon River* slogan: "You can fool some of the people all of the time, and that's enough."...

I saw *Newsweek*'s note on Ralph and Sorge. It can be a very good assignment. I think I understand Ralph's feeling about it as described by you. If I ever finish certain writing, I am going to devote myself to ten volumes on the incidence of the mousetrap in certain paintings of St. Joseph in the 15th and 16th centuries—or I would if one of my friends had not brilliantly done it already. But I will never finish if I write letters like this one.

Besides,

Savez vous pas que la nuit est profonde	Do you know that the night is deep
Et que le monde N'a que souci?	And that the world Has nothing but trouble?

Whittaker

21 July 1951
Dear Whittaker:

Repeatedly I have had the impulse to write to you. And repeatedly I have failed to do so out of a combined intellectual depression and a sense that I had nothing to say. What drives me to the typewriter is a feeling of loss because there has been no contact between us for some time....

I hold on at *Newsweek* because I must eat and my family must eat. The belief that I am doing some good there is dying fast. The victory of the liberals [on the magazine] is almost total. You will understand my mood when I tell you that I have written exactly one page on the

[Sorge] book. My escape has been in writing a couple of caustic pieces for the *American Mercury* and a piece on sacred music for the *Freeman*. John liked it but, mistrusting his judgment, showed it to Willi Schlamm. Should I be flattered or cast down that Willi missed the point completely?...

I imagine that you are approaching the moment in your work when you must cut the silver cord and cast the book into the world. From what I have seen of it, I know it is a sturdy child, and its first loud yell will do little to soothe the liberals....

Ralph

July 27, 1951
Dear Ralph,

...The day your letter came, I was about as deep in the dumps as a man can get. My first reaction was to reply at once. Then I thought: not in this mood. As I sat reading your letter, the telephone rang and the *Baltimore Sun*, the friendly paper, wanted to know all about Ellen [Chambers] and the VFW essay [contest she had won]. (I assume you know all about it.) Then Murray Kempton [a *New York Post* columnist] called up, etc., etc. It made me feel good, even though I told myself it had all happened a month ago and was of no importance anyhow. Then I went to the 4H fair at Taneytown. Sister [Ellen] had won first with a dress she had thrown together and the AP man had cornered and got her pix. She was quite set up and that also made me feel good. The next day I worked, milked in the evening and then went up to the fair again. Everybody very open and wonderfully friendly; and the children had won *all* the first prizes in the Guernsey breed. Well, that's a little shocking, but not the nastiest kind of shock you can have. The same day there had been a flock of mail (not bills as usual); a lot of personal letters from people who, like you, had not written for some time and suddenly all came through together.

Among them was one that, editorially and financially, was pretty terrific. Unfortunately, details censored; but I was set up again. And that made me feel even better because by writing twenty pages, I can earn all of Ellen's tuition and expenses at Smith for a year. It's not just the welcome cash. It's the vigorous thought that I can still do it. So I came out of the dumps and am waiting patiently for the next slam to the side of my head. Not long to wait, I presume.

I think I know just about what you are going through at *Newsweek*. Something similar happened to me for nine years at *Time*. You can't win the battle. But there are advantages to sticking around the battlefield. One of them, as you note, is money. Believe me, a dollar bill is a much more important weapon than a revolver. Another advantage is the connection. And on the battlefield, it's nice to have a few connections ("I work for *Newsweek*"). Then there's the business of being close to the news. It has its value too, and may one day have more. Then there's time and its chances. That softest paw of greediest time, e.e. cummings says, and it does the strangest and most unpredictable things for us as well as to us. Don't jump out of line. Meanwhile, the brass keeps its eye on you.

I had a pretty shrewd idea of where every *Time* writer was going, even when I did not seem to be seeing at all, and even he probably thought he wasn't going anywhere, and what a whoreson dog Chambers is. I, too, let off steam by writing for the *American Mercury*, and it was later developed interestingly by one Cross [Hiss's lawyer in the second trial]. I hope, at least, he won't be able to charge you with having taken the pen name of Luke Limestone [which Chambers had]. I couldn't write a piece on sacred music for the *Freeman*, much as I would like to. As for [Willi] Schlamm [an ex-Communist who had been editor of the Communist *Die Rote Fahne* in Vienna], he means no harm. Like Hamlet in another instance, I can only answer: "Sir, his definement suffers no perdition in you; though, I know, to divide him inventorially would dizzy the arithmetic of memory, and yet but neither in respect to his quick sail. But in the verity of extolment, I take him to be a soul of great article, and his infusion of such dearth and rareness, as, to make true diction of him, his semblable is his mirror, and who else would trace him, his umbrage, nothing more." He grew to maturity in the same Vienna coffee houses as Gerhardt Eisler and Hede Massing.

[Gerhardt Eisler had crossed the Atlantic to become one of the leaders of the underground CP and the *apparat*. Hede Massing had been recruited into the great Richard Sorge spy ring, and in the U.S. had known Alger Hiss as a Soviet agent. She testified for the government in the Hiss trials.]

The mode is not known here, and therefore Willi is taken for a mind of pith and iridescence. He has a good mind. He is very clever. He is in love with career. I like Willi. I have never taken him very seriously. Some day I will say more *viva voce*, I don't think he knows anything about sacred music. But is the *Freeman* a place for such a piece? Get you a literary agent and stop wasting your time on the pulps. As to your book, I can offer small comfort. To me, in my plight, the most sensible thing I can think of is writing only one page. I think you should polish off Sorge. But then, I think you should tack away from Communism and work in some other very different field.

Perhaps out of the Spanish flirtation will come a chance for you to go to Spain for *Newsweek*. How I shall envy you. I would give a good deal to spend the winter in Estremadura or Murcia, or even Madrid. Like the wife in the *Carnival in Flanders*, I am in the mood of "Ah, Venice! The leaning tower!"...

Whittaker

3 August 1951
Dear Whittaker:

Sunday night I told Nora, "Tomorrow we're going to get a letter from Whittaker—or else." "Or else, what?" she asked. "Or else we'll get one on Tuesday." The letter came Monday and set us up considerably. For whatever multitude of reasons, Mr. Chambers was feeling like Mr. Chambers—and that was fine. What's more, Mr. Chambers's family seemed to be doing pretty well, too. We learned of Ellen's shocking bad taste in winning the VFW contest by sheer inadvertence. I am on vacation, hence I read no newspapers. But [FBI agent] Tom Spencer called up on some routine business, asked after "Uncle Whit," and then told me he'd seen Ellen's picture in the *Journal American*. I was tempted to call *Newsweek* and tell the girl who writes "In Passing" [equivalent to *Time*'s "People" section] to include it and then decided against it. I felt she'd do it without prompting and then feel virtuous for it. She did include the item—and most handsomely, though I wondered how the "Pretty Ellen Chambers" would touch your Quakerish soul.

Your obvious satisfaction over the things you mentioned in your letter came through most clearly in your anticipation of the hit on the head to come. It reminded me so much of childhood guards against evil days. My mother, who combines a rather expansive sense of God with a lively belief in such matters as the evil eye, gave us a defense against *el ojo* [the evil eye] when we were children. It was one she had picked up from the Moors [though it is also common among Christians and Jews in the Mediterranean world]—the palm of the hand with the five fingers separated, waved in the face of the evil eye's possessor, plus a repeated *"Cinco, cinco,"* the five standing for the fingers of the hand. When politeness barred such an open invocation, we were to thrust hand in pocket where the sign could not be spied but still have the desired effect.

My mother was convinced that a cousin, now dead, bore the evil eye. She was a sharp-tongued but sentimental old woman, but my mother always warned us to ward off the *ojo* when that poor cousin was about. Whenever she told us that we looked well, my mother shivered. Even to this day, when someone compliments my children extravagantly, that old fear crops up in me and I find myself, hand in pocket, making the sign of the *cinco*. As a matter of fact, I have always felt that certain people have an unconscious evil force—as others have an unconscious good force. All this long exposition, and just to say that your note of pessimism in the letter seemed like a *cinco* to me.

...Your admonition to me to get out of the pulps may have been prophetic.... Against my better judgment I allowed myself to agree to do a piece for *Colliers* on speculation. It's finished and in.... I bear the weight of work to come, look uneasily at the pile of work on my desk at home, and wish I'd been brought up as a carpenter or a millionaire....

. *Ralph*

August 9, 1951
Dear Ralph,

It was a *cinco*. I am in a permanent state of *cinco*. For the bangs on the head come through with admirable regularity. I would that I could get copy out of that regularly. I have reached that point where the whole book [*Witness*] seems to me completely wretched, dull, flat, uninspired, and, moreover, I can't tell what it is and what it isn't. Well known occupational tizzy. That's where the regulars have it over the recruits. No doubt, it's all they have: the power to keep their feet lifting and dropping. Obviously this is the point to say that I should like to write another book. It's the book nobody wants. It's called *The Spanish Civil War*. It's never been written, or am I presuming? And what a story! Poor [Bennett] Cerf, found there in his office with the smoking revolver in his hand and the first few chapters on the Spanish Civil War scattered around his chair. We must talk about it sometime.

Very nice of "In Passing" to pick up Ellen and her essay. *Time*, the weekly newsmagazine, didn't. Yet, if I ever saw news, that was news.

I was sorry to hear about your wisdom tooth, clearly a misnomer. One of my neighbors strongly urged me to have all my teeth (a relative figure) out. Said he had had his out and never had a day's trouble since. It's the custom hereabouts. Out with the ill-created things and

in with the dentures. There's some comfort, though, in the knowledge that henceforth you and I will always be able to identify each
other by opening our mouths.

They're moving in on McCarthy, and, if the rumors that reach me
are at all true, things do not look too good. The real angle of the
[O. Edmund] Clubb story is wonderful beyond belief. Fortunately,
I testified before I heard about it. Before the House [Un-American
Activities] Committee, Clubb denied that he had ever been at the
New Masses [the Communist weekly magazine of which Chambers
had been an editor prior to going underground] or seen me. But, oh,
consummate conspiracy, Clubb kept a diary. When the Americans fled
China, they left certain possessions to be brought out by the more
staid British. Among the items left by Clubb was his diary. Now the
British are great readers of your whoreson diaries—or anything else
that they can casually leaf through. They read Clubb's diary. They
found an entry saying that in 1932, he had visited the *New Masses* and
talked with Whittaker Chambers. That was not all. Club also confided
to his diary that on the same occasion he had met with Mike Gold,
who called him "comrade" (giggle, giggle!) and they talked together
about overthrowing the U.S. government. With me he only got as far
as talking about the Hanyang Arsenal. And he did bring a message,
but I cannot remember, and I do not know, just what kind.

[During the confrontation between Hiss and Chambers before the
House Un-American Activities Committee, Hiss insisted that he would
not be able to say whether or not he knew Chambers until Chambers
opened his mouth and showed his teeth. He also asked for the name of
the Chambers dentist as a means of identification. O. Edmund Clubb,
a State Department official named by Senator McCarthy, and under
investigation for Communist connections, denied under oath that he had
ever visited the *New Masses* or spoken to Chambers.]

So the British sent the diary on to the State Department where, if
my information is correct, Clubb had rather miraculously been transferred from a fugitive consular official from China to the head of the

Far East section of the Secretary's (as we call him, *nous autres frères*) Planning Board. To my mind, one of the funniest stories of the year; and if I had time and space to cover all the details, you would see that it is even funnier. Low comedy, no doubt. But if the State Department does not drop him now.... It was the fact that I remembered his 15-minute visit 19 years ago, and his name and all that, that clinched the business, if it's clinched. I know it's wrong to dance around a poled scalp. But in the national sense, it's a good deed; and a man must take some pleasure in his work....

Whittaker

17 August 1951
Dear Whittaker:

Today is my 35th birthday, and if you accept the Biblical span and except the misdemeanors of trucks, planes, and Sunday drivers, I am truly *nel mezzo del cammin* [in the middle of life's journey]. I ushered out some of the waning hours of my 35th year having a long discussion with Jamie [my older son] on the nature of good and evil, God and the Devil, and the soul's immortality. I am very diffident about passing on my own rather complex and unorthodox ideas to my children. At the same time I do not want them to be Jansenists. When they are older I will pass on to them my belief in the inner sense of grace. At times like these, I wish I rested my life on a complete and closed system of doctrine. I am afraid that without it, children grow into Unitarians or Ethical Culturists or any other one of the bubble dances of timid materialists.

From what little you say about your book, I take it that a first draft is virtually completed. The "occupational tizzy" you are in, I know too well. I guess it is the function of the mythical brilliant and inspiring editor to fill you with new zeal at this point. The only person I know is Cap Pearce [Charles A. Pearce, who as editor at Harcourt, Brace &

Co. presided over the publication of T.S. Eliot's poems and edited
the earlier John O'Hara] who succeeds not only because his ideas are
sound, but because he's got antennae.... Unfortunately he works for
DS&P [Duell, Sloan & Pearce, struggling for survival] not Random
House. What's more, I don't think you need or want anybody's paws
on your MS at this time. I add hesitantly—and this is not phony pride
or phony modesty—that my affectionate and calculating eye is always
at your disposal.... I say "hesitantly" because even the deepest and
most intuitive friendship can sometimes be clumsy—and because I
don't want to place on you the burden of wondering what my reaction to a refusal might be. My reaction will be that you know best.

Joe McCarthy keeps bumbling along, but my private intelligence
is that things are not so bad as they seem for him. Tom Coleman, the
GOP boss of Wisconsin, is still staunchly for him and the plot to get
Gov. Kohler to run against him—murder for Joe since Kohler controls Wisconsin's patronage—seems to be getting nowhere. Kohler is
the only man who could seriously hurt Joe, but they tell me he's a
sort of Ferdinandish political bull who doesn't relish the thought of a
bitter and unpredictable [primary] campaign against the roughest
campaigner in these United States.

My two pieces for the *American Mercury* [on the stranglehold of
Communist and fellow-traveling book reviewers, flamboyantly titled
Gravediggers of America by editor Bill Huie] have caused something
of a stir, particularly in the hinterland where customers have come
into the bookstores with copies and growls. The booksellers have
reacted like the Bronx landlord in the old joke who told the tenant's
committee, "All right, I'll paint your bathrooms, I'll fix the kitchen
plumbing, I'll put new bulbs in the hallway, but how can I free the
Scottsboro boys?"

[Chambers never spoke out publicly on Senator McCarthy.
Privately, he remarked to me, "Joe is sometimes a rascal, but he's our
rascal." He felt that McCarthy had done a good job in arousing the
American people to the dangers of Communist infiltration of the gov-

ernment. His concern was that McCarthy left himself vulnerable to counterattack, particularly because of his association with Roy Cohn, who we both felt was one of the lowest forms of political life. And though Chamber was meticulous in what he said or wrote, he could argue that there are different methods of fighting.]

Colliers did take the piece, with great enthusiasm, and has promised to give it a cover line. It's called "Operation Storm… and the Four Red Fugitives" [the Party leaders convicted under the Smith Act who jumped bail]. Some of the [secret] Party directives I quote I bought from an idealistic comrade who loves a buck….

I usually spend my birthdays in the *temps perdu* mood of "*Dieu, que le son du cor est triste au fond des bois* [How sad, O Lord, the horn's call from the depth of the forest]." This year my mood is more akin to that of the Italian PWs I handled during the war: *Poco mene frego* [I don't give a ——]…. A man can have too much sense of the fate incumbent in the bone…. [Now] I must shower, dress, and get back to the life and times of Richard Sorge. I shall end this and lug my guts into the neighbor room.

Ralph

Oh yes. I mentioned casually to Cap Pearce that Whittaker Chambers might be talked into doing a book on the Spanish Civil War and he was much excited. So if Cerf doesn't have you tied down and you would care to discuss it with Cap, he'd be tickled to death…. Incidentally, I have a shelf of books on the subject which would be of some value….

August 17, 1951
Dear Ralph,

Awful, awful busy. If you are not the same, would you care to undertake my defense against a piece *Commentary* has just run on (as they put it) the Hiss case? Elliot Cohen, whom I know quite well, sent me the tear sheets in a letter beginning: "Dear Sir." I replied in a letter beginning: "Dear Elliot" to this effect. My first impression after a quick reading was that the piece was "strictly dishonest." But since I didn't want to think so, and hadn't the time or desire to check, I'd just suppose that the author didn't understand what the Case was about. Apparently he thought it was about "a fight with bowie knives between two species of dead-end kids in a darkened psychiatrist's office." I pointed out one factual error—the Third Period business [the beginning of the purges]. I broke with the CP in 1929, chiefly over the Third Period which I never accepted. I also pointed out that "the culture hero of our time" did not merely brush off [Ambassador William] Bullitt's warning [to Acheson about Hiss].... I closed, rather meanly, by quoting the refrain from the "Song of the Bandarlog": "Brother, your tail hangs down behind." I thought that, in my hasty reading, I might actually have missed some subtle point in the piece, which perhaps changed its whole meaning. Now I hear from some- one else that I did not.

Main point of assault, I think, is that the piece is dishonest. It's purpose is to hose out that Augean stable that is the liberal mind, by getting rid of both Hiss and Chambers—the first of whom makes them feel guilty, and the second makes them feel—an even less for- givable sin—small. That effort to lug out both bodies makes the piece different. To achieve their triumph, it has been necessary to denigrate Chambers even more than Hiss. All the old Hiss defense charges (plus some original sins of Fiedler's) are run off again with- out the slightest effort to discriminate as to what is true and what isn't. Such jabs as the Third Period untruth, on which quite a case is built, together with the quoted *New Masses* paragraph, which "he might" (but did not) write—those are gratuitous knifings.... But, above all, who ever heard of making an all-out assault on a man, by using a deliberately hostile legal mayhem as the basis for understand- ing his character? No attempt to search other records or get in touch

with Chambers. So far as I know, I have never seen Fiedler. The
attack on Hiss is almost as fantastic. But whereas Fiedler and I have
nothing in common (if only because I am a Christian and he a heathen) Hiss and Fiedler have certain ideas in common.

In the intellectual field (as for some reason it is called), the piece
performs exactly the function that must be performed in the political
field before [the election of] 1952: kill him....

Now, if you do not feel inclined to enter this dog-fight, very good.
Perhaps it is nothing to get enraged about, and I am writing a book,
which may well answer some of it. But if you do, my blessing. I do
not know this Fiedler, but I know these Fiedlers. As Hamlet says of
Osric: "t'is a chough, but spacious, as I say, in the possession of dirt."

To change the air, have you ever read the *Duino Elegies*? I have
used this incident in what I am writing. The story goes that Rilke
found himself on the tower of the Castle of Duino (circa 1911) while
a storm was tearing apart the Adriatic 200 feet below him. As he
stood there, he heard a voice utter what is the first line of the *Elegies*:

Wer, wenn ich schriee, horte mich aus der Engel Ordungen?

Who, if I cried out, would hear me from among the Orders of the
Angels?

It's nice to remember amidst the buzzing of *Commentary*, that,
when I was ten years old, Europe could still produce a man who
could, on the tower of Duino, hear such a question in a storm.

Whittaker

Perhaps it is pertinent that Duino was the property of the Princess
von Thurn und von Taxis-Hohenlohe. I know you reject German,
but the German line here is wonderfully powerful and beautiful.... I
cannot forbear to end with the same terrifying line that Rilke (whom
you see I have been reading) ends one of his letters: "The world has
fallen into the hands of man." I do not find that anyone has said it
more economically.

August, yet, 1951.
Dear Ralph,

The heck with Fiedler. I shouldn't have asked you. You shouldn't waste time on it.

I was delighted with your *Am. Mercury* pieces, and said to Esther, who was similarly delighted, that I wondered why I was wasting my time on the middle farm. For some reason, those pieces finally convinced me that we can work together, editorially I mean. I think we must have in mind the possibility of sometime finding us an organ. Incidentally, it seems to me that the *Mercury* is doing a better though cheaper job than the *Freeman* from which heaven deliver us. They are not merely Mr. Republican; they are still running Winfield Scott for president. That might not be so bad if it were not true that the man is the style; I can't take editorial sloppiness and lack of focus....

About me. I should like you to read [the manuscript]. And that so badly that I suspect my own motives; by which I mean that I think I'm doing badly, and so I look around for someone to say I'm not. Well, that's pretty shameful. After all, we have to sire our own children. Later, comes the pediatrician. Nothing disdainful in the term. When I've got this thing all, or mostly, in hand, I should greatly appreciate your sitting down with it. Then if you'll tell me what's wrong with it, I have no doubt that it will be a better book. I have my own suspicions of what's wrong. But it always helps to have an independent head at work.

I think that I should probably do the Spanish Civil War book, whether for Pearce or another. [At the end, he urged me to write the book.] I think I should try to go to Spain. All matters for later discussion. But I am looking forward to some radio colloquy in which I casually utter this line: "We cannot possibly begin to write the history of our time, until the simple fact is recognized that Franklin Roosevelt was an extraordinarily stupid man."

Whittaker

22 August 1951
Dear Whittaker:

I had picked up the Fiedler article, read a bit, and threw it down in disgust. But I shall dig up the copy [Elliot Cohen sent me] and write what I hope is a suitable reply.... But I do think you overestimate Fiedler when you call him a heathen. A little belief in small clay gods would be an improvement over his 180-degree negation.

In a sense, however, publication of the article took some courage. *Commentary* belongs to the American Jewish Committee, which is dominated by [Judge Joseph] Proskauer who still screams out his love for Alger Hiss. Recently, my mother was introduced to Judge Proskauer who asked if she was related to the writer of that "dreadful" book, *Seeds of Treason*. "Have you read the book?" my mother asked. "Of course not!" said the judge.

I put aside this letter for 15 minutes to hear Joe McCarthy. He did a fine job of putting Truman and [Philip] Jessup [a controversial Truman appointment to the State Department which McCarthy and other Republicans were trying to block] on the spot. They will yowl "smear" but Truman's attack on Joe entitled him to a nationwide hook-up on all networks....

Tomorrow I return to the salt mines, *les brodquin es pied, le flambeau dans la main* [Boots on the feet, torch in the hand], to quote Ronsard. Out of context, of course, but us anti-Communists always quote that way.

Ralph

September 17, 1951
Dear Ralph,

This has to be brief and to the point. Last night I had a curious call from Bob Cantwell [book editor of *Newsweek*, who had been deep in the underground Party. Once a close friend, Chambers had used the name Lloyd Cantwell when he broke with the *apparat* and was flee-ing from GPU (KGB) retribution]. I don't think it was curious just because I had already gone to bed and was partly asleep. Once or twice before, I have been on the point of mentioning him and certain relevant matters to you, but refrained on the theory that talking about unfortunate things only gives them a false life. He still seems to have some very odd ideas which do not conform to reality.

The burden of his call last night was that he would like to see me at once in New York, or come down here to discuss *Witness* with me. He had, he said, just had lunch with David McDowell [the book's editor at Random House] and the next day with Wilder Hobson [a former *Time-Life* editor who had moved to *Newsweek* as back-of-the-book editor] and they had left him with a feeling about the book that I found it quite impossible to get coherently from Bob. Now, ungener-ously, I don't believe they left him with any feeling about the book at all that was not first latent in his own mind. Long ago, he communi-cated with me and made it clear that he did not want me to say any-thing [in the book or in testimony] that could hurt his job. From what you have read of the book, you will recognize, I think, that I've actu-ally stretched a point to let him off the hook. Otherwise, he scarcely figures in the book. In any case, there's nothing I have to discuss with him *in re* the book.

Now I'm going to end up in a way that you will not expect; for most unkindly, I am concerned not so much with Bob at this point as with myself. I'm worried about his reviewing the book [and] I should much prefer to have you do it, or failing that, Raymond Moley [a for-mer Roosevelt brain-truster and a power at *Newsweek*, for which he wrote a column, because of his friendship with Vincent Astor, the magazine's dominant stockholder]—in which case it would go out of the Book section and receive treatment under politics. I suggest that as a protocol "out." I don't believe Bob can do a good review of it. By that I mean that I think the whole subject lies close to one of his personal storm centers and that whenever he approaches that field all the instruments begin to whirl around and the magnetic needle always points due south. I don't think I have ever been into his story with you; he was much more involved than I have ever admitted to anyone—and am trusting you to shield him too, for he needs his job and has suffered terribly. Lest there be any misreading of this he was never involved directly in espionage. But we were close friends throughout 1932 [to] '40....

Arthur Koestler [in correspondence with Chamber for years] offered to review *Witness* for the *Times*. No doubt worse could happen. But I don't want Koestler, much as I esteem him, for I don't think he has any apparatus for comprehending what *Witness* is about.

This is a disgusting kind of letter. Here I am caught up at once in the review racket. But in the end, I'll just say: the dickens with it— though Bob has given me a nasty turn. Yet there are few men to whom I owe so much....

Whittaker

18 September 1951
Dear Whittaker:

Nora has her nose buried in Betty Bentley's book [an account of her years as a courier for a Soviet spy ring]. I've read a few pages of it and find it, much to my surprise, adequately written and lacking the bad taste of the magazine pieces.... To my great shock, Bob Cantwell gave it an awful review, full of the kind of sneers you might expect from an [ultra-liberal] and implying that all this talk about spies and spy rings is so much nonsense. Fortunately, the review was killed for space.

I had intended to talk to Cantwell about it and then held off. It has gotten increasingly difficult to talk to him about anything. There is a fuzzy wall of cotton wool around him which I find it impossible to penetrate and often I don't even know what he is talking about. There is little I can do about it....

From your letters, and from things you have said, I have gotten a strong feeling that you have reached a point in your book—long past the point of no return—where you must find the radio beam and come in on instruments. I think you've been circling the field, waiting for the fog to clear, instead of bringing the plane down. I have had this feeling for some time. And for some time, I have debated the wisdom of speaking up.... It is only because your book is of such importance to me and to all of us that I venture to set down on paper what is, after all, only an intuition. But you will know whether I am right or wrong. There is an old, old Spanish ballad my mother used to sing which described a night so dark that *"ni pedro ladraba, ni gallo cantaba* [nor dog barked, nor rooster sang]." This, I think, describes the creative process. In that night, each man must carry his own torch.

If the Baltimore papers did not carry the item, you may be amused to learn that Angus Cameron [chief editor who had turned a great old publishing house into a semi-adjunct of the CP] has "resigned" from Little, Brown. The salesmen revolted, joined by John Marquand [Its most successful author], forcing the resignation.... One part of the story didn't hit the papers. The head of the firm, Mr. Thornhill, had been hearing rumors about Cameron. Being a proper Bostonian, he investigated by asking Cameron if he was a Communist. Some weeks ago, Thornhill told Cap Pearce, "Cameron gave me his word of honor that he was not a Communist. If I ever find out he's lying, I'll fire him on the spot." Which puts Thornhill several cuts above Dean Acheson, in integrity if nothing else. If Edwin Seaver [a Cameron associate at Little, Brown] and some of the other boys are eased out, then it will mean that the Communists have lost a major beachhead in the book field. I am not too sanguine. One grape of wrath is not a vintage.

Ralph

Sept. 20, 1951
Dear Ralph,

Everything about the gift [*The Poems of St. John of the Cross*, translated from the Spanish by Roy Campbell]—the saint, the poetry, the
translator, the giver and his tact, has given me a great contentment
from the moment I opened the unexpected package. Thank you very
much. Few books could have meant so much…. Though I am the
farthest from a sunny vista, I do not intend to concede the battle
until the last paladin falls. In this connection, I do not believe that I
ever told you, but the world will presently learn via *Witness* that
I tried to kill myself shortly before the grand jury indicted Hiss.

I failed for a curious reason, if one is interested in explaining things
only by natural causes. At the time it seemed outrageous to me that
with two infallible poisons growing wild on my farm, my need had to
fall within a season when both were gone. One of them is the water
hemlock, a pasture bane. The other is a mushroom, the *amanita phal-
loides*, commonly known as the Destroying Angel. Its principle is
phallin, from which there is no antidote. Curiously, I have not seen an
amanita since 1948. But yesterday, just outside my door where I write,
I found that two, and only two, beautiful specimens had grown overnight. A piece no bigger than a quarter will relax any mortal coil. I
picked them you may be sure, for in our age, the prudent husbandman
packs not only the fruit of the earth but its poisons against the brutality
of history from which our only safeguard is the intelligence of stupid,
ignorant, treacherous and wicked men. I have not only Acheson in
mind. It is also necessary to remind ourselves of [Clement] Attlee [the
socialist prime minister of Britain], from time to time.

Lest there be any question in your mind, I hope never to have to
use the Destroying Angel; but I do not mean ever to fall alive into
the hands of the Communists. It must have enabled Goering, alone
of the defendants, to follow the Nuremberg proceedings with a grim
humor, knowing that the capsule was concealed in the toilet bowl.

Two things I must ask of you: (1) never to mention the mushroom; (2) not to mention the suicide attempt until the book is out where it can be read in its proper context. It would do me much harm, I think, if known in advance.

I am now planning to drive Ellen toward Northampton on Saturday afternoon.... Somewhere on some shore or another we should be able to find a night's lodgings.... I'm told the trip takes 3 hours from Hamp (as we old grads say) to N.Y. If you still wish me to stop over, expect me about seven or eight as now scheduled. If you have other plans, don't worry. Dunc [Duncan Norton-Taylor, a close friend from *Time*] has asked me to stop over....

Whittaker

Sept 25, 1951
Dear Ralph,

I drove from Plainfield, N.J., to Northhampton, Mass., and back to Westminster in a day. And that day Sunday. Two (and sometimes four) lines of traffic sometimes crawled, and sometimes hurtled, from New Rochelle to N.Y. The same thing happened on the skyway. When I passed that vast edifice where you live, I felt like Odysseus driven from sight of Ithaca by the land winds. Actually I was driven by the obsession and urging of finishing this MS. I got in a pretty good day's work the next day, although I arrived home about 4 AM, physically cramped and shaken....

There can be no peace for me (or anybody else) until I am done with the book. Maybe there'll be no peace afterwards, but it will be a different kind of pressure. The book says flatly that the Administration covered up the Hiss case and that a part (but not all) of the Justice Department tried to save Hiss by indicting me! Not news to you, or perhaps anybody else. But probably grounds for those who do not like it said out loud, especially when I am the speaker. It also says that foreign policy (that is, survival), from which the Hiss case is inseparable, is the only issue facing the American people, and that it is up to them whether there is going to be a nation called the U.S., or a tradition called the West, in existence five years hence.

I think you are wrong at least as to the blind flying. Roy Alexander [publisher of *Time*] used to claim that as I writer, I am a natural instrument flyer. As a flyer, he should know. I don't. The real problem is fatigue—fatigue and interruptions. Then, the last yards to shore are always the hardest. But shore is in sight. Soon I want you to read the whole works if you have the patience. I doubt that it will be what you hope or want. It probably never is. I am not Augustine and I don't like Rousseau, and the times and problems differ.

Can you help me with a small problem? I want the Latin words for the sentence: "Paetus, it is not painful." It can be found in Pliny's letters, in a letter (I think the first) to Nepos (not Cornelius). There you can also read the story of which it is the great line. And you will see how it is, as now planned, the last line in the book. I do not mean to tell the story. Simply to quote the Latin without translation and without any exploratory reference. It is my one wilful obscurity. I think that it is justified and that a man who tries to be consistently understandable has a right, at least once, to be deliberately obscure. Let the world re-discover (it once knew) who Arria Paeta was, and why she came to say: "Paetus, it is not painful."

It occurs to me that it might be much simpler if you could find an opportunity to go to Brentano's and find downstairs a Pliny in the Loeb classics, with Latin and English....

Whittaker

October 2, 1951
Dear Whittaker:

The volume of Pliny which contains the letter you want is not available at Brentano nor at Scribner.... But I did go to the library and

the words you want are—*Paete, non dolet.* Any little acts of mid-
wifery you want us to perform return a magnificent glow of helping
at the *accouchement.* Incidentally, the whole Nepos letter spreads a
veritable panorama of interpretation, widely applicable to almost
every phase of the basic problems contained within the Hiss-
Chambers case, as they call it. Did your phenomenal memory record
that as well as those last words?...

Nora

October [?] 1951
Dear Ralph and Nora,

Lattimore a best seller and Pliny out of print! If Odoacer and Alaric
had not thought writing effeminate, I suppose our shelves would be
stacked with their *Ordeal by High Office* and *I Liberated Rome.*
Nora, thank you for the *non dolet.* I had no intention of giving you so
much trouble. I would not have thought it possible that Pliny would
be out of print. I sometimes think that the most revolutionary, I
mean counter-revolutionary, slogan we could raise would be: compulsory Latin in grade school; compulsory Greek in high school. Right
there the cultural arteries have been cut. How can a nation lead the
war against the Communist East when the nation has sponged from
its mind the culture it is fighting for, particularly when its only knowledge of it came from books; itself having missed the medieval experience? A somewhat tortured sentence, but I'm a classical illiterate like
the rest. How horrified Americans would be if someone said to them:
the difference between the Communists and you is that you want the
same things, only the Communists want them more so.

[In discussions of what was happening to American education,
Chambers noted that schools were increasingly doing away with their
cultural curriculum on the ground that students did not find it "relevant." The result was that in attempting to keep students amused with

"social studies" and other trivia—and reducing the work, and knowledge, load of teachers—schools themselves lost their "relevance" and
dropping out became increasingly prevalent, leading to the situation in
which it became fashionable for students to get low marks.]

   This is admittedly another one of the grey weeks. I do not ask
what underlies the mood, grey weather, perhaps. But I know what
precipitated it: a piece by J[oseph] Alsop [influential syndicated
columnist on defense and foreign policy, and putative conservative]
in the current *Sat. Eve Post*. Above all, a picture of Truman and
Atleeeee [*sic*] shaking hands. Despite what the news camera has
done for me personally, I insist that the photographic history of our
time is infinitely more honest and revealing than the written record.
Remember Eisenhower getting the news about [the firing of]
MacArthur? Or Mao Tse-tung (Mousie dung, my son calls him) in
Moscow. And that imperishable picture of Acheson and [Moscow
purge trials prosecutor Andrei] Vishinsky shaking hands in a kind of
Masonic grip. I think that perhaps just a book of such shots without
comment would be a shocker, that is, if there were more than a
handful of us to shock. The Alsop piece is worth reading for the
adjectives that draped the British socialists in it—multi-motored,
over-all-lands-prevailing [Hugo] Gaitskell; oak-ribbed, omnibenefi-
cent Atleeee; polouflosboisterous [Ernest] Bev*in*—to clown a few of
them. More restraint about [far-left Aneurin] Bev*an*, and even some
mean cracks about the left Laborites blackmailing the Gov't. But
then it's like that *New Yorker* cartoon with the strip-teaser prematurely loosening her girdle and the stage manager whispering: "Don't
give the plot away!" Aneurin is giving the plot away and slicing himself in, to boot. I am afraid Nye is a comer; he knows what Lenin
knew: in a revolution it doesn't so much matter who stands with you
as long as you know where you stand. Nye knows. The Alsop piece
also shows a holiday shot of the Bevans off to visit Comrade Tito—
"one must," as [T.S.] Eliot noted about another fortune teller, "be so
careful these days." John Chambers is turning into a wag with a gift
for understatement. "I suppose," he observes when P. Jessup and

Acheson or their likes have had a conference, "I suppose he had to deliver the microfilm in person."

It is much nicer to consider Ralph's piece on Sacred Music, which I have read through twice. I am astonished at its knowledge (I just didn't know you knew so much about such things), and impressed by the critical discernments. I am abashed also by my own ignorance; and when you add the *Colliers* piece (very good, of course) and all the rest that's appearing, amazed at the industry. I'm just a lazy chuck. You put me to shame. The piece in *Colliers* is not so much my dish, but it's very effective and tremendously important. One such piece in *Colliers* is worth a dozen in the *Freeman*, alas, and is not just running in place. One or two more of those and you will find all the takers you can supply with copy....

How I would like to sit down and talk to you both. What is your understanding of the McCarthy situation? I have a suspicion that there's something behind it that hath not yet come out, chiefly, perhaps, because each side is carrying a loaded revolver and therefore each hesitates to shoot first.

Whittaker

I guess the current depression is the reaction to Acheson on TV: "Well, maybe he did betray China and destroy the U.S., but he sure steam-rollered the Russians in Frisco—almost as good as Tammany!" I can only repeat what I said to the *Baltimore Sun* when it phoned to get my reaction to McCarthy's first charges: "Nobody can save a nation that will not save itself."

13 October 1951
Dear Whittaker:

The phonograph is playing a Bach suite for unaccompanied violin; the sign across the river keeps repeating "Spry" first in red, then in white. In my mind at the moment, the two have some kind of tenuous connection which makes me feel both sad and silly—as if I were reading a Louis Zukovsky poem. The great placid monomania of Bach to write music and the great itching monomania of Americans to make their mark on time with trade names perhaps stem from the same source. Does this mean anything? I don't know. But it's as good a way as any to start a letter.

For the past weeks, I have carried about a desire to write to you. But I have shied away from the typewriter because it has become an instrument of Chinese torture. The drip, drip of the keys in the office and then at home has worn thin the edge of my composure. Writing, as you know, is a compulsion, like rape or the bottle. And as with rape and the bottle, the craving is never satisfied. So here I am writing.

First I must tell you that the fine things you said about my music piece shamed me. I have always given people a sense that I know a good deal because I write with definiteness.... This is true particularly about music. Though I can compose in my head with some ease, I can write it down only with difficulty. And it has been many years since I could follow simultaneously more than a couple of lines of a score, I hold forth patly and authoritatively and then my sense of sin hits me between the eyes. I dig my foxhole in the no-man's land between the Bach suite and the Spry sign.

One point in a recent letter of yours I have never answered. That is, about reviewing *Witness* in the National Affairs section. Some short time before the book comes out, I will take it up with Ken Crawford. It should not be done too early. If it were dropped into the lap of a story conference right now, it would give Cantwell time to maneuver it back to Books should he so desire. Six months ago, I could have made an open fight. But right now, I am an "extremist" in case you didn't know....

I don't know how much of the Jessup [confirmation] business has percolated down to Westminster. My *Newsweek* stories were cut and re-written till all the pertinency was taken out of them—all for fear of giving aid and comfort to Joe McCarthy.... The State Department's

performance was so scandalous that even the Democrats in the
Senate realized it. But if we have won, the victory did not come for
want of stupidity on our side. For once we had the luck of children,
saints, and rogues. [Harold] Stassen did not crawl when the liberals
said, "Boo!" [and] if the Republicans had any sense now, they would
bind up Acheson's collection of lies [during the hearings], delivered
under oath, and insist that he be cited for triple perjury. They would
get nowhere, but it would have a tremendous effect. [Democratic
National Chairman] Boyle resigned tonight. In his last photos and
newsreels, Truman has looked haggard and confused. The attacks are
beginning to tell [and] the scandals will grow bigger, not smaller. One
topnotch fighter with a little knowledge of judo could finish Harry off.
But all we have in the Senate is a bunch of Hessians.

On a more personal level. Nora and I spent a couple of very pleasant hours with Anne Ford [an editor at Little, Brown who had
worked for Chambers at *Time*]. We liked her. We discussed the affair
Cameron at length. And she spoke of one Whittaker Chambers with
great affection. What particularly pleased me about her was the
slightly ironic air of the conspirator which so many intellectual
Catholics carry about them. "Conspirator" is the wrong word—but as
an approximation of what I mean it must do. Perhaps it might better
be described as the slightly mocking attitude of the man who seems
to stand alone but who knows that he stands in the center of an
armed phalanx. The Church is founded on a rock; they know it; that's
their little secret. I guess they're right to enjoy it.

Ralph

25 October 1951
Dear Whittaker:

...Thanks to Ralph putting the bee on Blanche [Finn, a researcher at
Time, who stood with Chambers in the old battles within the

American Newspaper Guild, and a loyal friend of Chambers] for *Time's* complete factual error on the Gustavo Durán case [in a cover story on McCarthy] we hear that they have undertaken a large research on the gent. Since Durán and [Indalecio] Prieto [foreign minister of the Spanish Republic and, in 1951, an exile in Mexico] both agree that Durán *was* in the SIM [*Servicio de Informacion Militar*, an adjunct of Soviet military intelligence] it appears that Mr. Bob Baker [the writer of the story] has torn the Luce pants.

Since he will read this, I shouldn't say so, but Ralph is doing a magnificent, if reluctant job, on *Spies, Dupes & Diplomats* [which began as a book on Sorge but had now moved beyond the story of a single Soviet spy ring to an account of its consequence and ramifications during World War II]. We hear that Major General Willoughby [General Douglas MacArthur's Intelligence chief] has called in John Chamberlain to edit his unpublishable manuscript, also on the Sorge case.

Nora

[In a cover story which was to demolish Joe McCarthy, *Time* made scores of factual errors, most of them contradicting the research prepared by James Shepley, the magazine's Washington bureau chief. One of the most grievous referred to the charge by McCarthy that Gustavo Durán, a veteran of the Spanish Civil War who was subsequently employed by the State Department, was a Communist. *Time* cited this as an example of McCarthyite smear. Though the magazine's research carefully detailed Durán's history and noted that he had served in the SIM, making him both a Communist and a Soviet agent, *Time's* story stated that not only was he not a Communist but that, in fact, he was an anti-Communist. Durán's admission that he had been in SIM, which carried out Stalin's purges in Spain, was corroborated by Sr. Prieto. Despite this, *Time's* editors refused to admit that the magazine had falsified the record in order to counter the "McCarthyism" of McCarthy. The whole story was told by Nora de Toledano in *"Time Marches On McCarthy"* which was published in the *American Mercury*.]

Nov. [?] 1951
Dear Ralph,

When I was alone, you walked beside me. And when I was without a roof, you sheltered me. You gave me yours. That makes a difference in kind between you and most others. There were a few who were with you—a man and wife whom I do not believe I have ever mentioned to you, and in proper time, Tom Murphy [the assistant U.S. attorney who was prosecutor in the Hiss trial]. But that was the innermost circle, and not many names could be added to it. That is very good, too. Others occupy widening circles raying out from that. Maybe there will be more and more circles. That, of course, is what I am talking about—what now seems the distinct possibility that there will be wider circles, all or most of which must be received as if they had been there always. No one must whisper that the newcomers were asleep in bed on Crispian's Day. But you must know, and that is why I am saying it, perhaps a little prematurely, that the distinction lives in my mind and that it is well rooted there. I know who was with me in the dark; and I know something about how men shift and surge, like sheep when a hurdle has been opened to them. If I am right in supposing that the tide has turned, and that a small but important part of the enemy is coming over, then, this is the moment for renewing my memory of gratitude to you, who do not have to come over to anything because you were always there. In my groping way, I am trying to say: Thank you, and I remember.

In part, this is apropos of the Book of the Month business, of which you heard no doubt as soon as I. It takes me a little while to

absorb such things—not that I did not see it off there in the distance
or that I did not understand its importance. But between seeing and
being there is quite a difference. I do not think that Esther is much
more stirred than I was, but it comes out in a different way. She
wants to holler, decorously and within four walls, of course. I want to
retire into my turtle shell and lock the door. I think John caught my
feeling best at the supper table when he suddenly said: "We're going
to stay right here in these hills and take care of our sheep." It exactly
echoed what I had written the day before, of which he could not possibly have known.

[The selection of *Witness* by the Book of the Month Club was so
important to Chambers because it marked a tremendous change in the
BOMC's orientation and way of operating. Though *Seeds of Treason*
was the third biggest seller of 1950, the Book of the Month Club did
not even list it in its Book News. For the BOMC reflected the generally liberal coloration of the publishing business and the book-review-
ing fraternity. That it selected *Witness* came as a shock to the
still-dominant Hiss forces and a tremendous surprise to conservatives
and anti-Communists. Selection was a more important indication of a
creeping change than the serialization by the *Saturday Evening Post*.]

Anyhow, this is my mood on the morning of what appears to be an
important change of affairs. Perhaps Nora was right when she said
that this is another period of history. I hope so; I'm tired enough to
welcome one. I'd be very happy if you read the book through. Most
of it is in bound galleys now, which I am correcting; and there are
important corrections coming from elsewhere. One apology I must
make: No *Paete*, no *non dolet*. It was the last line of the book, and it
survived through the submitted copy. But the day after I sent it in, I
telephoned to kill the line and the line before. My editorial rule is
that if there is the slightest sense of doubt about something, it is
wrong; then: kill it. I had a slight sense of doubt about *Paete*, so, poor
fellow, he's killed for the second time. But I'm sorry to have given
you both so much trouble about it.

I'll be in New York, so I trust. Clothes chiefly are holding me up.
I suddenly discovered that I need a whole outfit. Of course, I put off
getting one; in part because I have been busy; in part, because I
dread few things as I dread buying clothes. But I guess I must go to
Baltimore today and fancy up. I'm glad to see that the dawn has not
broken. A few hours of grace.

I'm not saying anything about your book today, beyond this. I'd
like to read it, and I think that now I have time, if you wish. I committed myself some time back to write an essay on St. Benedict for a
book [*Saints For Now*, edited by Clare Boothe Luce] in which
Graham Greene and E. Waugh are also hagiographing. The publisher is poking me up, and while the essay will not be overlong, it
requires a good deal of reading, and a good deal of careful work.
I hope to write a book pitched to the same historical area, to be
called something like: Benedict and Hildebrand—From Subiaco to
the Air Raid Shelter. A little unwieldy, perhaps, and I doubt that
most publishers will know that it is the book their readers are waiting
for. It is. For the crisis of history has much longer roots than is commonly supposed. All this began by way of saying that Benedict stands
chiefly in my way of reading Toledano: chiefly but not seriously.

Whittaker

14 December 1951
Dear Whittaker:

Your letter arrived this morning and I read it hastily over Nora's
shoulder before leaving for the office on the run. I am answering the
spirit of it now, since it remains at home.

It came as a gift to me in this Season when modern man does
penance for the birth of Christ. It came as the best kind of gift—the
undeserved gift. In the deeper ways of living, I gave you nothing, and

you gave me much. Or perhaps "giving" is the wrong word. I do not know how much you gave, but I know how much I took from you.

Few men are chosen to pass through the dark night of the soul. But there are some of us… who clank about in our skeletons in a grey twilight. In the murkiness, there is no certainty of the Good and the Evil which lurk. Until I got to know you, I had known only one other person who truly lived in confidence of God. That was my grandmother, Estrella. During her last years—the years in which I knew her—she prayed in her closet, to use an archaic but true word, and she brought security to at least one of her grandchildren. But that was a long time ago. And a child's faith, unless it is molded to ritual, vanishes easily.

It vanished more easily with me because I was born of transplanted cultures. From the moment when my maturity began I struggled in the grey twilight. Somehow, through you, I returned to my belief in God. It was not the God of comfort I had known as a child. The vague forms of Good and Evil acquired some definition. Perhaps I was ready, at the moment you stepped through my doorway and shook my hand. Perhaps you cannot believe in God fully until you take one great preparatory step of understanding. You must know the Devil—and before I came to know and love you I had seen the Devil. So I accept the gift of your letter, though I do not deserve it. God bless you.

Ralph

1952

January 22, 1952
Dear Ralph,

I haven't time for more than a line to note that on my last visit I
certainly wasn't much help to you. I was sick and it took about all the
strength I had left to get up to Riverside Drive. More important, my
own wars had left me so close to the snapping point that I had no
comfort or courage for anyone else. A bad way to be. But that is how
the struggle leaves me sometimes. Especially when we are collecting
our forces to rise to a new situation. Specifically, I am rallying mine
to re-enter the active struggle which my book must precipitate on all
sides. The lawyers talk in terms of libel. That is almost beside the
point. The problem for the C.P. and other exalted powers is how to
destroy an active opponent—myself. It is a simple political problem.
How it will take form, how it will turn out, whether I shall have
strength to meet, I do not yet know. At heart I have always sensed
that the cause of the West is a lost cause so it is a hard cause to
defend, for it keeps defeating itself.

Whittaker

April 6, 1952
Dear Ralph,

There are few things in this world that I so little like to do as wound you. But I think that I am elected because nobody wants to do it, and everybody is looking at me and I must act to save you possible embarrassments. Perhaps I have been too tardy, anyway.

So here it is, straight-edge: the *Chicago Tribune* has switched reviewers of the book I wrote. I have heard the new man's name, but do not recognize it and have forgotten it. In any case, it scarcely matters—somebody in Washington. I am certain that this is not Babcock's [editor of the *Chicago Tribune* book section] doing. I have seen enough of the correspondence to make reasonably sure. Apparently, the Colonel [Robert R. McCormick, owner and publisher of the paper] acted. Apparently there was nothing that Babcock could do. There isn't much that I can say, either, except that I am sorry to be the occasion of this. I am also the real loser, of course (not that that weighs), for you are, obviously, the one man in the country from every relevant point of view uniquely fitted to review that book. And you are shut out! It is, as if you did not know it, a most curious world, and not one that a man would willingly take up his quarters in, being happy enough to shuffle through the dance to the end.

I am very sorry to have to be the one to bring this to your knowledge on top of all the disappointments that you have had. I can, however, make a very self-serving suggestion to you, which for my sake at least, I hope you will entertain. It is to treat the book and interview me for the *American Weekly* [the Hearst syndicated Sunday magazine] or whatever it is called. I believe that you and I could give them quite an interview and it would let your voice be heard. Moreover, the *American Weekly*, for my purposes, is worth many *N.Y. Times* Book Review sections. Please consider it, and, if it is not offensive to you, consult [David] McDowell about it.

During the day I came up to visit with the grand jury [investigating further ramifications of the Hiss case and the infiltration of the government by Communist agents], and I stopped in at *Newsweek* to have lunch with you. I did not realize, until the receptionist said you were at home, that it was Tuesday [a "weekend" day on news-magazines]. The grand jury business seemed to me strictly silly, signifying little or nothing—my presence being due chiefly to the fact that I write for the *Sat. Eve. Post*. Winston [Churchill], too, now. My family asks: "What will the *Post* do when they lose both of you?"

Bear up. It's all an unweeded garden. But there are greater matters than the *Chicago Tribune*, and we may come to them, though at the moment I don't know what they are, either.

Whittaker

[I had sought to review *Witness*. But all doors had been closed to me. The *Chicago Tribune*, for whom I had reviewed books in the past, was a last resort. Willard Edwards, the Washington Bureau chief, who had covered the congressional hearings and was the paper's expert on Communist activity, wanted the prestige of reviewing the book. The *American Weekly* proposal was overruled by William Randolph Hearst, Jr., who had always stood in opposition to me, for reasons personal.]

16 April 1952
Dear Whittaker:

Since yesterday, I have been reading at that book you wrote. I have reached the section headed "The Hiss case" and so I stop for the time being. By now I know how much of yourself you have put in the book, and perhaps how much of myself I can find in you. There have been passages which touched me and others that have brought tears to my eyes. And there have been moments when I was glad that it has not fallen to me to review the book. For how could I have resisted the temptation to start my piece with "Diamonds, diamonds you are throwing out of the Party." [What the mother of Benjamin

Gitlow, a Communist leader, had said at the Party conclave which
expelled her son.]

You should have been a Spaniard. For you have in you that linkage
of pride and humility, that dignity encompassing emotion, which
comes from the sense and knowledge of place, that faith which moves
not mountains—steam shovels can do that—but the soul. And you
have what may be the most important thing of all—and the thing
which will perhaps save humanity—the sense and cognition of continuity. By its very nature Communism is a form of cannibalism which
must destroy and eat its past. There is poetic validity to the fact that
we shall never know if the Communists or the Falangists murdered
Garcia Lorca. Perhaps it was this I meant in a poem on his death
when I wrote: *Esta noche / en el ruido bruto / de los fusiles / se corta la
plata / voz de Espana. / En el polvo de la carretera / se apaga / la luz
de Espana* [This night / in the brute sound of rifles / the silver voice / of
Spain is cut, / in the highway's dust / the light of Spain is extinguished].

Like a Spaniard you know that death is never ahead of us, but
always behind us. The voice of Spain is the *saeta*, for it mourns not
the Death but the Resurrection of Christ: the singer stands not
before the Cross but at the empty Sepulchre. The soul of the voice is
Iberian; the accent of the song is of Jew and Arab, and it passes
between gypsy lips. When the heathen pick up your book, they will
feel the vibrations of the *saeta*, just as they will smell the faint breath
of incense. They will not be deceived by the purely American ring of
its laughter or the power of the American earth.

Ralph

April 29, 1952
Dear Ralph,

I have been trying to find a way to tell you how much your letter
after reading the first half of the book meant to me. But there come

weeks when almost without any relief, I am beset by the awful stupidity of everything. Weeks on end, I mean, and perhaps "beset" suggests too much life. The feeling is more like being caught in rising, tepid, brackish water in which drifts whatever noisomeness you choose. One is waterlogged and pulped in that and occasionally swallows a mouthful of it....

And that is why I do not write. I have never quite overcome my sense of shamelessness with which, particularly just after the second Hiss trial, I inflicted on you my glum reactions to that shocker. I do not want to do that again. But you, Spaniard, are the only person to whom I am tempted to do so.

Whittaker

There must be six fully adult men and women in the U.S. Is it too much (to echo Nietzsche) to ask that they should communicate with one another?

11 May 1952
Dear Whittaker:

So very belatedly I answer a letter which should have been answered immediately. But I have been out preaching to the heathen—in Chicago and at Dartmouth, among other places. And though this has not taken up all of my time, it has drained me of energy to a remarkable degree.

And then, in some ways, your letter was unanswerable. For what it said I could only accept mutely, as all love and friendship must be accepted mutely. Only on one point can I speak up—to reproach you for feeling that anything you may write me could possibly be a burden.

As you know much more than I do, in any deep relationship there is no distinction between giving and receiving. Both are one. I have never given without a sense of receiving; I have never received without a sense of giving. This, perhaps, is life's third law of emotion. When the night has closed in and you have written, you have done me honor. At night the heart speaks true....

I remember some nights during the war, walking guard, the rifle heavy on my shoulder—pacing hour after hour among the looming cannon and hearing the light scuffle of small animals. I remember other nights, standing in a gun embrasure of the old Spanish fortifications and hearing the surf wash against heavy stone. Under the feeble Virginia moon or the deep night brilliance, I learned many things about the voices that speak and the voices that answer. And I learned that these voices must be captured on paper, if only to be exorcised.

I dwell on this because your ordeal by book review has still to come. When the friendly reviewers and the unfriendly reviewers have had their say, you will wonder why you wrote the book. And you may be angry and you may despair.

In advance of those bad hours, I can say this: You wrote the book for those who love you, for those who cannot put into words their time's anguish, for those who feel but cannot utter. They will not write book reviews, but they will bless you.

If the spirit moves you, write to me then, *aunche es de noche* [though it be night (from a poem by John of the Cross)].

Ralph

May 23, 1952
Dear Ralph,

Cantwell's review [of *Witness*] is truly a shocker. It seems to me that if the least responsible editors of *Newsweek* had put their heads together to devise how best to blur the meaning of the Hiss case and the book, and do the maximum disservice to both, this is what they would have come up with. In the *Saturday Review* it is to be expected. In *Newsweek* it is paralyzing. It leaves the mind with the hopelessness of a struggle which cannot get an intelligent, let alone clement, hearing even in a part of the press which is not supposed to be hostile. But the same fatality dogs the literary stage as dogged its legal stages. It always flew in the face of history. For nobody can save a society that cannot save itself.

Excuse me for shouting. It does me good.

Whittaker

[The review by Robert Cantwell was not only unintelligent but disingenuous. It was motivated largely by Cantwell's fear of being linked to Chambers or to his own Communist past—which he kept well hidden from his editors—and from deep trauma and a discordancy of emotion. For this reason, he withdrew from those of his fellow editors who had strongly anti-Communist views—and he subsequently reviewed a novel by me, *Day of Reckoning*, with such obvious unfairness that it was killed and another review substituted by *Newsweek's* top editors. Cantwell was close to a nervous breakdown and left *Newsweek* not too long afterwards.

Whittaker Chambers had been given an honorary Doctor of Laws degree by Marquette University in Milwaukee, and I had been invited to the ceremony. Victor Lasky, riding on the fame he borrowed from *Seeds of Treason*, had moved on to Hollywood with an assignment from Hearst to do a wrap-up of the Communists-in-Hollywood situation but spent his time getting sandwiches named after him and hobnobbing with the bigwigs, as the columnist Murray Kempton with happy malice noted. The "Forrest" mentioned below was Forrest Davis, a freelance writer of some note (and a friend of Chambers) who had invited him and me to an evening at his New York apartment.]

27 May 1952
Dear Whittaker:

...This is my third attempt to write you since that evening at
Forrest's. There has been much to say but little heart to say it....

First: The *Newsweek* review. The very blankness with which my
first objections were met discouraged me from pressing the point.
Cantwell was not around, and he would not have understood me
anyway.... After the review had appeared, I bumped into him in the
corridor. There was a look of pleasant anticipation on his face. I said
nothing more than a "hello" and walked on. To reason with the hopeless is hopeless. Second: The *American Weekly* piece. Results are
zero. I proposed it to the Hearst people and there it died. Since my
relations with them are at present of a delicate nature, I have not
pressed the matter....

It has been inexcusable of me not to write immediately to tell you
how we felt about the Doctor of Laws. The Church does itself honor.
I had hoped to be able to accept the invitation sent me. I tried to find
some kind of assignment in the vicinity of Milwaukee, but with no
success....

Fourth: Victor Lasky writes from the Coast that he "bumped into"
Walter Wanger at the race track, that Wanger wants to make a movie
of *Witness* which would start out with you doing a reading of the
"Letter to My Children" [the opening of the book], and that I should
ask you if you are willing. As an inducement, he offers to do the
movie treatment himself, with my "help." I am writing to Vic, even
before hearing from [him], and answering with the Hollywood translation of *jamais de la vie*.

And now about the reviews of *Witness*. I know they must be caus-
ing you pain and anger. I know how full of distortion, stupidity, and
viciousness some of them are. But you never hoped to reach people
by reviews. And as bad as some of them are, they will cause people
to read the book. It stands inviolate.... It will do what none of us

have been able to do in years of trying. Its greatness is untouched.
The impact of the book can already be measured by what [Lewis]
Gannett [of the *New York Herald-Tribune*], [Orville] Prescott [of the
New York Times] [Professor Sidney] Hook, and others will say about
it. They are visibly shaken, and it shows. Ironically, Granville Hicks
[a former member of the Communist *intelligentsia* and in the 1950s
a professor at a women's college] comes closest to revealing what the
impact on him was. I have not read all the reviews, nor will I, but the
pattern is clear.

Ralph

June 12, 1952
Dear Ralph,

I will not write you. I must not write you. I must finish writing St.
Benedict by tonight. I will write you. That is because I had the bad
luck to read the *Newsweek* review of your book [*Spies, Dupes &
Diplomats*] at breakfast. (Esther insists on leaving these things
opened to the pertinent page at my place.) I think, perhaps a word,
any kind of word, from a friend might come handy.

   On the whole, I think you got off better (though not much better)
than I did. I presume that the same writer wrote both reviews, the
same editor tinkered them. In *Newsweek* in 1952, we are up against
the same Bog that I beat my head into so long at *Time* in 1939. It
isn't the Communists, though they make use of it. It's the little circle
of oh-to-take-serious-anything-but-the-authentically-serious-things-
of-life, by which they mean the ballet and New Orleans jazz. Also,
novellas about decay under the magnolias, off-side history of the
Civil War (Did Lincoln murder Stonewall Jackson?), and the Oregon
pioneers vs. Big Chief Running Water. These nasty jabs come, I suppose, under that stricture Harry Scherman [head and founder of the

Book-of-the-Month Club] sometimes scratched at the side of my copy: "Unnecessary spot of hate not in tone with the rest of the book."

I searched my soul about that one and was sorely troubled by it. But only the other day I noted that St. Jerome was in the habit of referring to St. Ambrose as "a deformed crow." Since then, I have taken heart again. I cannot however avoid the impression that some subtle shift in feeling has occurred at *Newsweek* and that there exists there one of those quietly functioning *axes* whose little group has only to sit in shelter and knock off the ducks as they fly over. The ducks never know what hit them and few can detect the operation because the operators use Maxim silencers, and, if questioned, say: "Firearms? Is that the new Stravinsky ballet with Marmaldoff's marvelous *entre-chat*?"

[Chambers, of course, sensed what was happening at the magazine. Little by little, the writers who had pulled *Newsweek* into the black and given it status as the "honest newsmagazine" had been eased out or lost influence. With the Yale-oriented Malcolm Muir, Jr., taking over as executive editor, the magazine began moving into precisely the orbit described by Chambers, and like *Time, Newsweek* became a journalistic jungle. Editors like Kenneth Crawford were being shunted aside, and top writers like me given "the treatment"— that is, seeing their stories written and rewritten, then killed.]

I haven't read your book (with its beautiful unearned inscription) beyond the foreword and the first chapter, which I found the absolutely right way to begin the book. At that point, the world closed (in some rather pleasant ways in part), and my reading has been saintly exclusively, for Clare [Luce, editor of *Saints For Now*, the book for which Chambers was contributing a piece on St. Benedict] is on my neck. Poor woman, she has cause to be. Once I am out of the woods, I hope to return to Toledano.

Henry Regnery very kindly came to Milwaukee while I was there and we had a long talk. We discovered that independently, we had both concluded that the important book, from an enlightenment and marketing point of view, was a glimpse of Felix Frankfurter. We had also concluded that R. de T. was the man to write it. I strongly urge you to. The problems are enormous and the importance of it I don't have to spell out for you. This is only one of several matters I should like to discuss with you, for that is not only what Henry and I talked about that touches you and others. Also in Milwaukee, I had several talks with others who know you or of you. I should like to tell you what we said. I believe that by now Henry will have written to you about a meeting of minds well-screened for compatibility. I put it this way: "a small group of right wing intellectuals who, intellectually, do not eat with their knives." With another mutual friend, I discussed another small meeting of minds on a slightly different plane. On these matters I think we, too, should sit in shelter and use Maxim silencers, such being the climate of the time.

[None of these meetings ever took place, in most instances because "right-wing intellectuals" were either too fragmented or too busy with other matters. Chambers, however, continued hoping that he could bring about such a mobilization, but with no success.]

Where are you going for vacation? If you should care to rough it, there is a choice of two empty houses here…. It would be highly primitive, and, I think, highly peaceful….

Whittaker

Later: While Esther and I were West, John dutifully wrote on a calendar the names of people who telephoned. There was one that meant nothing to me. But since I am seldom eager to receive calls from strangers, I passed it up without asking about it. But yesterday my curiosity got the better of me. "Who," I asked John, "is Mrs. 'Delabanana'?" He was hurt as usual when his spelling problem arises. "Why," he said, "Mrs. de Toledano, of course."

21 June 1952
Dear Whittaker:

...It was good to hear from you, and good to know that the combined
flood of bile and well-meaning stupidity which washed over *Witness*
had not gotten you down. Whatever may have been said by the critics
of your book, I'm sure it kept them nervously awake. And when they
slept, they probably muttered, *"Vicisti, Galilae"* ["You have won,
Galilean"].

My own book, as Cap Pearce [of Duell, Sloan & Pearce, the pub-
lisher] predicted, was poisoned on page 20 of the *New York Times*
book section—a nastier job than the one perpetrated on *Seeds of
Treason*. But this time, most of the people who might have rallied to
its support were elsewhere detained. People like [Arthur] Krock,
[Eugene] Dooman, and [Richard] Allen wrote warm and flattering
personal letters, with a "no quote" injunction. They made me feel
like the mother of a stillborn child who must derive comfort from
those who assure her that its toes are perfectly formed. I have tried
to lock the whole thing out of my heart, but Nora and Cap persist in
their belief that [the book] is alive. [They were right, because *Spies,
Dupes & Diplomats* made the best seller lists.] The *Newsweek* review
did not bother me as much as it might because I know that Cantwell
has gone quietly mad; he lives in a world of dervishes.

The Frankfurter book which you mention would, I think, be a bad
idea. It would require tremendous research. It would not sell, or
even find a publisher. And it would jeopardize my already shaky position at *Newsweek*. No matter how carefully documented and delicately written, it would be branded as anti-Semitic. At the first clap
of B'nai B'rith thunder, most of my friends would run for the storm
cellar, leaving me defenseless. If I were disposed to destroy myself, I
would write a book on Mrs. FDR, to be titled *The Madame*.

Regnery wrote me about the meeting of minds. He did not say on
what ground these minds were to meet or what language they would

speak. At the moment I tend to share Karl Hess's preference for long knives—but perhaps the mood will pass.

My mother used to sing me a sad, old song of the *Andaluz*: *Pariome mi madre, / N'una noch' oscura, / Ni pedro ladraba / Ni gallo cantaba* [My mother bore me / On a dark night / Nor dog barked / Nor rooster sang]. Until the dog barks and the cock crows, I shall be useless. But I envy you your Benedictine task....

Ralph

June 25, 1952
Dear Ralph,

...I pass hours of bitterness which can only be called crippling. While they last, and they come unexpectedly and last for long times, half a day, a whole day, I am unfit for any good use. I woke at dawn the other morning, and, half asleep, felt a sense of pain and distress, and slowly realized, as I wakened more, that it's because I was sorry that another day had come and I that I must live through it. At that point I knew we had entered a new plane.

One of these bad times overtook me, at Medfield, the other day, and I lay down, thinking: "It's just because I'm tired." But, of course, it wasn't just because I was tired. Presently, the thought came to me: "I'll drive to Berryville, to the Trappist monastery there, and stay overnight with the Brothers." I wondered why I had not thought of it before and regretted that I couldn't get into the car at once but must wait a few days. An hour or two later, I wondered: "Why did that seem such a brilliant idea? The Trappists will be just like everything else. What can they do? What can they know?" [Chambers had taken temporary refuge with the Trappists on previous occasions and had, in fact, a correspondence with Father Thomas Merton, coinciden- tally a classmate of mine at Columbia in the 1930s, and my art editor for the college magazine.] For there's nothing wrong with you or me that a little comprehension couldn't cure.

It's the realization, as they spell it out over the years, that this side is in its plight because of its stupidity, and cannot get out of it because of its stupidity, and cannot help anybody to help it because of its stupidity—it's that that's killing us. And the stupidity of well-meaning friends is far more destructive than the malicious mischief of outright enemies. When you have to face the fact that they cannot, simply are unable, to act like grown ups, then you know that it's hopeless and all that we have tried to do is for nothing. The Spartans on the sea-wet rocks sat down and combed their hair. After our braver fashion, we wear ours short, and, as my pictures show, I never manage to comb mine, anyway, so I guess we'd just better sit and brood. Now that, I submit, is a low-spirited page. Don't imagine that I don't mean all of it....

Listen to me: the Hiss case has not ended. It will end in tragedy for me. I knew it from the day it began because I know, as an irreversible truth of history, that situations such as the case highlighted, cannot exist unless the stupidity that causes them also makes it impossible for those involved to solve them or help others to solve them. The stupidity is of a piece and it's a smothering blanket. It's the token of the doom that everyone connives at because he can't really grasp what he is doing. No one is so doomed as the handful who understand what is happening. The simple fact is that the great tide of feeling was always with Alger Hiss, at least among literate people. Even yet, the slightest hint that he may be innocent brings it quivering to the light. Give them Barabbas. They want what they can understand, and they understand that his hair is always combed. *Your* Barabbas is different, but it's the same mob shouting, and the same sage rabbis egging them on. I suppose you know that those two great Pennsylvanians, Judge Musmanno and Clarence Pickett [ultra-leftist head of the American Friends Service Committee], have each

denounced me; Musmanno because I called Communism a great
faith, and (the one term such minds can understand) made some
money by writing a book; Pickett because I don't represent the
Quakers, or so [Senator Richard] Nixon tells me. [At the time, Nixon
turned frequently to Chambers for counsel and support.]

On second thought, I agree with you about the Frankfurter idea,
at least at the moment. But this isn't supposed to be a helpful letter.
This is a letter to exchange honest low spirits—a prolegomena to the
possibilities. The letter that issued from your mummy-case was so
toneless that I thought you should see how brisk we can be at the
end of the night. A Baltimore doctor said to me not so long ago: "The
trouble is that all the brains are on the side you deserted from." He's
a violent anti-Communist, but, as you see he's not stupid. Nothing, I
gather, has so upset people as a line in the book that I scarcely
thought twice about: that I had left the winning side for the losing
side. Did they have to wait for me to tell them that? *Circumspice*
[look around and see]. Meet me in the crematorium.

Whittaker

3 *September 1952*
Dear Whittaker:

If I have not written before, blame it on New York, blame it on
Newsweek, blame it on the gloom which has permeated everything
since we got back [from four weeks on the Chambers farm]—but do
not blame it on me. I have tried to write…. The fact of the matter is
that we are both de-gutted…. We live *senza infama e senza lodo*
[without shame and without praise], as Dante put it. But now that I
am writing, I can say that we were very happy in Maryland with
Whittaker and Esther. For me it was a time of peacefulness in which

much bitterness slipped out of me. For Nora it was a time of positive
and active joy. For the boys, it was a liberation.

You will forgive our rudeness, I know…. In this tremendous room,
even a whisper has the sound of doom.

Ralph

10 September 1952
Dear Whittaker:

This cold night will turn us all to fools and madmen. That says it
much better than my last letter—and it has a slight patina. What I
did not say, so full was I, can only be said baldly and badly. Not that
we are grateful for the month of shelter—that's easy and obvious—
but that we can understand the effort on your part and Esther's in
getting the house ready and as comfortable as it was… and in making
it seem as if nothing was given which is the most generous form of
bestowal. I did not say this in my last letter, nor will I say it now.

Lasky, to move to simpler topics, has gotten married. The girl is
pleasant to look at and seems to have the less complicated of the
Protestant virtues. The wedding ceremony itself was something else
again. Marriages should be made in strict religious fashion or quickly
at City Hall. This one was held in a blocked-off corner of the cocktail
lounge of the Weylin Hotel. [Federal Judge Irving] Saypol officiated,
Angela Calomiris [a witness against the Party at a Communist trial]
set off innumerable flash bulbs, and the chatter from the nearby bar
drowned out the responses. [*New York Post* gossip columnist]
Leonard Lyons came appropriately late. The Black International, for-
tified by [movie actor] Charles Coburn, and a few stray newspaper
people, minor celebrities of the publishing world, etc., were all on

hand. At one table, off to the side, Vic's parents and family sat quietly, neither abashed nor aggressive but proud. They seemed like good people. There was much champagne. I left moderately sober—I had to get back to *Newsweek* to finish a story that night—but the mood of the wedding remained and poured out in an acidulous poem [the last line of which had ended my previous letter].

Joe McCarthy's overwhelming [primary] victory will come as a shock to the official GOP. He swept everything before him and left Uke [John Chambers's nickname for Dwight D. Eisenhower] high and dry. Now both the general and Dick Nixon will have to eat crow. Dick has behaved very badly not merely toward Joe, but toward himself. After he ducked on the McCarthy issue, Dick met with me and Frank Conniff [advisor and ghost to William R. Hearst, Jr.] and Jack Clements. At this meeting, it was decided by all of us that Dick would correct his former weaseling statement. I was to write him a couple of pages which he would incorporate into his speech before the Connecticut Republican convention. Dick ignored what I had written, ignored the McCarthy issue, and has never explained to us why he went back on his word. I'm not particularly important, but Clements swings a lot of weight [as vice president for public relations for the Hearst Corp.] and so does Conniff. These people are no longer happy about Dick. If the Republicans win [in November] it won't make any difference. But if they lose, Dick is going to find himself minus a good many friends—including most of the [anti-Communist] California crowd which elected him [to the House and Senate]. They, too, are furious.

Fortunately for all of us, everything seems to point to one of those upsurges in American feeling. If I can read the signs, this will be a Republican year despite Uke and his advisers. All the great liberal targets of the conservatives seem to be doing badly....

Ralph

September 17, 1952
Dear Ralph,

When I went to bring back some of the stuff at the Creek farm, I was
a little shocked at its barrenness.... But I'm glad if you were at all
tranquil there.... Besides, we're not good hosts. As you saw, we carry
a work load. As I may have observed to you before, we're not very
sociable; at times we're rather savagely unsociable. I get scores of letters assuring me that I was mistaken in supposing that I was alone
during the Hiss case, or that I am so now. Good souls, they miss the
point clean. It isn't a sob for my loneliness, but an amazed comment
on a society in which nobody came forward, in particular, no one
from the churches. Being alone doesn't disturb me.

You are the only person I know who supposes that the Republicans
are going to win. Oddly, I think you may be right. I sense it, and I may
be wrong. I also think you worry too much about Nixon. If he wins,
everybody will be for him. If he doesn't, it doesn't matter.

Incidentally, [Bill] Arnold in Nixon's office phoned while I was
milking. I got to the house, hot and interrupted, to learn that the
Penna. Republican Women had requested the Senator to get me to
address them in November. "In *November*," I asked, not sure that I
had heard right. "After the election," said Arnold. I said that, *after*
the election, my cows would regrettably be claiming my full time and
that I must decline. So runs the world away. So long as it runs fast
enough, I do not see why I should be displeased.

Whittaker

5 November 1952
Dear Whittaker:

At a time like this, we can only say simply that we love you and need
you. This is too much and not enough, yet in its own way it sums up

the deep and lasting bonds which have tied us together these years. In the raging turbulence of these times, we have seen you lash yourself to the wheel. We have clung to you; we have drawn strength and courage from you....

I say "we" meaning Nora and me. But there is a much greater "we" who have huddled fearfully below decks. Consciously or unconsciously, they know what they owe you. Consciously or unconsciously, they took cognizance of this debt in the polling places yesterday.

For the first time in many decades, we have a fighting chance. The enemy has lost a battle which began on the 3rd of August, 1948 [the day Whittaker Chambers gave his first testimony before the House Un-American Committee]. All these weeks of the campaign I have wanted to write you these words. I have known all along that the New Dealers would lose. But it has been an inner conviction, an intuition I held virtually alone. The only guarantee I could give was that I *knew*. And I could not peddle this faith indiscriminately. I knew because I also knew that, paradoxically, there are times in history when the free will of men moves inexorably to an inexorable conclusion. As each phase of the Hiss case unfolded, it brought its own consequences. Eventually, they added up to the slow stirring awareness among Americans of the [forces] that lurked behind [Adlai] Stevenson [the Democratic presidential candidate].

For all of this, you are paying the price.... God love you.

Ralph

[Shortly after the election, Whittaker Chambers suffered a serious heart attack. It was at this time that he was called upon to make cuts of some 150 pages in Witness for an English edition and to decide whether to permit a French edition which took considerable liberties with the book. I was asked by Esther Chambers, at Whittaker's request, to take on both responsibilities. "Tell Ralph," Whittaker told Esther, "that he is the only one I would trust to do the cutting."]

Nov. 13, 1952
Dear Nora,

I hope Ralph won't regret taking on this big order for the Chambers.
It is a great deal to ask of you. I enclose [the letter from Nicolas
Bentley, editor at Andre Deutsch, the British publishing house]. The
more I think of it, the less I like cutting the foreword ["Letter to My
Children"]. It seems to me something should remain whole. Also it
should remain as Whittaker placed it. [Bentley had proposed, for
some reason, that the "Letter" run at the end of the book, which
made little sense.] Still the pattern of the whole should be as
Whittaker conceived it....

Esther

[undated]
Dearest Esther:

We have the letter from Nicholas Bentley with its suggestions for
cuts in Witness. I must say we were delighted with the whole tone of
it—the attitude toward Whit and toward the book. This is not merely
the courtesy of an editor toward an author.... Your note about the
"Letter to My Children," with which we agree, gives me the feeling
that you may be uneasy about the nature of the suggested cuts in the
book generally.... But since [Bentley's] whole feeling is of such deep
understanding and deference to Whit's needs and desires in respect
to the book, I'm sure there will be no boggling at whatever we feel
must remain in the English edition and which he thought safely
expendable. Remember, he says, "I hope I shall have avoided cutting
anything which might seem to diminish the force of your argument
or lessen the book's spiritual appeal." Also, "If you feel that the
removal of these passages in any way affects the balance or signifi-

cance of the sections concerned, I hope you won't hesitate to restore them."

Dear Esther, our only regret in taking this on is that anyone should have to do it for Whit.... You and I know that the love Ralph bears Whit, the identity of their interpretation of the case, the intimate knowledge of the events and their significance, together with the technical skill necessary, which I don't think come together in any one other person who might be thought to qualify for the task, assures that the job will be done scrupulously, efficiently and with humility. And with gratitude that we are allowed to "help" at a time when no friend of yours can feel anything but helpless.

Nora

[The cuts made by me left the "Letter to My Children" untouched and as a foreword to the book. Certain passages, such as those describing the erratic behavior of Chambers's grandmother, which I had originally advised Chambers to cut from the American edition, were deleted. So were references to matters which would be lost to British readers. Other cuts were made, a paragraph here and a paragraph there, basically not vital—in all some 150 pages. Through it all, Nora and I felt that I was cutting living flesh, but the job had to be done. What the editors of the proposed French edition had in mind was a mangling job, with whole sections of the book clumsily rewritten, and the moving "Letter to My Children" gutted. I offered to cut the book down to the length sought by the French publisher but refused categorically to allow the proposed rape of the text—and the deal fell through.]

1953

San Juan, Puerto Rico
1 January 53
Dear Whittaker:

I held back from writing to you during your illness because I did not
wish to intrude myself at a time of pain and withdrawal. I could
rejoice at your recovery and perhaps communicate in ways other
than on paper.

Sitting here, looking at the blue water of the Condado lagoon—in
a land so crowded by its vegetable nature that the soul shrinks—I
suddenly felt very much alone. This note is a reaching out of hands as
we enter a terrible and hopeful New Year.

Ralph

Feb. 4, 1953
Dear Ralph,

They let me write a little, lying on my back. The result, as you see, is
not very different from my usual script, which some people suppose

that I write with my toes while standing on my head. I have not only
been bedded for three months, I have been pretty well fenced off
from the world—a blessed state that I have happily connived at. This
is by way of saying that I have lost track of you, too. Since that bleak
letter at Christmas from the Caribe Hilton [in Puerto Rico], I don't
know what has happened to you. I hear rumors, but I hope they are
not true. I think that you should dig in at *Newsweek*, that the more
unpleasant they become, the more blandly busy you should become.
I know it is a difficult role and mine may be a counsel of ignorance.
But these jobs on the established journals are the only ones worth
having. They pay best in prestige and money. They offer the best
base from which the Right may utilize the changed climate to infil-
trate and practice a little cell fission. They enforce a standard of performance, too. Those others—the *Mercury*, *Freeman*, etc.—they are
not in it. Nor will anyone like them be until somebody comes along
with the idea which will capture and give voice to the change of
mood in the country, if it is as authentic and permanent as the ripples
which reach me seem to portend.

I don't know how to go about thanking you for what you did in the
English edition of *Witness*. There were no others to whom I could
turn to with such trust. And so the heavy task fell on you. I expect to
come back to this later. Now let me just thank you.

I'll spare you the critical notes except to say that it's been up and
down and rather disheartening. The worst was rather recent, sudden,
and without apparent cause. I suppose the miracle is that such a tear
in such a place ever heals.

Whittaker

6 February 1953
Dear Whittaker:

Now I am alone—at *Newsweek*—with only the small, shy noises of
the cleaning women around. This kind of pleasant desolation always

makes me itch for the typewriter, for it was in this kind of quiet that I did my freest writing when the words poured out easily and full of emotion. The mind begins to pick at words, to sort out too much, when we grow older.

Is there news to send you? Perhaps I am inhibited because it has been so long since we spoke. I have wanted so much to go down to Westminster, but I've known, too, that any visit would put too much strain on you. And this wish to see you has bottled up the words.

There is much to pass on. Andre Deutsch—through Nicolas Bentley—seems well pleased with the cuts I made in *Witness* and even more pleased by the stirring of interest in England. They have increased the press run on the first edition and I foresee some rousing times on the sour little island. Rebecca West is girding up her loins for action and reports that the Jowitt people are running into difficulties. Someone there read his MS and put his foot down, so his lordship was forced to do some re-writing.

Nora is busily conspiring with [David] McDowell and others. Bob Humphreys [former National Affairs editor of *Newsweek* who had moved on to take over the public relations of the Republican National Committee] has promised to put any congressmen or senators on the floor to deliver speeches denouncing the Jowitt book. [George] Sokolsky [then one of the most widely syndicated columnists] got INS [the Hearst International News Service] to interview Jowitt and the worthy peer delivered himself of several provable lies. My one concern is that we stir up so much fuss that the book will be noticed where it may have passed off in perfunctory fashion had none of us taken the trouble to agitate against it.

Closer to me, though only because I am involved actually… is the revivification of the *American Mercury* under Jack Clements [vice president for public relations of the Hearst Corporation] who did not impress you but is, in an uncomplicated way, a terrific guy. With money at his disposal, he has begun to give it direction and to print some of the right things. If he can push up the circulation, he will double the number of pages and pay writers more. This will help further in bringing in readers. If by July—and this is off the record—it shows signs of real success, I may step in as editor.

[Earl Jowitt, a former British Lord Chancellor under the Labour government—a post somewhat analogous to Chief Justice of the United States—had embarked on a book, financed by friends of Hiss in the United States and Britain, attempting to demolish the case against Alger Hiss. Rebecca West, author of such political books as *The Meaning of Treason*, had become a strong partisan of Whittaker Chambers after reviewing the British edition of *Seeds of Treason*. It was Rebecca West who had alerted Nora and me of the Jowitt project and helped to dig up a considerable amount of information involving the Labour peer and disclosing how he became involved in writing his book.]

Meanwhile I languish at *Newsweek*, which gets worse and worse for me. I do my work, write the stories as I am told to write them, and go home. This is not precisely the kind of role I had hoped to play or that I was repeatedly promised by [publisher Malcolm] Muir, but it has become a question of open rebellion or a well-sealed mouth. So far, I have kept my yap shut. This sounds grimmer than it is. It is not grim at all, merely a little grimy…. None of this is very meaningful, and perhaps that is my real problem. I have reached that point in my life where I need something to do, but no one else seems to think so. So I turn out pieces to order for Clements and scratch myself.

The death of Stalin… has made the wrong kind of dent on the consciousness of the government. The newspapers are full of nonsense, some of it inspired by the enemy. There is confusion everywhere. Our masters in Washington are acting as if the idea that Stalin might die had never entered their minds. We have moved from an era of scurrility to an era of platitudes. Only the terrible and destructive rationality of the Russians saves us. God love us all.

Ralph

10 February 1953
Dear Whittaker:

I returned this evening from a flying trip to Palm Beach—there, speech, return—to find your letter. Nora announced it to me with a great surge of joy, and I felt it, too, for contact has been reestablished. That you should feel concern about me, at a time when all concern should be over you, caused me a... twinge of remorse. I have tried not to write to you, and particularly not in specifics, because I did not want to burden you with a weekly or monthly fever chart.

Fever it has been, for my position at *Newsweek* remains the same. I've been passed over on money and place; and even when fulfillment follows hard on prediction, my judgments political and otherwise are ignored.... I do well to be angry, but not unto quitting. All the reasons for staying on are, of course, operative. But the most important is financial. It is bad enough to cry out in the wilderness without tossing away the knapsack and canteen. I shall remain.

This may amuse you. For my sins, I was sent up to Bronxville [New York] to interview Allan Nevins [historian and Columbia professor]. I was pretty certain that he would be hostile to me. Once he had ushered my into his living room and sat me by the fire, he said, "You're the young man who wrote that book about Awlger [*sic*] Hiss, aren't you?" "I am," I said, and here it comes, I thought. "Very good book," Mr. Nevins, said. "Many of your colleagues at Columbia wouldn't agree," I answered. "Why not?" Mr. Nevins, said, as if the idea had never entered his mind. "They think Hiss is innocent," I said. "Really?" Nevins said, seeming surprised. "Why even old [Professor James] Shotwell [one of the aged stalwarts on the Columbia faculty who had defended Hiss in the early days of the controversy] admits Hiss is guilty." So perhaps a new wind blows through Columbia.... Certainly the Republican victory is having its effect.... Eisenhower is showing... less of a tendency to compromise than many of us thought possible. Even Joe McCarthy seems to be developing some sense. Perhaps it's catching.

[I spoke from experience. After *Seeds of Treason* appeared, I was on the Columbia campus and dropped in to see Professor James Gutmann, my old adviser, who refused to shake hands with me because I had written "that terrible book about Alger Hiss." Subsequent to this, I was enlisted to write for a newly formed book-review syndicate which included Irwin Edman, head of the philosophy department at Columbia who had remained a very good friend of mine over the years. When Edman's colleagues learned that he was partici-pating in a venture that included me, they put sufficient pressure on him to cause him to resign as a contributor, though he did so with apologies to one of his former favored students.]

I have left until the end two things: (1) *Witness*. I do not deserve thanks, for the feeling that we were being of service, at a time when we could only stand by, more than made up for the service itself. If we did a passable job of cutting, it was only because we were so thor-oughly convinced that not a line should be cut. Procrustes, I imagine, was not a happy man. (2) You. Here I have no words. If you have heard Marian Anderson sing, "But the Lord is mindful of His own. He remembers His children," then you know....

Ralph

Feb. 13, 1953
Dear Ralph,

Our letters crossed. Yours told me all I needed to know—and, of course, a bonus of much more. The kind of hanging on to a limb you're having to do at *Newsweek* is scarifying to the mind and proba-bly very good for the soul. At least, it teaches a military virtue—how to out-patience and outlast the enemy. I went through about two years of it at *Time*. During much of that time the managing editor would not speak to me. It's tough but it teaches a man to be ascetic. And you sometimes win. There are intangibles and unpredictables.

I'd batten down the hatches and express few opinions while writing the unexceptionable copy.

The last thing I said to the vice president [who made periodic visits to the Chambers farm] as he left us was: "No one will know from us that you were here." For I hold that the second head of the state must be given freedom to speak or remain silent on such matters. He was seen at Westminster where he stopped to buy gas and sign a ten dollar bill for the attendant. But to all public guesses that he was here, we answered nothing, or "not to our knowledge." Now, I discover that the vice president has told Victor Lasky about his visit. Let the trumpets sound!! So I guess I am free to tell you that he did a very nice thing and dropped up with his wife the Sunday after Inauguration. Naturally, the doctor's orders could not apply here and we had a long talk.

That "let the trumpets sound" line is the echo of a passage which I recently read and which seemed to me quite good: "The bank of the Rubicon is crowded with men imploring to be bought. Let the trumpet sound!" Author: Benito Mussolini. Almost like Washington.

[In his early days at *Time*, Chambers had to cope with the large Communist cell on the magazine and its friends among some in the upper echelon. My problems at *Newsweek* were of a different nature. I had risen rapidly in the magazine and had brought it both attention and money with *Seeds of Treason*, a *Newsweek* Bookshelf book and a recipient of part of the royalties. *Newsweek*'s publisher and chairman of the board, Malcolm Muir, had always resented those members of his staff who achieved independent fame. In my case, moreover, there was an element of "social" anti-Semitism involved which had led to the firing of other staffers. And it should be noted here that Chambers felt that Richard Nixon stood between him and a reopening of the Hiss case. He was convinced that a Democratic victory would put him in jeopardy.]

All the rest I know is about snowdrops blooming and lambs being dropped and cows milking. In two months, the geese will be heading back north, and I will hear them in the night—if I can hear. The Liberals! What have the Liberals got to do with life?

Whittaker

[undated]
Dear Ralph,

...If you are not in a laughing mood, this will scarcely amuse you. But there is something wonderfully uproarious about [Victor] Lasky's doing a book on Mrs. Eisenhower [a gossip column item]—perhaps because I suspect that he is just the right man. I still think you should do one on Mrs. Roosevelt for which I now have a brand-new title: *My Daze*.

I think the Republicans are almost caught up with the realization that it is hard to reverse a revolution—especially if you don't know what the revolution is about, and they wake up in the middle of the midnight realizing that *la révolution, c'est moi-meme*.

Whittaker

Feb. 16, 1953
Dear Ralph,

...Let's really give Lord Jowitt the old heave-ho. His book is in galley proof now. Let Nora consider herself a committee of the whole to see just how much hard fact can be gathered about milord here and in England. Let's see if we can influence the reviews of his book.... I believe we can. I believe it's a little test. If Owen L. [Lattimore, chief Soviet "agent of influence" on U.S. Far East policy] could, why can't we? I'm sick of lying here doing nothing. The Redcoats are coming. Let's pepper the pan.

Whittaker

11 March 1953
Dear Ralph,

I have vowed to restrict my letters to a few lines. More than that goes to words and gloom, which is well founded perhaps, but must be a great bore to those who are not even invited to share it, but have it forced on them.

Let me try to take up briefly the main points you raise. Andre Deutsch etc. Oddly enough, nobody has ever told me who Nicolas Bentley is. I assume he is Deutsch's editor. Independent reports reach me of a stirring interest in *Witness* in Britain. Do you have Rebecca West's address? Many thanks to Nora for her activity in the matter at issue [the Jowitt book]. I think it goes so far beyond any personal interest of my own, that a campaign is justified. I also think that good hard facts about Lord Jowitt, his biography, personal and political history and connections, are worth yards of unkind comment, however justified....

What could I have said to you that made you think Clements did not impress? He impressed me as a man of a good deal more force and directness than one commonly meets. I also thought that he was happily without the pretensions that wrap most intellectuals in grave clothes, and that he was kind, a virtue not popular now, but that I find important. What his horizon is I do not know....

[John A. Clements, Kentucky-born and with County Clare antecedents, had at age sixteen enlisted in the Marines during World War I, and had been commissioned in the field at Chateau Thierry. After the war, he and other ex-Marine officers organized a small but highly effective Intelligence operation which, though technically unofficial, reported only to the highest level of government. As I knew from some of its reports I had seen, the organization had even penetrated the Kremlin. I had, in fact, even taken on several small assignments from Clements, including one which involved Igor Gouzenko, the Soviet code clerk who, on defecting, had brought documents out of the Soviet Embassy in Ottawa, which broke open the spy ring operating in Britain, Canada, and the United States. While with Hearst, he took over the editorship of the *American Mercury*, building up its circulation and its prestige. He resigned when the owner and publisher, Russell Maguire, insisted on publishing an anti-Semitic editorial he had written.]

I think I like (from your point of view) the *Mercury* editorship idea. I am not quite sure because I am not sure of the *Mercury*, of which at all ages I have had a poor opinion. But, perhaps this is an inevitable next step for you, above all because you must step somewhere. I still think that the infiltration of the big journals has it all over membership in the little clubs. I also appreciate the difficulties and believe the struggle will be long. No doubt, a combination of both tactics is the answer.

Need a Books editor? I do not mean a book review editor; I mean somebody to run a Books section—always, in my opinion, the No. 2 spot in any well-kept journal. Well, I don't know that I would want it, even if you wanted me—I'd have to know more of what is planned and possible, political and otherwise. But I'm for sale for certain kinds of things. I doubt that even the *American Mercury* would buy me, so that I hope I shall not seem unduly acrid if I mutter with Robinson Jeffers, "Shine, perishing Republic." It is perhaps simpler to say with you that "I have reached a point in my life when I need something to do, and no one else seems to think so." There seem to be a number of us, not the stupidest men abroad, either, but at war with our environment. That teaches the tough virtues, but also estrangement....

One trouble with the Right is that, few in numbers, we are as scattered as wild flowers—you in New York, [Willi] Schlamm in Vermont, Regnery in Chicago, I in Maryland—to mention only a few. I still think that we have to take to the simple congress method that the Bolsheviks used. We have to meet together, somewhere, at some fixed place, if only to disagree. We might also find that we had some common grounds of thought and action.

Whittaker

13 March 1953
Dear Whittaker:

This will not be a full answer to your letter; Friday morning [on a newsmagazine] is no time for that. But just to take up a few points you make:

Bentley is a novelist and mystery writer who doubles as Deutsch's editor. He seemed fairly knowledgeable on the Hiss case—and what he lacked in facts, he made up in intellect. We intend to smite the Earl of Jowitt hip and thigh.

Clements is an old newspaperman and a fighter. He has more intellect and subtlety than he will admit, but he is not a topnotch editor, mostly because he lacks the sense that a magazine must be, with each issue, a unified thing. But he is doing wonders with the *Mercury*. From time to time, he has asked me, very tentatively, if you would write for it. The tentativeness stems from his tremendous respect for you; you are very high in his pantheon of Americans. Last week, he called Nora to ask if you would write a piece on the raising of blooded cattle. I think he got the idea from *Witness*, a book he reads and re-reads. He would be delighted if you would write about anything for him, but he is diffident.

For the time being I have put aside all political things and set myself to reading the *Quixote* from beginning to end. So much of it I had heard quoted and discussed in Spanish as a child—and so many of the tag lines were family language—that the Samuel Putnam translation's gentility does not get in my way. In one of the very funny scatological passages, Sancho, who had lost control of his sphincter, tells Quijote, who was urging him to bestir himself, *"Peor es menea'llo"* ["It is worse to stir it up"], and this gives me a slogan for these days. Next week, I'll take up my lance again.

Ralph

Mar. 15, 1953
Dear Ralph,

...A couple of months ago, I decided to read *Don Quixote*. I had read about a half of it at other times. I thought I would never have a better chance to go to the end of the road with the knight of the Rueful Visage. I got into the third volume, enjoying it all the way. But then I bogged down again. One of those long incidental tales stopped me. I decided I might as well leave this Manchan world, without facing *Quixote* step by step. I think I had the rather uneasy feeling at times that perhaps all that I had succeeded in doing was to tilt at windmills. I have the wonderful Shelton translation—an Elizabethan job—so that it's free of latter-day gentilities.

Whittaker

[Starting early in March, Nora and I with the assistance of David McDowell (of Random House), Hearst columnist George Sokolsky, Rebecca West in England, and others, began a campaign to expose a book then in the works by a British Labour peer and former Lord Chancellor, the Earl of Jowitt. The book purported to be a legal analysis of the Hiss case and trials, but was an ill-disguised effort to vindicate Alger Hiss and a frontal attack on the American legal system—as well as an artillery salvo on the person and reputation of Whittaker Chambers. We and others had been alerted of the Jowitt effort and some of its curious ramifications by West and others in England. Most of the correspondence with Chambers—and the brunt of the counterattack—was carried by Nora who set herself up as the Committee for the Defamation of Lord Jowitt.]

March 14, 1953
Dear Whit:

I had planned to wait until I had a solid body of facts re: his lordship, and then to astound you with the tangible results of my diligence.

But I suspect that a little of David McDowell's enthusiasm may have led you to feel that the sum would be merely organized vituperation. We will have plenty of that, I'm sure, when the time comes.... But at least the people or acts I motivate will be based on facts.

I got McD into it for the simple, and I think essential, purpose of getting our hands on the galleys [of the Jowitt book]. Because without them, the Chamberses and the Toledanos and such are merely speculating. Speculating from a sure instinct, it is true, and from a deep understanding of the meaning of this book (I call it the Fourth Trial). But in this case, we can enlist even the anti-Chambers but open-minded groups, provided we can demonstrate that among other things the book is an attack [à la Alistair Cooke] on the American judicial system, the press, etc. I have no doubt from [Jowitt's] review of *Witness*, and other source material, that the book will be just that. But I want to have the proof, of course. Galley proof, if possible. McDowell has not succeeded yet....

But in the process [of attempting to get the galley proofs], several interesting things have come to light. The main thing is the extraordinary secrecy with which Doubleday is surrounding the book. The word we got from England about the "damned nonsense" opinion may be one explanation. Others, of course, leap to mind in droves. Incidentally, it would help me if you could tell me the source for your original statement that there were galleys at the time you first wrote us about Jowitt. Doubleday, you see, claims there aren't any yet!

In preparation for the real work, however, a number of important facts have been reestablished. (1) Jowitt is demonstrably a liar, and a poor one, on how he came to write the book. I have established this beyond question and we can give him a real blow with it to start off. (2) He does not have, nor admit to having, the government briefs and judicial rulings [in Hiss's attempts to claim "forgery by typewriter" in his move for a new trial]. Since the Hiss lawyers do their case no service in the handling of the facts, Jowitt will be completely off base there. We plan to make the facts available to all parties....

For the time being, we are not making public use of this because
Rebecca West is very touchy about being quoted, but she [writes] a
number of the details we have had, including that "somebody" in the
English [publishing] firm "had kittens" on reading the MS, etc., etc.
From another source we learn that Jowitt was very hard up, received
a large lump sum.... The second informant is being coy because he
learned about the book while a house guest of his lordship. But if we
put this together with the peculiar Doubleday behavior, not only in
response to requests for galleys, but in announcing the book originally, and with [Horace] Mangies's [the Random House lawyer]
remark to [David] McD the other day that Jowitt is "in the depths of
senility"—well, what is your feeling?

Nora

Mar. 19, 1953
Dear Nora,

...Sokolsky now has the galleys on the book, so that point is covered,
I presume. For your information, a friend of mine had the galleys
and reported to us on them about a month ago. I also have a live
hunch, again without access to facts, that much of the trouble coming
from the New York Bar Association [passed on by Nora] stems from
Stephan Duggan, who was angry when I would not omit mention of
his brother [Laurence Duggan, named as a participant in the Soviet
apparat, who jumped or was pushed from the window of a New York
office building prior to the trial when it was rumored that he would
testify for the government] from *Witness*....

A woman named Hannah Arendt has written a vicious and distorted attack on the ex-Communists using me as the butt.
Commonweal is lending its columns and has sent me tear sheets and
asked for comment.... I won't answer the letter at all since I suspect
[the magazine] wants to use my reply to print my name on the cover

in heavy type. Miss or Mrs. Arendt appears to be one of those
Central European women who has read too much and has nothing to
sustain it except an intensity which shakes her like an electric motor
that is about to shake loose from its base. This piece seems to me
very unjust, the premises largely flimsy, and the conclusions largely
preposterous. What did I ever do to her? I never set eyes on her.

Whittaker

Mar. 19, 1953
Dear Ralph,

Nora telephoned tonight and suggested a tactic that featured threatening Doubleday with a libel action over the Jowitt book. I need not
tell you that bluffing (the point of the tactic) is very dangerous unless
you are prepared to go through with your bluff. I do not intend to
sue Doubleday or anybody else anywhere, at any time, for anything.
No intimations of any kind or degree that I intend to sue are desired
by me and I must disavow them should they be made.

That's one point on bluffing. Point two must be on the worth of a
tactic in which you are trying to bluff the enemy into thinking you are
going to do exactly what he wants you to do. If I were Doubleday, I
would pray for a libel threat, because it might jack up a book which
may well be a commercial dud, or at least have little sale, to a considerable sale. Let's block that talk about libel actions, here or in
England, before it makes us look very sorry, indeed.

I think that equal care must be used in the matter of congressional
speeches, though here the danger is less, I think, because the only
interest I can imagine a congressman having in the Jowitt business is
to twist the lion's tail. Besides, my initial alarm about the matter was
quieted when you said that you would write the speeches. But I do
not think that a speech by Senator McCarthy would help anybody
except Senator McCarthy. I have no objections to helping him, of
course, but not, I think, on this occasion.

My original prospectus called for assembling *facts* about Lord
Jowitt and the circumstances of his book and its provenance, and perhaps, his review [of *Witness*] in the *Journal* of the N.Y. Bar Ass. These
facts I supposed, could then be fed out to reviewers, columnists, publishers, and others who might find them helpful in dealing with Lord
Jowitt's book. This, in my opinion, still sets out the frontiers of what
should be done. Beyond that is a no-man's land where only the
extremely imprudent will venture. The pleasant land of book reviewers and columnists and books about the Hiss case is very different to
that dark and bloody ground where the Hiss case itself begins, where
the multiform toils and lairs of the law begin. It is one thing to have
observed it; it is something else again to have been through it.

So forgive this letter if its tone seems peremptory and brisk. These
are great affairs, and my inclination to bluff them or otherwise play
games is to trifle and may lead to trouble. Let Sokolsky fire off a salvo.
Let whoever will follow suit. But do not threaten anybody, in any way.
And, in any case, it must be borne in mind that one danger of any strategy is to make important a book which, outside the intellectual gopher
warrens of New York and similar sinks, will pass almost unnoticed.

I know how generous your indignation is, and what personal loyalty prompts your proposals. But it is the function of general staffs to
be cold-blooded. Even you do not know just how cool a head I had to
keep in the Hiss case, how many things I had *not to do* or say.

I have made an effort to spare you the darker moods of the last few
months. Do you think I care whether I get out of this bed again or not?
I would like to see my children started in life, and they are close to the
line. But I know that we cannot take care of all such matters and must
leave an unfinished job, sooner or later, in any case. We never really
know what is best. I would like to spare my wife.... Moreover, I don't
like the mere physical sense of dying, not the pain, but having my
breath choked. And I love too much the earth and its creatures and the
evening and morning light.... Do you think that, otherwise, I care

whether or not I die tonight or tomorrow?—but not the slightest bit.
What, then, do you suppose I care about Lord Jowitt?

You see, there is one land for which we need only the simplest of
passports. God has given me one out of infinite mercy. It is in my left
side. I have only to run upstairs to use it.

Whittaker

COMMITTEE FOR THE DEFAMATION OF LORD JOWITT
22 *March* [1953]
Dear Whit:

Sokolsky, who has already given two columns to his lordship (and as
usual missed the point in a couple of places) let me read the galleys
under dire promises to keep the fact secret. We will be able to do so
and still get some factual information based on the reading out to
where it will be useful by referring to our advices from England.

You are quite right in your hunch that Stephen Duggan enters
under the cloak of the N.Y. Bar Association. But far more directly
than you suspected. Horace Mangies was asked by Whitney Seymour
to see that Jowitt received *Witness* [for review]. Much as I hate to give
this devil his due, he seems merely to be the catspaw. You see, one of
Seymour's partners is—yes, Duggan. Also of interest is this. Tom
Murphy [the Hiss case prosecutor, now a federal judge] told me that
in all the years that he has been familiar with the *Journal* of the Bar
Association, this is the first time he recalls seeing a book review....

We already have Jowitt well hooked on his motive for writing the
book. Sok had an INS [International News Service] man in England
interview him, and the results were as follows: Jowitt said that during
the second trial, "someone" in America, he doesn't know who, sent
him each volume of the trial transcript [one by one] as it was published. A nice fat goose-egg to the contestant who first spots three
clear lies in that one sentence.

Of course, no volumes were published during the trial. The ten volumes of trial transcript were not published (printed) until the case had passed the Court of Appeals and moved on to the Supreme Court, many months after the Hiss conviction, and then were published all at once. He may be able to defend a claim that he did not know who caused the 10-volume transcript to be sent to him. But he certainly knows what return address there was on them, required by the U.S. mails and the British customs service....

The genesis of the Hannah Arendt attack should interest you. She first delivered it at an American Committee for Cultural Freedom Forum [an organization set up presumable to wean liberals from their ambivalence and moral equivalence on Communism but which frequently played into the hands of the anti-anti-Communists.] The sickening story of the ACCF aside, Mrs. Arendt is married to a man whose ex-ness is in a very dubious state. As a result, in attacking ex-Communists, she is protecting a vested interest.... You were absolutely right in your interpretation of the *Commonweal* request for comment. And as a matter of fact, the attack on you has produced a great swell of protest, which I am sure you will hear about directly.

Not too peripherally, our friend Frank Meyer, who testified in the trial of the eleven Communist leaders, and whom we place in a very special category of intellectual and spiritual substance, has told us repeatedly of his wish to write to you. At my urging, he is doing so directly, and I think anything he will tell you will be very meaningful.... He is at present doing the Books section for the *Mercury*.

If a friend read the galleys, you must have a good notion of what balderdash the book is.... Ralph told you, I think, that Rebecca West wrote that it is being revised in England. We may be able to do a little psychological warfare with that against Doubleday by inquiring if the American and British editions will differ. This affects the areas where Jowitt tries to theorize away the handwritten notes and other "immutable witnesses."... A great deal of his book is based on so-called quotations from *Witness*. These are distorted where they are not out-right falsehood. Further, there are *ad hominem* attacks on you....

Incidentally, Rebecca West's address (which Ralph says should be set to music):

> Ibstone House
> Ibstone
> Near High Wycombe
> Bucks
> England

At the moment we are seething at our friend Joe [McCarthy], having read of his visit in the papers. I pray that it was someone else's stupidity and not his this time that allowed the matter to be made public.

Nora

[The mention of a McCarthy visit refers to news stories asserting that he had conferred with Chambers over the appointment to an important post of Charles (Chip) Bohlen—an appointment that McCarthy was opposing on the grounds that Bohlen was a security risk, if not worse, and on the basis of Bohlen's record. McCarthy had previously consulted with Chambers, but secretly. In this case, he wanted to create the impression that Chambers corroborated his attacks on Bohlen, without any open mention.]

3 April 1953
Dear Whittaker:

We read by the papers that Joe tried to pull another fast one. His publicized trip to Westminster shocked us—although we are not quite certain so far that the publicity was intended. Now that Jeanie Kerr [engaged to marry McCarthy] no longer works for him, everything that goes on in his office is subject to blatting. But we were pleased, reassured, and admiring over the statement you issued [denying any knowledge of Bohlen's alleged dubious past], which put Joe in his place and gave the newspaper boys no excuse to do you any damage.

Things are moving along just a little bit better these days. The conservative coalition is beginning to take shape despite [Senator Robert A.] Taft's defection to the [Thomas E.] Dewey-Ike gang. The Bohlen fight, no matter what the liberals may say, was more a victory for us than a defeat. For one thing it has put [Secretary of State John Foster] Dulles in a spot where he must walk with great care. A solid group of senators [Republican and Democratic] are waiting for him to make the least offside move and then they will pile on him. This will force his hand to keep steering right—if I can muddle the metaphor—if he wants to hold his job. It's tragic that Joe has to be the vehicle for much of what has been going on—but as in the Commie housecleaning fight, he's been the only one ready to take on our dear Uke's camp followers. And Uke has shown that he is less ready to fight than was Harry Truman. McCarthy has him completely terrorized. It would have been good to have a firm president at this time—but barring this, we may as well have one who can be pushed into line. All this is very vague and schematic unless you have been reading the newspapers and magazines with a great deal of care. And maybe you'll think this is nonsense.

Your last letter shook me so that I refrained from answering it—at least for a while. I realized that the suggestion that you threaten suit must have been a trying one for you to receive. In a sense, we were prodded into making it, mostly by Rebecca West. Your wisdom in forbidding the bluff is clear.... We find ourselves in a position of being intermediaries who can only feebly evaluate what we are called upon to transmit. So I can only say that we are sorry and add, somewhat Pollyannaishly, that the world is never so bleak we cannot fight for it.

You must know that whatever errors I make are errors of judgment and that all I do, however misguided, is motivated by the deepest affection and friendship. If my recent letters have seemed wooden it is because in the last months I have lost any driving sense.

The measure of my creativeness has been the pieces I've been writing for the *Mercury*. Spraying bushes with bullets is hardly warfare. The liberals have placed me *hors de combat....*

All this explaining is unnecessary. You know how I feel.

Ralph

April 6, 1953
Dear Ralph,

Yours was, of course, the first letter I read this morning and the first I am answering. I was so afraid that my outburst had hurt you.... There never was, there never could be, any question of your motivation. There was only the question of the expediency or hazards of a tactic which seemed to me to complicate dangerously an overall strategy which you could not be expected to know. Nobody knows it all because no single person knows all the enemy's plans or threats, and, what is quite as disturbing and disastrous sometimes, the cross-purposes of our uncoordinated allies—witness Senator McCarthy's raid. Then you have the problem of a harassed man, myself, trying to get well in the deliberate and relaxed way that alone does anything for coronaries. Meanwhile, it sometimes seems to me, the Indians are hollering under the window, arrows quiver in the wall, every so often a newsman knocks at the door and sends up a rattlesnake skin stuffed with powder and shot, while live snakes slither down the chimney and up the stairs. And, *O ces voix d'enfants, chantant dans la coupole* [O those voices singing in church]: "We want Ike."

This troubled image must do service for the facts that I do not mean to write. It is a pity that we cannot talk face to face. Because there are many facts—most of those worth discussing, in fact—that I do not mean to write. Of Senator McCarthy's "publicized" visit let me say only that, as he stepped inside our door, the telephone rang. That was the *Washington Post*, asking to speak to Senator McCarthy.

I asked how it happened that the *Post* knew he was here. The Senator, in that soft hurried voice that sometimes accompanies the flash of his hand out of the cookie jar, said that he had told an INS girl that he had one date he would not break—a visit to me. And so the news leaked back to the *Post*. The Senator's remark to the INS girl I take to be unexceptionable: his visit here was certainly one date that he would not break. The fact having been certified by his speaking to the *Washington Post*, from our telephone, the Senator and Jeanie, who was with him here, then vanished completely until Monday night or Tuesday—that is, from Saturday evening until late Monday or Tuesday, the baying press was left with no McCarthy but with the terrifying impression that McCarthy had come to see me about [Chip] Bohlen (in fact we had a long talk on the subject), and that I knew something damaging about Bohlen. I say "terrifying impression" because, of course, the press, by and large, was pro-Bohlen.

One of the recurrent oddities of my situation is that the press, which has consistently tried to discredit me and all I may say, clearly believes in its black heart that I know everything about everybody since time began, and was probably a witness to the event and have, in some pumpkin, a tape recording of those great words: "Fiat lux!"

It was pushing noon on Monday before I discovered the position I had been left in with respect to Bohlen. Hence the statement [in which any knowledge of Bohlen's secret past was disavowed]. Esther tried to restrain me, pointing out that I would seem to be letting the Senator down, and the [Republican Senator Styles] Bridges bloc, while I gave aid and comfort to the Acheson set and other natural enemies. I pointed out what the moral dilemma was and why Senator McCarthy had left me no choice but to speak out....

Item: Taft has not sold out. He is a shrewd politician. There are matters about which he is temperamentally, and I am afraid, permanently blind. Everybody is blind about something. So long as Taft retains a gift for rising above his blind spots, or for turning them to advantage, he's not doing too badly. This and the Bridges-McCarthy axis, etc., are among the matters I will talk, but not write, about: I think that tactically, you should (at least in public) keep as close to the Taft line, whatever your ultimate views may be. It gives you an opportunity to make some important distinctions about your position with respect to both chief factions among Republicans. I feel that Taft himself is making these distinctions on moral grounds. I think it is necessary to scrutinize those grounds very closely. I raised a warning finger about them in your apartment about a year ago. Recent experiences have not changed my views.

I should like to know very much what you think of [Ludwig] von Mises—as theoretician, first of all. I think this is very important, that it is the first thing that you and I and several people must make up our minds about. If we don't make them up, at least we must know very well what the alternatives are. I have in mind that group meeting which Henry Regnery and I discussed the first day we met, and which I think may now come off.

Tired. I have to stop. Tell Nora I'm less a brute than a man with no heart—in the clinical sense....

Whittaker

[Chambers was talking about the rather complicated position on Taft, as conservative, and Eisenhower, as political chameleon, taken by me. In the pre-nomination process, I had gone along with Nixon on the Eisenhower vs. Taft confrontation, arguing that Eisenhower alone could win and that the important thing was to dislodge the Democrats from the White House. For this I had been roundly criticized by conservative Republicans who believed that it was better to lose with Taft than win with Eisenhower. The Chambers position through the primary battles and during the campaign and its aftermath was similar to

mine—though based on a fuller knowledge of what was happening in
Washington. When, in the early period of the new administration,
when it became clear that Eisenhower was (1) perhaps the most astute
politicians of his day, and (2) totally bereft of any real conservative
principle, I hoped that Taft would use his powerful position in the
Senate to ameliorate the opportunism of the White House. Taft,
instead, tried to establish a working relationship with Eisenhower,
seemingly jettisoning the conservatism for which he was noted.
Chambers was warning those who stood with him to hold their fire, for
strategic and tactical reasons.]

May 8, 1953
Dear Nora,

I still don't know exactly what sudden move caused Doubleday to
[call back copies already in the hands of reviewers] of the Earl of
Jowitt's book at the eleventh hour, and I shall not ask too closely. I
am sure that the country owes you some kind of debt, and I know
that I do.

Just before you called me yesterday, the post brought a review by
the British Books in America or something of that kind. I read the
first few lines and filed it away. I thought: Is there never to be an end,
ever, to this business. I know, of course, that there isn't. But I can
only live by acting as if it were. At that moment, it really did not seem
worth carrying on. The persistence of those vipers. And I cannot fight
the whole Socialist International—and that's what it is. That's what
it's always been.

Then came your telephone call with the news that I could not at
first believe. Today, its official. Now the whole picture changes, and
what was merely harassing to me in a personal way turns into a major
reverse for the Hiss people. There are certainly enough of them
posted high and low, but mostly high. The Lord Chancellor of
England to have his book withdrawn because of egregious errors!

Perhaps nobody but me knows how extremely funny a great many episodes of the Hiss case have been, and I cannot enjoy them. But this one, now that it's over, if it is, is surely the supremely preposterous and fantastic high mark. No, that is still the typewriter construction. [Chambers was accused by Hiss and his lawyers of having constructed a typewriter which would duplicate the Woodstock on which the State Department documents were copied, though the most skilled typewriter mechanics had failed to do this.] But the Earl of Jowitt stands very high.

So please accept my thanks—and thank Ralph, poor fellow, with his own load of worries. And will you thank George Sokolsky for me.

Whittaker

May 12, 1953
Dear Whit:

The providential nature of certain events in the case was never more apparent to me than in this last matter of his lordship. My first surge of elation at the news on Friday was supplanted immediately by a shadow of what you must have felt when you opened that envelope [containing papers proving Hiss's espionage activities], and even in delight which small further episodes have brought, that very humbling knowledge has not been very far off. Thread after thread, demonstrably, leads back to a Source—and some of the threads become manifest in actions to which I was opposed. Which has reinforced my sustaining belief, that though He will not make it easy for any of us, you least of all.... He does not intend us to lose, provided we stir ourselves a little to demonstrate that we are worthy of victory....

Start out with the fact that Ralph and I and others who love you were not happy that you were moved to tell in *Witness* of the suicide attempt. But it was on that story, as told in *Witness*, that Jowitt was broken. He "misread" it in time sequence... and proposed a theory

of the forgery of the documents predicated on his claim that the
attempt was made before the 17 November session in Baltimore
[where the typed documents that convicted Hiss were produced].
This he made "use" of seven times in his book....

Take the idiot proposal which we made that you threaten suit.
Even that, hurtful as it was, was a necessary part of the operation, for
without the strong reaction I got from Esther and you, I would not
have had enough reserves to keep us tunneling with bare hands,
blindly, until we broke through to daylight, and might have lain back
and allowed that mountain of dirt to suffocate us all. Sokolsky, who is
a good man but understands little about the case, was horrified when
I admitted that my first motivation was emotional and only my second political. Though I think he has come to understand that emo-
tionalism, too, serves a useful function in harness. But enough of this
now. Let us revel in the gory details. But not too many of them.

The book was published in England April 30 and various wire service stories appeared which seemed to bode no good for our side.
The same day I learned that review copies of the bound American
edition were being distributed. And so that afternoon, very simply
and directly, I wrote to [Pyke Johnson] the publicity man at
Doubleday, a non-polemic letter stating that I had read the English
edition and inquiring if they were publishing the same MS, since I
had found over 100 errors of fact in the English edition. I gave no
details, beyond a reminder that although there were very few people
with access to the trial transcript, some 280,000 copies of *Witness*
had been sold.

I mailed the letter Thursday afternoon and on noon the next day I
had a reply delivered by messenger. It was a strange letter, because
although it showed real concern, there was the hidden razor edge of
a challenge to let Doubleday see my "list." I took my time about
answering that one, and when I did I politely declined the suggestion
but agreed to give them examples of the kind of thing that was

wrong. Whereupon I laid it on the line about the suicide attempt and followed it up with a dozen or so other examples put in such a way that they had to research on the basis of my comments. I said that Jowitt was wrong, as to the matter of such and such, and left it to them to discover what was wrong.

They received this second letter from me on Tuesday night or Wednesday morning; Wednesday afternoon Sokolsky's column appeared; Wednesday and Thursday the English reviews arrived here—Rebecca West, Colm Brogan, D.W. Brogan, all quietly rending Jowitt limb from limb and each one pointing out a different batch of factual errors and logical deficiencies. (Incidentally, that must have been the last thing D. W. Brogan wrote before he died and I was struck by the fact that he remarks the absence of "world enough and time".) This is not to say that others, Lord Beaverbrook for example, didn't love it, but the panegyrics were mightily ineffectual against the facts.

On Friday Doubleday sent out telegrams recalling the review copies and the bookstore orders. Ralph spoke to the editor there when *Newsweek* planned to do a story (it was killed for space) and he told Ralph that it was so kind of me to write them, as well as admitting—off the record—that that did it.

Nora

May 16, 1953
Dear Nora,

I am writing (elsewhere) against a deadline so that this is chiefly by way of an IOU on your moving and informative letter. It seems clear that a sizable victory must be racked up. But it cannot end the war; only give it momentary check while strategy is reformed. The war must go on because the issues remain at stake, and the forces remain

embattled. The next major drives will be expressed to try to discredit
Witness, and to discredit, or otherwise destroy us. I am the stumbling
block. I wish that it were not so. But it is so. Hence no peace for
me....

Whittaker

27 May 1953
Dear Whittaker:

I have not written before—and perhaps should not write now—
because for the past months I have been in the grip of what best can
be described as a complete spiritual exhaustion, with physical complications. During this time, I have done my work at *Newsweek*, and
turned out a certain amount of copy for the *American Mercury*—in
the latter case under pressure from Jack Clements and my bank
account. Apart from this, I have burrowed deeper and deeper into
myself, participating minimally in the Battle Against Jowitt, virtually
stopping publication of that miserable book.

The impact here of Doubleday's withdrawal has been tremendous.
The Hiss forces had staked a great deal on Jowitt's Jumblings and
now, to mix the metaphor, the wind has been taken completely out of
their sails. There has been one other by-product of the Jowitt fiasco.
The people at Doubleday have taken to fighting and bickering among
themselves, and I expect any day to see a small trickle of blood on
their doorstep. Even Alistair Cooke [who had also taken liberties
with the Hiss trial record in order to question the jury verdict, and
who had less pointedly impugned the American judicial system] has
taken cover. The only thing that stirs now in the Hissite world is
rumor. There are rings within rings in this, and whorls between
whorls including the involvement and the financial backing of high-
ranking Democratic figures such as Senator Herbert H. Lehman and

the family's Wall Street firm, Lehman Brothers. The neatest irony is
that Nora stuck the knife into Doubleday so delicately that Ken
McCormick [the editor-in-chief] turned, bowed, and thanked her for
scratching his back….

We have been thoroughly bedraggled by the cold, wet spring. I
hope the sun has been shining in Westminster.

Ralph

June 1 [1953]
Dear Whit:

This will refer to business of the Committee [for the Defamation of
Lord Jowitt]. Ralph will attend to other matters which concern us all.

First, you were quite right that the tactic—for the time—was not
to tell the whole story [behind the withdrawal of the Jowitt book].
But, as detailed in the enclosed [tearsheets of *The Strange Case of
Lord Jowitt*, an article in the *American Mercury*], two things took
place which forced me, I believe, to tell the story: a *London Times*
despatch and a *Daily Worker* article. Jack Clements pulled a piece
from the July issue of the *Mercury*, and *voila!* Reprints will be sent to
all book editors.

Since getting the article into type, I have learned several things
which sustain the wisdom of having done it. For one, Doubleday
maintains that a "corrected" version of the book will be coming out
"late in June" (one version of their story) or "during late summer," or
some such. Manifestly, if they correct the errors they have on the
book. I don't see how they can put it out if they don't correct the
errors, since almost every week brings out a fresh batch. The
Sokolsky column (enclosed) will be followed by at least one more,
dealing with certain malicious distortion of *Witness*. Today we got a
review from the *London Times Literary Supplement* of May 15

which outdoes West & Company [in cutting up the book] to an aston-
ishing degree.... These things all together confirm, I think, that the
time to tell the story came far sooner than anyone would have
expected....

Incidentally, proof of the degree to which this was a put-up job is
mounting. I have internal and external proof, which cannot yet be
made public, that the book was very carefully checked. (For tactical
reasons, I imply that it was not.)

Nora

[The following letter crossed in the mail with Nora's report, above.]

May 29, 1953
Dear Ralph:

That is a sad letter. And it has the effect of making whatever I wrote
you just before sound merely impertinent. Wrapped in my ills, pretty
well insulated too, I have not quite understood what is happening to
you. Or how deeply it is affecting you. I am used to thinking of you as
the intrepid agent, and of myself as the man who has slipped in his
own blood and finds it very hard to stand on those buckling knees, or
even to grasp why he should try, since he knows that, as often is
counted, a hammer blow will hit him somewhere. There are good
souls, I suppose, who would call this an anxiety neurosis—perhaps in
both our cases. But to me it merely seems like fighter's fatigue—particularly in a losing fight.

I want to talk to you about these things (and others)—talk, not
write, because the spread between the spoken and written word per-
mits too many misunderstandings. Turns of phrases, which are meaningless scratches in haste, take on false intonations, leading to false
readings, on the written page. I want to talk to you *à deux*. I should
like to talk to you at Medfield for a day, the house I write in, where

there is complete retreat, and try to reach some conclusions about you and me. Once I should have hesitated because I would have said that that would be important only to me. Your letter makes me wonder if it is not, for once, more important to you.

I have just finished and sent an article to *Life*. It took me six weeks to write it because I have about two hours a day of writing in me. If I try to do more, I pay for it. I want to write the way I used to wrestle, doggedly dawdling along, conserving my strength while sizing things up, move by move, and then coming through in that terrific fight at the end. Now I haven't got what it takes for that last effort. It's gone. It just isn't there any more. And I suppose it was the succession of those last terrific efforts that took heart out of me. I want to tell you, sometime, for I think it bears on Toledano's situation, too, at what moment I decided that I would go on living. It wasn't very long ago, and a man named [Father] Luigi d'Apollonia had a lot to do with it. But that's not for a letter.

Life may not accept the piece—it has one subhead, "The Liberal Neurosis," that will make things sizzle, and Luce, as usual when needed, has fled the country and is in Rome. But, anyway, I have done the impossible and written a piece, and am still alive, though very weary. I have also contracted to do two more. There is also, as you guessed, a book. That's why Carl Brandt will be here shortly, followed by Bennett Cerf.

When I lay on my couch in the living room last election day, fading in and out of consciousness, I had to make one lightning decision— could I just fade [W.C. *implora eterna quietà*] or must I still go on because Esther needs me and the children are not yet 21 and must still be provided for. You know I chose to go on. So I am doing what I stayed to do. Catholics very kindly keep telling me that that is just why God gave me a heart attack—so that I could write and couldn't do anything else. I don't know. But I am writing. So must you. In all this autobiography, I am writing about you. I hope you realize that you and I belong among those writers who write for the same reason that birds sing in the dawn—let's not explore it farther. There are not many such writers around. To talk as if you doubted yourself is mood, or fatigue. It is true, of course, if you feel it to be true. But it need not be final. I think that practical details are highly important here, and that, in large part, is what I want to talk to you about. One of the things [Arthur] Koestler told me, that when he has completed a book, he always feels suicidal until he has begun another. There is just enough in this to make it seem worth quoting.

I cannot ask you down here in June—in part because of other visitors; in part, because of matters I will report on later. But when is your vacation? Soon, I shall be able to turn over to you, I understand, the first payment on the British rights to *Witness*. It may not seem much to you, and it cannot repay you for your labor on that job—that can't be paid—but it may help out.

Is there any question that Nora did a superb job in the Jowitt matter? It is hard to know what to do about it. It is hard to know what to do about it because the story should not be told for tactical reasons. Not yet. But that time will also come. Meanwhile, let me say that she had a far firmer grasp than I did of the importance of the whole business, and she handled it better than I feel I could have done. I can't write more now.

Also, please tell *nobody* that I am moving around a little and even writing. The news will leak soon enough. And people, in particular the Justice Department, may leap to conclusions that I am therefore fit to fell an ox. I want grace until autumn at least before I emerge to public view and activity. After all, it would be rather stupid to invite a second thrombosis now, and might be fatal.

Sursum corda [Lift up your heart].

Whittaker

1 June 1953
Dear Whittaker:

Yes, we must talk. But precisely for that reason, I have stayed away from you all these months when I would have merely given in to my wishes by going down to Westminster. I wrote as freely and as miserably in my last letter only to let you know, by indirection perhaps, what caused my absence and my few, inhibited letters.

You are, of course, right in your understanding of my state of mind. And that includes the fact that I should be writing a book. But there is always the lurking ghost who peers over my shoulder and says, *A quoi bon ecrire* [To what good is writing]? For another book, unless it kindles some coals, is just a vanity. To wave a sword in an empty room is merely gymnastics. I have sharpened that sword for two decades, and I think it is a good one. At the moment, I prefer slinging it into the scabbard.

There are two novels I wish to write—one political and the other about sin. But I am no [Andre] Malraux and wish to be no [Alberto] Moravia. I would like to do a book about Yalta, but who would care to read about an old betrayal when Panmunjon reeks in the newspapers. Regnery wants me to write about myself, but at this stage of my life, that would be the ultimate vanity. And Quixotic, too, in a most literal sense, for like the Don I would end up being brought home in a cage. And like the Rueful Knight, I would be accused of having confused shadow with substance.

But I am happy that you are writing once more, for what you have to say is of consequence—even when written for *Life* magazine. And a book which sits by the side of *Witness* is of importance to more people than you realize. Man is mutton, but God has purposes which he doles out to a few men. You are one of those, and you have suffered for it. You know that the real suffering of Christ did not begin until he was taken down from the Cross. I know what it must cost you to write, but I am still happy that you are writing.

You say you thought of me as an "intrepid agent"—and there you
may have touched on my malady. For, intrepid or not, I was an agent,
and it was the sense of being an instrument which made all the difference. And this takes me to something else you write. You say you
will turn over to me the first payment on the British rights to
Witness. Because you were unable to do the job, you turned it over
to me and I did it gladly and humbly for the love and respect I bear
you. At that moment, when I stood helplessly by, it was a gift you
made me—one more of those which began with the gift of your
friendship. If I did well what you would have done better, that is one
more gift. So we will say no more about turning over anything to
me....

Ralph

June 8, 1953
Dear Ralph,

Chiefly a note to keep the record straight. I hope to answer your letters when *Life* and others let me up.

Nora's piece [on the Jowitt episode] was, of course, excellent and
just what was needed, I should think. I was interested to learn how it
had all worked out. My information is the Jowitt book *will be published.* How it can be published in view of what has happened to it,
I do not understand. But I can agree happily that there are lots of
things I do not understand. I thought that if a Lord Chancellor wrote
(in gratuitous review of a foreign case) a book shot with errors that
would have shamed a cub reporter, that henceforth no one of intelligence could take the gentleman seriously. I thought so because it is
pleasanter at times [not to think] that we are living through a revolution (which has hired Lord Jowitt) and just fancy that we are comparatively rational people. In fact, I succeed in doing this so often that I
constantly find myself sitting in the dunce's cap. And, do you know,

age and the wars are so hardening me to it that, sometimes, I scarcely mind. But it is early in the morning, just past the dawn, and the sour day has still to curdle my temper. Still, for a few hours, say till 11 AM, let Lord Jowitt fuss and fust, but let me take my morning tea while a hundred birds more pleasant than His Lordship waken my body in this most gloriferous of springs. It is something, isn't it, to have lived to see it. By noon, I shall fuss and fust myself....

Whittaker

19 June 1953
Dear Whittaker:

This [an attack by Father George Higgins to a piece on Walter Reuther which I had written for the *American Mercury* and my rejoinder, as published in the *Florida Catholic*] may amuse you. I'll be answering your letter soon. But for this one, only a word that I read your *Life* piece with huzzahs—both for the piece itself and for the fact that you wrote it.

Nora and the kids are out on the semi-inhabited end of Fire Island for the summer, far from the New York grime and isolated from the Comintern and the Homintern centers on the Island. I spend weekends with them and will take off the month of August. With luck, I may even write something during that time. [I did, my first novel, *Day of Reckoning*.]

Ralph

June 24, 1953
Dear Ralph,

In [Father Higgins's article in the *Florida Catholic*], I especially admire the reference to the "golden" Middle Ages when all the world was at peace. The period of the Crusades and the Hundred Years War, if I remember correctly two disturbances of the time.

In your reply to Father Higgins, I especially admire the phrase "economic Jansenism." That is very *juste*, very good and to the point. And so, of course, is the whole riposte. [I had answered the sharp criticism aimed at me by quoting Encyclicals—"very wicked to do to a priest," another priest told me with a grin]. These leftist Catholics (or with the order of accent reversed, as I often feel that it is) are so troublesome, and worrisome—and also so inevitable. Nobody else, except the socialists and Communists, has any program for action, least of all Washington. For this, we cannot blame them too far since the only rational program for the Right must be straight reaction. And that is not only unfeasible. It isn't even politics. So for the Right it looks like out-Caesar out-nihil. More likely, it's just out.

I'm glad that Nora and the boys are at Fire Island…. The sea will be a good change—and it is always the sea which I greatly miss. I can scarcely have been older than Jamie [our older son] when I first saw Fire Island—then an hour or so across the Bay—the Bay that Whitman loved. I guess that was the only time I was ever on the Island though I used to look across the inlet at it in later years— rather fearsome, the inlet, too, with the rollers breaking on the still water of the lagoon….

I'm glad you liked the *Life* piece—the dead cats should be sailing in soon. There's another piece locked up in *Look*, so I presume it is due soon. I've been asked to do one on Senator McCarthy; *deo volente*, it could be a decisive piece on him. But I think not. I don't think that that's for me right now….

Whittaker

26 June 1953
Dear Whittaker:

I always know when a letter from you is on its way, so I am not surprised by this morning's mail. There was, however, the unfailing
splutter of pleasure at seeing your handwriting on the envelope.

You have been more in the front of my mind on weekends. What
you wrote in *Witness* of the sea struck a chord in me. And it comes
back to me now that I can hear the sea again. We are very far from
the Bohemian crowds, in a tiny community of perhaps a dozen
houses with the unlikely name of Kismet. So far, the beach has been
deserted. There is scarcely a footprint on the packed white sand. In
the quiet of the night, we can hear the breakers pounding—and
there is no sound more full of comfort and longing.

The Long Island I knew as a child was not yet broken up by superhighways and the urban nomads had just about begun to build those
endless rows of wooden tents along the beaches of Rockaway. The
jetties which tamed the surf and the boardwalk which destroyed the
beach had not been built. Sometimes a high-riding sea would form
great pools on the wide [Far Rockaway] beach, and it was in one of
these that I learned to swim. Lillian Russell's home had not been
turned into a boarding house, some of the estates were still intact, the
Edgemere Club Hotel (later to burn down) had not become a seaside
Grossinger's. There was Jamaica Bay, with its great oozing smell, and
the houses on stilts in The Raunt. I remember that sea, as I remember a bluer, deeper-running sea which I saw as a small child in
Tangier. And the Atlantic, too, as it raced by the deck of a Cunarder.

We took the Fire Island place because I wanted the boys to have
some sense of this before the ocean around this country is divided
into lots and rented by the week. The longest they have been away
from the city has been the one month they spent on your farm last
summer. And that was wonderful for them, for Nora and for me. You
speak of making the Creek farm "more habitable" but we found it in

no way non-habitable, though you refuse to believe us when we say it. We were happy at the farm and we will, I am certain, be happy there again. But it would not have been good for you and Esther this summer.

If you will have me, I would like to go down to Westminster for a day late in July.

Ralph

The news about Ellen's marriage is heart-warming. Nora and I say, "Congratulations, *auguri!*"

July 8, 1953
Dear Ralph,

In the whirl around of wedding plus the literary life, I can't remember whether I wrote to say, of course come when you can get away. If I didn't, it was simply because that was what I thought when I read your letter....

Grandmother goes home today. With her, the last member of the wedding will have departed—and we shall be left on the tidal beach with the gulls, the shells and the seaweed.

I hope, Sir Knight of the Rueful Countenance, that you will not get mixed up, out of motives of gallantry that chiefly you possess, in the current imbroglio between the Enemy, the Senator [McCarthy], and J.B. Matthews. No gallantry there.

Whittaker

[J.B. Matthews, former research chief with the House Un-American Activities Committee, had been appointed to take charge of research on the Permanent Investigations subcommittee of the Government Operations Committee, both headed by Senator McCarthy. Prior to that appointment, Matthews had written an article naming several hundred members of the Protestant clergy as being fellow travelers of Communism. There was some irony in the controversy, as when Senator Harry Flood Byrd, Democrat of Virginia, who had not read the article, rose up in high dudgeon accusing Matthews of smearing the clergy without naming a single name. Matthews, whose article was based on newspaper stories, the advertisements of Communist front groups, etc., was forced to resign. Had he remained, he would have been a counter-influence against committee counsel Roy Cohn, whose penchant for making wild and unsubstantiated charges was a factor in the destruction of McCarthy.]

August [?] 1953
Dear Ralph,

...No news except that we sell the cows Sept. 18. I had always said of the oldest brood cow that she would end her years on this farm. In my mind, I had set aside a field (Legonier), where there is a spring and shade, and where she would decline in comfortable uselessness. But much has changed, including my children. When there is no continuity in the children, there can be none in promises to cows. I hope she finds a comfortable barn and a kindly owner for a couple of years before they bundle her into a truck and down to Blackshear's, and the mallet drops between the horns.

Did you ever read Jim Agee's story called, I think, *A Mother's Tale*? It tells how the young range calves plague a cow to tell them the legend about the bull who came back. Reluctantly, she tells how, long ago, lost in the mists of time, the freight cars still pulled east in the fall, carrying their loads of lowing cattle that never came back. Nobody knew where they went. But one day in those far off times, so the legend goes, a bull, a bleeding carcass with the hide flayed off, dying of hunger and exhaustion, stumbled back to the Plains. He told his horrified herd how he had been taken to a place called Chicago and described the horrors of the stockyards and slaughter-house. He had been struck on the head with a mallet, strung up, and partially flayed, when he broke loose by a superbovine effort and had struggled back to bring the terrible warning. Only the hope of doing so kept him alive. "But we," says the mother cow in conclusion, "are enlightened cattle, and know that such things are just myths."

'Tis writ in choice English but appeared in a Roman magazine called, I believe, *Bottighe Antiche* (Second-hand Shops).

Whittaker

[In the reading he was doing preparatory to writing another book—he had two tentative titles, *The Losing Side*, with which he thought to drive Bennett Cerf to drink, and *The Third Rome*, which alluded to a Russian and Soviet dream of world hegemony—Chambers asked me to get for him or lend him a number of books, among them Hilaire Belloc's *The Servile State* and Ruth Fischer's *Stalin & German Communism*. Ruth Fischer had been Member #1 of the Austrian Communist Party, right after World War I.]

Aug. 17, 1953
Dear Ralph,

Thanks for the books, of which Belloc's seems surprisingly slight and, intellectually, not quite honest. Not only by contrast, Ruth Fischer's seems a monument of a certain kind of mind and scholarship. I am ashamed of the snap judgments I have made about her in the past. No doubt, in the last instance, this fat record can be summed up as a kind of revolutionary gossip; and, no doubt, Miss Fischer has a somewhat lofty view of herself as a socialist theoretician while her opinions of others, [Rosa] Luxembourg for example, or [Karl] Radek, are

less than charitable. It also has the readability of gossip about important things. And how else are we to know them? Those who knew
them at first hand are now so few. The ad hominems are plain
enough to make discounting them fairly simple; and they invoke the
exercise in charity that she shirks. Moreover, whatever awe she lacks
before men and women, she renders unto history, and has the great
merit of having recognized it for what it was while it was happening
to her. So that one has the rare impression of being in the presence
of an adult mind. If she is arrogant, she has a better right to be,
surely, than most. And she must be lonely. Here is the first book I
have read in some time which gives me the feeling that I must read
every line carefully and slowly, and go back to make sure that I have
read it right, or to fix what I have read in my mind.

I cannot well say how grateful I am to you for taking days out of
your vacation, or making the long trip down here, or how much I
enjoyed talking with you. I have had a most unusual letter from
Schlamm—no pyrotechnics or sprightly thrusts and jabs, but a sad
intellectual humility, transient, I suppose, but disclosing a side of
himself that I have never known before. I hope you will be able to do
something re: *Colliers*.

Whittaker

Willi goes to the hospital for a week or so soon—he does not say why.
Piles are understood, I believe.... Do you have a copy of the *Golden
Bough*? I can't find mine. The priest of Nemi now uneasily prowls
the Kremlin.

One of the oddments that stands out in Ruth Fischer's book, in
contrast to the hitherto almost exclusively masculine reporting of
these events, is the role of The Women—Luxembourg, [Clara]
Zetkin, [Maria] Spiridonova, [Dora] Kaplan, [Kathe] Kallwitz. Most
exciting is a long quote from the theses of the (then) Left
Bolsheviks—[Nicolai] Bukharin, [G.I.] Lomov, [G.L.] Piatakov,

[Mikhail] Uritsky, [Vladimir] Smirnov *et al*—which shows how clearly they had foreseen, as early as Brest-Litovsk, exactly how the Communist state must develop—though Stalin was still an unobtrusive figure. I had never seen these theses before.

Kismet, Fire Island
[?] August 1953
Dear Whittaker:

I'm glad the Fischer book arrived and was of interest. I found it somewhat overserious, but valuable. As for the Belloc, I only stuck my nose into it years back, but I know what you mean when you say he is dishonest. He was a writer and a wit, not a deep thinker. I always felt that his artsy-craftsy medievalism was more than a little put on....

Poor Willi. Hemingway used to refer to himself during the war as "Ernie Hemarrhoid, the rich man's Pyle"—but to be laid low at what might be called the seat of the humors. It is just as well that I haven't spoken to Paul Smith [editor of *Colliers*] about him. I had decided that it would be more effective to bring up the subject [of a job for Willi] in conversation. If Smith makes concrete the offer he held under my nose [a high-level editorship on the magazine], I will be in a good spot to push the suggestion. I do hope the offer is made. [It was not.]

When I returned from the farm I learned that the two Muirs had almost succeeded in firing Karl Hess [a skilled and effective Press editor whose only crimes were that he was strongly conservative and friendly to Joe McCarthy]. Only [former Chambers associate at *Time-Life* and at the time a *Newsweek* top editor] Frank Norris's flat refusal to fire him saved the day, but it is a matter of time. I am fairly certain that I am next on the Muir list—although it will be a little more difficult to dislodge me....

Do I see in your word about The Women another article—from Pompadour to Pauker, with a comfort stop at the Finland Station? It would make good reading and appeal to the editors of *Life*. And what a movie, with Lionel Barrymore playing the role of Ruth Fischer.

I do not have *The Golden Bough*, but the abridged edition is readily available. Shall I get it for you? And what other books?

Ralph

Aug. 22, 1953
Dear Ralph,

...There seems to be little doubt that a second clot is forming—or something of that order. I have known it for several days, but have at last had to tell Esther about it. So I find myself lying around again with all those delicious medicines. I daresay we shall head it off. I should like you to keep all this quiet. I have strong personal reasons—practical reasons. Not much other news....

Whittaker

Sept. 5, 1953
Dear Ralph,

Your silence troubles me, particularly in view of what you wrote about the attempt on Karl Hess. A line saying that you are intact would be nice.

At the time I wrote [my last note] I thought I was racing time, and my chief concern was getting it off to you while I could. I went to the hospital yesterday for a brief check-up. The X-ray shows the old scar healing nicely, but the heart somewhat enlarged. In the last fortnight there has been a slight new attack; what they call a warning. Nothing to worry about; all that is necessary is to avoid worry and effort. And I have two new medicines to take. A very solemn doctor was telling Esther about my case in my absence. He found the just analogy. It was about the troubles of an over-aged used car, and how, part by part, it goes to pieces. "Until," said Esther who was getting tired of the image, "we trade it in for a new one." Heaven knows what she will be charged with if this story reaches the Earl of Jowitt.

I wish I could express myself more solemnly about all this. But it so happens that this solemn moment has coincided with one of that other kind in which I cannot help smiling because I cannot see anything about the world beyond an elaborate *bétise*. It isn't cause and effect. The prongs of the discrepancy have been sharply separated.

It also seems to be *Botteghe Oscure*, not *Antiche*. So much for complacency.

Whittaker

13 September 1953
Dear Whittaker:

I did not answer your last letter immediately because I could not trust myself to express what I felt. I still can't. Nor could I find a way to write about something which has been on my mind ever since you drove me to Baltimore. You spoke then of your concern over what might be done for John (college expenses, and so on) should you have another and fatal attack. I did not know how to say that you could count on me in any and every way—and not only in regard to John.... I was afraid that, in some ways, my saying so would burden you.... If it does, ignore it.

Hess's situation, which gave you some concern, remains the same. I suspect that only Muir's fear of the [American Newspaper Guild, of

which I was vice chairman of the *Newsweek* unit] has kept him from
firing Karl. My troubles are the niggling kind, for the time being.

Ralph

Sept. 17, 1953
Dear Ralph,

Thank you for what you write about John and the rest in case I go
away. I won't comment on it beyond saying that I believe you implicitly. Do you know how many men there are in this world of whom I
would say that? Not three. And yet I count some dear old, dear and
very close friends. But in this I believe and trust you....

When I saw you were still using *Newsweek* stationery, I was reassured before I opened the envelope, and felt like No. 508 (or whatever his number was) in *Blindness At Noon*, rejoicing at Rubashov's
return from the barber shop: "Ha! Ha! I feared the worst!" I have a
feeling, which I am sure you share, that something must change;
only, you must do nothing to precipitate change. But until change
comes (by better ways, let us hope, than "the worst"), you will be
simply marking time. I wish there were some way for you to para-
chute into Books [dangled before me and then withdrawn because of
opposition by Malcolm Muir, Jr., whose father had catapulted him
into the executive editorship]—and perhaps that is alone worth waiting for. K. Hess will soon have some other changes to write about in
the publishing world—or a couple of its better rumens. In which
connection, what about you and *Colliers*? Or *der arme* Willi?

I have worn thin the edges of the dust jacket of your Ruth Fischer
book. Back in 1933, Valentin Markin (the murdered Herman Oskar)
explained to my continental ignorance in great detail the pattern of
National Bolshevism and many related things. From him, and others
since forgotten, I learned the role of Karl Radek in 1923 and the

famous *Wanderer ins Nichts* speech about [Leo] Schlageter and his like. I knew the roles of Bela Kun [head of the short-lived Bolshevik government of Hungary] and Heinz Neuman and what [N.N.] Krestinsky [one of the Left Communists purged by Lenin] was up to, and later on, Kandelaki (Walter Krivitsky told me that "K" stood for Kandelaki in [Ignatz] Reiss's notes [found after his assassination by the Soviet secret police]). And someone (Ulrich, I think) told me of connections between [German General Hans von] Seekt and the Reichswehr [created by Seekt] and the Kremlin. From (still) someone (what German does to my English!) else (someone who figures briefly and importantly on our side in the Hiss case), I learned about [Karl] Goerdeler and [Colonel Klaus Graf von] Stauffenburg and von der Schulenberg [all three part of the plot to kill Hitler] and their connection with Allan Dulles, Arthur Schlesinger, Jr., etc.

So that I had a rather complete, but wonderfully patched up picture of the whole decisive story of German-Russian relations in their inward meaning. But it was not until I read Ruth Fischer's book that I saw it spelled out, step by step, play by play. And she is almost completely right. She only steps off the curb, it seems to me, at those moments when the brackish knowledge sweeps her that the history of the human race would have been so different if it had followed Ruth Fischer's directives in 1923 *et seq.* Perhaps it would have, though not in a way to please you and me. As far as I'm concerned, she can indulge all the foibles she pleases since she has written that solid book. For she has added to our understanding; and what she effaced of herself in doing it, is infinitely more than what she indulged. And that is a great triumph for anybody. All the more so perhaps for Ruth Fischer.

I picked up Delgado's book, *J'ai Perdu la Foi a Moscou* [which I had sent him] to finish reading it (I laid it down more than a year ago). In it I found a brief letter of yours, quoting Rilke's lines:

| *Heilande muss man in den* | Men should quarry saviors |
| *Bergen schurfen,* | from a mountain |

> *Wo man das harte aus dem*   Where they hew the hard
> *Harten bricht.*   from the hard.

Because Rilke could write poetry like that, I must not write it at all.
The barns are empty. The cows have been trucked away.
Tomorrow they go on the slave block. Ellen came up to see us
through the sale. I found her weeping in the pen with the old brood
cow. Years from now, she will return to the land. If John does, it will
be a long and, I am afraid, a hard way back. I will try to hold things
together with the sheep and beef cattle against the time when the
children may be drawn back. [To his expressed sorrow, they never
were.] But there are really no more beginnings left in me....

Whittaker

If you come on El Campesino's book [he was a Moscow-trained general in the Spanish Civil War, who derived his *nom de guerre* from
the myth that he was a peasant who had sprung up from the land to
defend the Spanish Republic], will you get it for me? Also, a year or
three ago, there was a book on the organization of the French CP by
a former member—his name and title forgotten by me.

[Valentin Markin was one of Whittaker Chambers's associates in the
underground apparatus, and so was Ulrich. General Krivitsky had
been head of Soviet Intelligence in Western Europe and defected after
his friend Ignatz Reiss, who had written a letter to Stalin denouncing
the *Vozhd* for his betrayal of the Revolution, was gunned down in
Switzerland. The events about which Chambers writes involved the
attempt by Radek to bring down the Weimar Republic and replace it
with a National Bolshevik regime. It also deals with the deal that Lenin
made with the Imperial German General Staff to turn over much of
the Russian economy to Germany and the Reichsbank. This collapsed
with the defeat of the Kaiser, but secret political and economic ties,
embodied in the secret clauses of the Treaty of Rapollo, continued,
under the secret guidance of Seekt, until 1939 when they were tacitly
proclaimed in the Hitler-Stalin Pact. The documents corroborating the

existence of these deals (and the fifty million gold rubles transferred by the Reichsbank to Lenin, plus the military help to overthrow the Kerensky regime) were buried away by the State Department, and for years my attempts to unbury them were blocked by "scholars" and the media. My account of them was published in *Chronicles* in 1955.]

Sept. 25, 1953
Dear Ralph,

Can you take a letter from me in script and in pencil? Somehow, I don't feel up to typing, or working. My strength ran out before I got to the morning's task although my head is full of what I want to do. Besides, something curious happened to me this morning that also acts as a short circuit. You know, I take breakfast by myself in the kitchen while Esther is in the barn. I get up, take my pills, boil my eggs, make my tea, light the fire in the big fireplace, and spend an hour or so soaking up the tea before the fire. All he needs, you will say, is a cat and a parrot. But this is the interval in which I do what passes for thinking, at least, this is the time when I try to arrange my thoughts for the day's writing.

Well, this morning, as I sat there, there suddenly came into my head, I don't know why or how, an idea. Or rather there first came into my head the jingle from an old German fairy tale, of which Scherezade, that marvelous practitioner of our craft, also spun her version. As the jingle sifted aimlessly through me head, it suddenly struck me: "This is what I have been looking for; this is what I have been waiting for." For I have long been laboring to squeeze from my memory and experience some little story, as common as the wind or rain, and as unassertive, that would free me from the bondage of fact—but one strong enough to bear the burden of imagination and meaning since the only kind of "progress" that matters occurs when the reality of meaning transcends the reality of fact, and paints the

distinction between fact and truth.

A Catholic philosophy professor, who has been teaching for 50 years, told me the other day that effect can never rise above cause. I asked him: "Has none of your students ever asked you: 'What happens at those moments when effect *does* rise above cause?'" "That," he said in his tidy Catholic way, "would be a miracle, and would no longer be in the field of philosophy. It would be in the field of theology." I said: "My mind makes no objection to miracle." He looked at me as if he smelt a Left deviationist.

Perhaps some ferment of that conversation was working in my mind when the jingle came into it. I pray that I have found my Faust—but, then, alas, I am not Goethe. I can only do what I can. (All of this means, of course, that I have been looking for a fable on which to rig my reactions to experience in our time.)

But, at least, I can now write one of those wonderful, simple and disarming leads—and indeed, nothing more may ever come of all this. I have very strong feelings about leads. I hold that they always tell us whether it is worth our while to read further. They are the chords that disclose the whole symphony. They tell us whether the author knows what his work is about in its fullest, most inward meaning. I often repeat to myself the great first lines:

> *Would God that pine had never grown to height on Pelion!*
> *There was a man in the land of Uz and his name was Job.*
> *Halt, who goes there? Nay, stand and unfold yourself.*
> *I thought the king had more affected*
> *The Duke of Albany than Cornwall.*
> *Amendum genetrix, hominum, divumque voluptas,*
> *Alma Venus, quae mare navigerum, quae*
> *Terras frugiferente concelebras*

But, of them all, the closest to my temper is the prosy line that leads us into the most terrifying story of our time: "Someone must have been telling lies about the engineer K. because, one morning before he got out of bed, he was arrested."

But enough of that fiddle.

It's been nice chatting with you. Now I've got to get back to work—or try to....

Whittaker

1 October 1953
Dear Whittaker:

Your letter arrived today and brought with it a warm and happy-making feeling. It was the kind of letter you might have written me had we known each other before the Hiss case changed your life so dramatically—if that is the right word—and mine more subtly—if, again, that is the right word. It was the right letter for me to receive on this particular day. Why is this night different from all other nights, the young boy asked Rabbi Eliezer. The bearded gentleman had an answer—and so have I.

For the past weeks, I have been struggling mightily to go along with Nixon on his Far East trip. First the answer was, No. Nixon was only taking representatives of the three wire services. Then he decided he could take one other man, and he asked me. But *Newsweek* said, No. It would cost the magazine the vast sum of about $2,500 to send me. Then I cooked up a deal with Paul Smith at *Colliers* whereby they would pay my expense in return for a series of articles by Nixon which I would ghost. Once the articles were done, there would of course be a substantial payment as well. On Tuesday, Nixon agreed to this. Today, *Newsweek* grudgingly agreed to the arrangement.... I was all set. Then, this afternoon, Nixon's secretary [Rose Mary Woods] called to say that all bets were off. Nixon had discussed the possibility of doing some articles with the president, and Eisenhower had disapproved. It was not seemly for the vice president to exploit an official trip by writing for a magazine. There is one glimmer of hope. *Reader's Digest* called Nixon to ask him to do a

piece for them on the trip, he explained the situation, and he suggested that I do the piece for them. It is now in De Witt Wallace's lap and I am to be notified tomorrow. But it will have to be approved by *Newsweek*—and Chet Shaw [the nominal editor] will be reluctant.

I made a flying trip to Washington last Tuesday to watch Joe McCarthy being bound in matrimony to Jean Kerr. I won't attempt to describe the festivities. But there was a certain pleasure in watching the tall hats of the Administration suffering. Allan Dulles sat in a front pew, Sherman Adams was shunted off to a rear seat. Dick Nixon and Pat made a quiet entrance, accompanied by Alice Longworth who was restrained enough to put aside her usual mammoth hat and wear one which only blocked the view of half the altar. (Nora asked me: "Who were the altar boys, Cohn and Schine?") There were 1,200 people at the St. Matthew's cathedral and 1,200 at the reception and a good rush hour was had by all. Joe in cutaway looked like a truck driver at his wedding, but there was dignity to the low nuptial mass, despite the popping of flash bulbs.

Such other news as I have is unpleasant. Karl Hess was fired. Frank Norris refused to do it, so the job was passed up to Shaw. No explanations, no complaints about his work, just fired with three weeks' extra pay and his severance. I am doing what I can to get him another job, but my resources are limited.

I have ordered the book you wanted by Rossi on the French CP. I will send it to you with the El Campesino, which I have.

Ralph

Oct. 5, 1953
Dear Ralph,

More records came this morning. I haven't played them all yet (time! time!). But Bach was Bach and Beethoven Beethoven, and Esther

and I were delighted and grateful. More out of curiosity than anything else, we put on Shostakovitch. We particularly liked the cho-
rus of female left Mensheviks and the basso solo, which we took,
for our Russian is not quite up to these capers, to represent the
entrance of the *Zemlia i Volya*, chanting: Over the hill and through
the woods to Beria's house we go. I would get to play more of the
others, if I didn't keep re-playing the Couperin. This is riches. I
hope it doesn't make you poorer.

I am assuming that you did not leave through the overcast with
the vice president this morning. I don't see that anything would be
gained by any comments of mine… on the story of your disappointments…. I only hope that the business with poor Hess does not
point the gun at you. What will he do now? And for that matter,
what will any of us do? By the waters of Babylon, there we shall sit
down; there we shall weep and eat matzoth, if we can charge
them….

When the young Count von Einsiedal (whose book you could do
worse than read) was captured at Stalingrad, the Russians first shot
at him, laughed with him, beat him, and sent him to pass the night
(under armed guard and with no blanket) in a hen coop without a
roof. Glancing up at the freezing stars, he was reminded of a line of
Kant's: "The eternal stars above and the moral law within me." But
the wonderful mischief is a spirited account of General von Seidlitz
and the Stalingrad brass thickly and unsteadily cavorting with the
German Communist quislings and their commissars at a typical
vetcherinka. When Seidlitz groped for a suitable analogy for Petrov
(a commissar) and Marshal von Paulus by invoking SS. Peter and
Paul, Petrov simply cut him short by emitting three cheers. And
they wonder how the Communists were able to convert 23
American boys out of an army of how many—500 thousand?
Whittaker

Oct. 22, 1953

Dear Ralph:

I have just finished a number of letters, all scandalously overdue, which I could no longer put off writing. So I cannot refrain from adding a line to you, to hope that all goes well, happily and prosperously with you. It does not here as you may have observed from that press for which we continue to provide so much ubiquitous and profitable copy.

Of course, I am assuming that you are still opposite the Alcoa sign and not somewhere among the emus and platypuses with the vice president. After all, there are lots of emus and platypuses right in NYC. We have just sustained, in breathless succession, visits from Dr. Ruth Alexander, Frank Hanighen, Henry Regnery, Douglas Hyde. At this moment, I am waiting for the tone of the gong that will announce the arrival of Frank Meyer and family. Tomorrow: Henry Fuller and Isabel Paterson. Meanwhile I am trying to write what turns out to be the most difficult job I've attempted. Whoever wrote that business about the better mouse trap left out one point: that the inventor would find himself inside the trap. I note an awkward transition above. Unintentional. I do not mean that any of these people who make the hard trip here are (with two possible exceptions) either emus or duck-billed platypuses. And we love the Henrys, Regnery and Fuller. But, you know, most of our visitors do not come to see us or the better mouse trap. They are just twisting and turning to escape the trap themselves; and one of the turns is marked: Westminster, 32 miles. So we can't really help them. But, Lord, what hob they play with our full working days!

Whittaker

27 October 1953
Dear Whittaker:

Frank Meyer reports that you looked well and that he had a pleasant visit with you. I hope he was not too awed to put his best foot forward. It is a good foot, and I am very fond of him. He is one of the few intellectuals I know who also has intuition. So we can communicate. Frank also brought us the bad news about [John's injury]. Having children of my own, I know what you must have gone through. And I have a sort of remote-control father-feeling for John. Nora tells me that Esther says he is mending well. Is there anything we can do from here?

Jack Clements has been threatening to call you. He wants something, anything, for the *Mercury*. He has asked me repeatedly to intercede on his behalf, which I have studiously not done. Now he has asked me if he might phone you directly. It's not up to me to say him yea or nay, so I merely say, "If you want to call him, call him." If he asks you what you think of the *Mercury*, I hope you are frank— but not brutally so. He has found a good formula for pushing up the circulation, but this has meant pushing down the calibre of the message. Frank Meyer is right, we need a serious quarterly. You are right when you ask, "Where do we agree?"

But I don't think many answers will come from the group Henry Regnery is calling together. [It never met.] Certainly, there must be a few less tired minds on our side than some of the people he has included. Your name is listed (no sequitur intended). Do you intend to come to New York for the meeting? Or will you be with us only in spirit? From a purely selfish point of view, I hope you do come.... But from your point of view, I can only say that it seems like a footless errand.

Henry Holt has accepted my novel, on the basis of four chapters submitted. So far, the arrangements are oral. But the Commies [in a book publishing cell] have flattered me by meeting secretly with a

Holt editor to plot ways and means of sabotaging the project.
Fortunately for me, a [non-FBI] informant was present at the meeting, and the top people at Holt (who are strongly conservative and anti-Communist) have been alerted. I was amused to note the slight flicker of the eye of the bad boy in the firm when I was introduced to him. This was before I had passed on my information to the Holt vice president with whom I am dealing. If we can nail my story down, there will be one less Commie editor in the business. But he won't starve. C.D. Jackson will undoubtedly give him an important job in psychological warfare.

Ralph

Dec. 21, 1953
Dear Ralph,

If I were a smarter man, and several other things, I should have found some perfect Christmas gift for you. As it is, I think it better to leave this, like so much else, up to you. So forgive the form and know the spirit that sends this crass Christmas gift [a check for $100]. Perhaps it will buy a shingle on the roof at Fire Island. Much gratitude to you and Nora goes with it. [I never cashed it.]

Merry Christmas to you both and the boys— and a good New Year—from all of us at Pipe Creek.

Whittaker

1954

1 January 1954
Dear Whittaker:

...Our Christmas was quiet and satisfactory. The boys spent most of
the day playing with the games Esther sent them, and now the castle
and the western town occupy VIP positions in their room.
Charlemagne, I am afraid, would ponder the sight of a medieval
knight sitting in a cowtown barber chair or of a cowpuncher astride
the battlements. But the kingdom of childhood knows no
anachronisms.

I saw Dick Nixon in Washington the day before Christmas and had
a long talk with him about his trip. What he had to say I wrote in the
current *Newsweek*'s lead National Affairs piece, planted among a lot
of Panglossisms which, in referring to the Eisenhower Administration,
are *de rigueur* in our copy. The optimism which I am forced to
assume in print gives me acute flatulence, but if man does not live by
bread alone, it is still somewhat of the essence. At any rate,
Newsweek has rewarded me with a (small) raise and bonus, an apology for their minuscule nature, and the reassurance that I was the
only writer on the staff to receive both a raise *and* a bonus. Sitting

tight and letting the controversy flow over me has paid off, but I still feel that my experience could be better employed elsewhere. Incidentally, a big wind has swept across *Look*, [the top brass is] out, and Dan Mich has returned from *McCall's* to become top editor. What this means in terms of policy, I have no way of knowing. Mich [then managing editor] tried to get me on *Look* in 1941, when I was already politically identified as an anti-Communist, but the editor-in-chief's wife (very pro-Communist) nixed the whole thing. If Mich has not been taken by the liberal afflatus, things may not be too bad on the magazine. Do you have any pieces cooking for them? And will this make a difference?

Ralph

January 8 [?], 1954
Dear Ralph,

...It is about time that Newsweek recognized that it has in you a writer of the kind editors pray for; but commonly find their prayers unanswered. There are wars which sitting tight and keeping quiet can win, and nothing else can win. Nothing else is much harder, as a rule. So your success is the more meritorious.

I know about the new *Look*. It amuses me that, with my built-in sonar equipment, I caught the sounds of fission well in advance and repeatedly warned my friend, Mick McCullough. When I last heard from him, the day after the great *coup de main*, he was still surviving. I have been too cowardly to find out if he still is. The change affects me only remotely, if at all.... I had sworn off *Look* before the blow-up. Of course, it was not necessary to tell them that I don't think I can meet its editorial standards.

More important, I think you should reflect long and narrowly before you make any move in *Look*'s direction, regardless of your relations with Mich. He is not the key to the situation there. There is a hidden situation personified in people, some of whose names you may not ever have heard, who would like to support you as Lenin said he would like to support the British Labour Party leaders—"with a rope."

Whittaker

Since this was written, I have heard commentators picking up ex-President Truman's denial that he made the "red herring" remark [about the Hiss case], and his assertion that *he*, and only he, has jailed any Communists. He and Drew Pearson will broadcast this stuff Sunday. But though it is stuff, it shows that as usual, Truman is incomparably more sensitive to political dangers than the Republicans, who hulk all over the lot, gossiping and bitching, and wondering what that small object was that flew by. It was a forward pass and usually Truman & Co. intercept it, sometimes for a touchdown.

Even in its battered condition, [my recent piece] in *Look* did certain things. One of them was to direct attention for the first time (so far as I know) of a mass readership to the maneuver of the basic Democratic strategy about subversion. As you know, it was to attack the open (and relatively ineffectual) CP and distract attention from the Communists in gov't. It was done in the first instance, by swinging the first of the spy grand juries to indicting the 12 CP open party leaders the minute the jury got interested in Miss Bentley's explosive revelations. It is this maneuver which [my Harry Dexter] White piece levels on, and it constitutes its war-head. It is the more dangerous because the charge brings into wide public view two hitherto obscure figures—John J. Brunini and Thomas J. Donegan....

An alert Jenner Committee [the Senate Internal Security subcommittee] would have Brunini in Washington tomorrow because, even if he did no more than say: "As foreman of the grand jury, I cannot reveal what happened in my grand jury room." He could (and, since he has gone on record in print, *Catholic World*, March 1952) tell what he believes happened with the other two juries. Spotlighting either would have the effect of an electric eye, touching off a charge that should blow up the house. This is what terrifies Truman and the Democratic Nat'l Committee. If it were not so, the latter would never have honored me with a denunciation and the ex-president would not be back on the "red herring" which so astute a politician knows would otherwise much better be treated in silence.

Even if a congressional committee simply read the Brunini piece into the record, a charge would be planted. Why can't they see this? Why is it that every time I move in at the risk of my skin and drop a grenade through the slit in the pill-box, our side rushes off into the bushes, or does nothing at all, while the others, who at least know what a grenade is when they receive one, swarm out shooting? The answer is: our side does not know the nature of the enemy, therefore, the nature of the war he enjoins, therefore, the nature of the tactics. So the simple tactic of exploiting an opening is inconceivable to them. Only the vice president [Nixon] has an inkling of this and he is otherwise employed. Senator McCarthy's notion of tactics is to break the rules, saturate the enemy with poison gas, and then charge through the contaminated area, shouting Comanche war cries. Can't someone besides Truman be made to see what is at stake?

[Donegan, a former FBI agent of some standing, was assistant to Tom Murphy in prosecuting the Hiss case. Brunini was the foreman of the grand jury which attempted to investigate charges of widespread Soviet/Communist infiltration of the government. Despite the intense efforts of the grand jury to hand up indictments, it was frustrated at every step by the Justice Department. I had some direct knowledge of this. Brunini had called me and spent an afternoon, speaking for publication, telling me of how the Justice Department had acted to prevent a presentment. I had returned to *Newsweek* and written what was an electrifying story, but my editors had spiked it. "If we run it," I was told, "we will all land in jail."

The case of Brunini was nothing new. When an earlier grand jury had heard the testimony of Elizabeth Bentley, courier for a spy ring in Washington which included Harry Dexter White—later to become an Assistant Secretary of the Treasury, and Secretary Henry Morgenthau's Svengali, in the Truman Administration—it sought to make a devastating presentment. The Truman Administration, however, shunted the jurors aside and indicted the leaders of the open Communist Party under the Smith Act, a piece of legislation which it was believed would be declared unconstitutional by the Supreme Court. The Smith Act barred any "conspiracy to teach and advocate" the overthrow of the U.S. government, though such teaching and advocacy were not illegal if openly undertaken. Efforts to move against the Communist leadership under the Foreign Agents Registration Act, which at least made a minor point, were blocked by President Truman.]

[The following letter was typed with a ribbon so worn that it was very difficult to read in the original, and even worse in its Xerox form. It concerns a libel action filed against Chambers (as author of *Witness*) and Random House. In the book, Chambers had written that Joe Pogany, a Communist operative, was related to Willy Pogany, a fading artist. Willy Pogany filed suit, claiming that there was no relationship— and Chambers turned to Nora and me for help in defending himself.]

Jan. 17, 1954
Dear Ralph and Nora,

Dockets in the New York courts have been so changed that Willy Pogany's suit against me is due to come up this spring. (Last spring it was Lord Jowitt; this spring Pogany.) Pogany, as you know, is an old gentleman who is, apparently, a cat's-paw in this action. He appears to have been pushed into it by his lawyer, a man named William Hyman. Who pushed Hyman? I do not know. There is highly informed and expert opinion which holds that Hyman is moved by nothing more mysterious than a desire for fees. This view holds that the Pogany action is one more libel action like many others. For the present, I shall act on this premise while waiting to see. I sincerely hope that it is true. For I do not think that Mr. Pogany has a very good case, and, if gain is the chief motive in play, he may be induced to drop it.

But I am sure that your fears, and Ralph's, will at once meet mine in quite a different view of the matter. There is Larry Duggan's brother [L.D. was named by Chambers as a member of a Communist cell in the State Department and was defenestrated from a high floor of a New York skyscraper under circumstances which made suicide impossible]—partner of the president (or past president) of the N.Y. Bar Association; friend of Horace Manges [who had figured in the Jowitt business] and sworn enemy of mine. There is the Truman gang [which included Max Lowenthal, arch leftist, bitter enemy of the FBI, and friend of Mr. Truman], extending, let us say, from Mr. Justice Clark [who as Attorney General engineered the *Amerasia* spy case cover-up] to little hard-shell groupings in the Democratic Clubs. Of these, the bigger birds are made very uneasy by me (with good reason). Some of them are on record as disliking me a great deal more than Alger Hiss. I do not need to labor the sweep of power included in that encirclement, or why I should once more feel that I may be encircled. All these forces share at least one emotion: an intense distaste for me. It is beyond question; they have been completely forthright about it. How much pleasanter (and more expedient) to get at me on some grounds far removed from the Hiss case. And nothing in their conduct, past or present, suggests that they would be above stirring up an action against me; or that they would find it beneath them to help out such an action (at least discreetly) if only somebody else could be got to take it up.

We have to remember, too, Budenz's testimony that, in 1945 or thereabouts, the Politburo decided that henceforth concealed Communists and their allies should press libel actions wherever possible; not for the sake of winning them, but as the quickest way of bleeding to death financially those who must defend them. That, I fear, or something close to it, is the strategy behind the Pogany action. And that is why I am afraid that it will not be dropped. For those who may be behind it have nothing whatever to lose and much to gain by wiping me out economically.... Besides, there is the great gain to them of publicizing the fact that I have made one mistake in recollection which can be expanded by their legion of busy, hostile publicists to further a public doubt of my reliability in other matters. It was one of Cromwell's captains who said: "We may win twenty battles against the King; but, if we lose one, we are all hanged men." For the Hiss coalition, that is high stakes.

There is, too, the possibility that just the strain of the action might break me; that I might have another heart attack which might prove more effective. You know, as well as I do, that the very fact that I exist is a challenge and a danger to many people; just as Alger's mere existence, so long as he continues to deny everything, is of enormous use to them. In the nature of the struggle, they must further the pleasurable possibility of removing me physically in ways that will not directly involve them. This is an ABC of the Communist doctrine of war, whether waged against an individual or a nation. At least, we must, in the light of experience, assume that they will not overlook that one.

In fact, a heart attack is the simplest of solutions. Let us note this without sentiment, as cold-bloodedly as would the Politburo itself. Moreover, the Politburo, knowing me (we can be sure that they have carefully studied my reactions to pressure as I disclose them in *Witness*), knows that I, too, will see that this is one solution. The Politburo must also hope to make me feel that it is the only feasible solution; they will work to make me see it that way. Do you doubt it?

Some such motives are what I fear is the dark background of this affair, or part of it. My fears may prove unfounded. But I am sure that neither you nor I would find it realistic to leave them out of the account. Nor does any of this imply that I suppose either Pogany or Hyman to be Communists. I don't. How much better for the purposes of the others that they should not be.

But these people are not going to get their heart attack if I can help it. It is true that I am tired past my power to describe how I feel. So tired that Esther and I have been discussing the possibility of our going to Spain, Portugal or the Dominican Republic, just so that we might lie on a remote, warm beach for a month or so to recoup the lost stamina that there does not seem to be any other way to get back. When home-bodies like us go that far, you know that we are pretty beat up. But this action makes anything like that impossible. We must fight even as we are. This is how I propose to begin:

Last year, I was reliably told that the Pogany libel action was "cooked up" in Fannie Hurst's apartment. [Fannie Hurst was a writer of best-selling "romantic" novels.] Pogany was reluctant. But pressures may have been exerted on him through his fears that my statement may harm his son who is (or was) in Government. Pogany, moreover, has been messing around with younger women, and, he is, above all, afraid that these facts might come to light.

Therefore, our strategy for the present is to try to scare Pogany out of pressing suit. Our first tactic is to try to gather all possible facts about him, but with particular reference to his specific fears. No, it isn't nice.... But he has chosen to fight, or let himself be pushed into fighting; and his choice dictates our strategy.... Are your Bren guns oiled? Last year, you and Ralph turned back Lord Jowitt and much high and mighty mischief centered around him. Willy Pogany may seem tamer game, and more sordid. Will you undertake it? If you can get it under weigh, we can take counsel on the next steps.... The thing is to keep it from being a battle at all....

The more I learn about it, the more I am sure that Ralph should be very careful of [Dan] Mich; and should be especially careful of what lies around Mich. My information [is] still in the raw stage, but pretty good.

Whittaker

I think that the researches into Pogany, past and present, should be conducted discreetly, though it might do no great harm if sounds of people moving in the bushes did reach his ears—but with finesse.

Sunday night [1/25/54]
Dear Whit:

I hope you know without my having to tell you that of course we will do what you ask.... As a matter of fact, as much factual stuff as you gave me in your letter, agrees with what we collected when the business first loomed.... Consider it in hand, then, which it is. I have some material already gathered [and] several good sources for more. The bushes will be very lightly rustled at this point.

Nora

Jan. 31, 1954
Dear Nora,

I have changed the typewriter ribbon. I always put this off until the last moment because (I hate to confess this), despite my internationally known skill at forging typewriters, changing a ribbon is a feat that usually takes me an hour, and ends up in two snarls—the ribbon's and mine.

My last letter to you may have seemed oddly labored, setting forth some pretty obvious stuff all of which I should have credited you

with knowing long since. That is because it was written not only to
you. It was also written for my lawyer.... I have great confidence in
him as man and lawyer. He is a Catholic, a life-long Republican, a
former assistant to the Attorney General (who isn't?). But, as you
know, it is difficult for those not in the Communist fight to grasp, or
even believe, how it is waged. I am greatly relieved that you are at
work on the business.... Random House and I would not share an
adverse verdict. The suits against us are separate; [Horace] Manges
[Random House's attorney who, as noted, was anti-Chambers in spite
of the money brought into the publishing house's coffers by *Witness*]
is not defending my interests....

Esther's arm [she had sustained a fracture] is much better. It
would be more accurate to say that she never complains about it now.
But then she seldom complains about anything. I still have not told
her of the fun Pogany *et al* are planning for us. I am afraid that it will
be the drop too much for her.... But in general, I think she manages
to be happier than I can. Then, every once in a while, a little flap is
lifted and I glimpse how much desolation she is dissembling for my
sake. Still, the children give her a strong grip on life whereas I worry
chiefly about ways and means to get them started on their own roads
so that they will need me less, in case. But, perhaps because I am a
man, I know, too, that there is a point beyond which all contrivance,
whether completed or half done, abruptly ends; and nothing more
in that way can be done or said than can be summed up in the wave
of a hand. From there, whatever the odds, they have to take it
themselves....

Whittaker

Feb. 9, 1954
Dear Nora,

My attorney's name is William F. McNulty. His address: 295 Madison
Ave. He has my complete confidence and warm personal regard. I

have made free to give him your address. I think he would be happy
to hear from you if you do not first hear from him.

I have been in bed for a few days. I got up, in part to write this; in
part, to see what will happen. Not much else to report.

Whittaker

I note that Prof. [Robert Gorham] Davis has been made head of the
English Dep't. at Smith. It is all right to be an ex-C, even to testify, if
only you denounce the investigation. [In the investigations of
Communist infiltration of the colleges and universities, Davis had
testified against the Party, but he had managed to keep one foot in
the anti-Communist camp and the other in the anti-anti-Communist
camp. I had debated him at a curious meeting at New York's
Museum of Modern Art, sponsored by the Committee for Cultural
Freedom, at which Norman Thomas, perennial Socialist Party candi-
date for almost any office, was moderator, and which included *New
York Post* editor James A. Wechsler, onetime head of the Young
Communist League at Columbia University and later a strong anti-
Communist when it suited his purposes.] So shall the world go, as
the Dutch say.

Mar. 15, 1954
Dear Ralph,

"Two Requiems," I said when Esther unwrapped your last gift of
records. "One would have done me." This was not ingratitude, but
my way of kidding finales. I haven't heard the Requiems, or anything
else, because we have been having a series of attacks rather like a little earthquake. The earth has not yet settled, either. We're waiting
to find out if it will. If the thought has crossed your mind that there
is something expedient in my illness, dismiss it. This is real. The

condition is like Nov. 1952. But instead of working it to a thrombosis by hard labor, I've been trying to prevent one by lying still. For later news, listen to your Esso reporter.

That's about all I know. Senator McCarthy seems to be in trouble. What a honking and hooting.

Whittaker

Mar. 17, 1954
Dear Ralph,

That's very fine, giving the adjective its true value—I mean your autobiographic *Mercury* piece ["The Road to Anti-Communism"]. *A la fine pointe de l'ame.* An uncommon Catholic priest lent me that phrase not long since. I have never met him. He wrote me briefly about the Beatitude: "When men revile you." He wrote: "It is self-evident that this beatitude resides essentially in the will, *à la fine pointe de l'ame*, whence it softly radiates, giving in the end a joy and a light-heartedness that the world cannot give and cannot understand. At this point, a far greater miracle has been achieved than the change of water into wine. For it takes place not in a stone water-pot, but in the heart of a man."

There are such priests in the world! Earlier, this one had written briefly as usual, to ask if I knew the answer which St. Bernard gave to Cardinal Haimeric, who had asked him: "*Quare et quomodo diligendus sit Deus* ["Why and how is God to be loved"]?" "Saint Bernard," wrote my friend, "replied with a short treatise, *De Diligendo Deus*, which opens upon this admirable phrase, as upon a mystical garden: *Vultis ergo a me audiere quare et quomodo diligendus sit Deus? Et ego: causa diligendi 'Deum, Deus est; modus, sine modo diligere'* [Do you want to hear from me why and how God is to be loved? And I said: 'The reason for loving God is God; the way to love Him, without measure']."

You will, of course, recognize your tone of voice; and that is why, in part, I quote this to you—to let you know that in the lonely world, there are actually other voices of your own tonality, by which, not by words, they know each other. The priest's name is Fr. Luigi d'Appollinara. So one may only guess whose shrine in Magna Graecia his forbears served, and caught the tone of those unusual strings.

On the least important level, your piece sets out much fact about you I had sensed, but did not know in detail. It was not necessary, but I think it is helpful to know it. Incidentally, my excitement about your piece was stirred before I reached and was stirred higher after I had passed your salute to me—a matter about which history may well not bear you out. It is your authentic voice, reporting your authentic course, that stirs me. At the moment of your course at which you reach me, and thenceforth, our courses coincide, I am bent by an annihilating humility, which, I think, no one else can truly comprehend, and which, I know even to mention, sounds like a vanity. The annihilation comes at the instant when it is permitted me, such a man, to sustain the grace which, independently of me, in turn becomes in you the grace that carries you on. It is here that I have always sensed (though we have never discussed) that your conservatism and mine are at one. For conservatism is truly this, *à la fine pointe de l'ame*, the chain of grace, the evidence of things unseen, working out, in the world, in chains of succession and authority. Too many who suppose themselves conservatives have forgotten, or never knew, that the chain of the spirit alone has binding force, and that the mere chain of authority with which the other is no longer interlinked, binds only to kill....

Whittaker

Speaking of forbears: There is a monk near here named Fr. di Venere who claims unbroken descent from servitors in a temple of Venus, also in Magna Graecia. At least the world is old.

6 April 1954
Dear Whittaker:

This has been a long silence—a longer one than usual—and particularly inexcusable since you have been ill and in need of such small comfort as a letter can bring. But letters to you are hard to write unless I am moved by the spirit. I was moved to write you when I got your letter about my *Mercury* piece, but perhaps I was too overwhelmed by a combination of fierce humility and joy. In so many ways, I am your creature, exactly that, and in the laying on of hands I am left robbed of motion.

I am glad that you liked my piece. Unfortunately, it is a piece which of necessity must say more between the lines than explicitly. Fortunately, you read the interlineation. When I am at the typewriter, an angel sits on one shoulder telling me what not to say, and the Devil sits on the other whispering phrases in my ear. It would shock many of my friends to know that I mean this almost literally, but it will not shock you. Someday, I shall write a piece about the Devil, and it will be taken as an allegory. It will begin somewhat in this fashion:

"When I was five years and five days old, I saw the Devil standing by my bed. He was a pleasant-looking young man, wearing a brown suit, not at all frightening, who smiled at me. I have never forgotten him, and I hope he has not forgotten me." [I used that scene in my 1979 novel, *Devil Take Him.*]

Very few people approach God directly; they are introduced to him by the Devil. I am certain that it was from this encounter that I drew my sense of Grace, and much later my sense of the meaning of Grace. It is a deeply heretical sense for one who believes, as I do, in free will. Something of it must have come through in my piece, because you touched on it so deftly. [I once explained it in great detail to Karl Hess who passed it on to his instructing priest. Karl expected anathema, but the priest told him that perhaps there was something in it. There must be more enlightened heresy in the Church than I suspected.] Very baldly stated, it is this: I believe that most men may attain Grace, but there are some men, a very few, who have it no matter what, and another few who may never attain it, no matter what.

There is a scene in [F. Scott Fitzgerald's] *This Side of Paradise*— and I am a little amused at the number of people who read the book but do not remember it—in which Amory Blaine sees a face peering in through the window and knows it is the Devil. This scene, I think, explains Fitzgerald and his crack-up. He knew he could never escape the Devil, no matter what. He tried to drown the Devil in alcohol, but given the Devil's specific gravity, this was a self-defeating endeavor.

I don't know what started me off on this—the angel must be taking the evening off—and I don't even know that it makes sense. The newspapers are full of nonsense, sound, and fury. I hope you're not reading them. As a matter of fact, I've taken to a strict avoidance of the papers, or at least everything in them but what I must read to write the routine stories I have been doing for *Newsweek*. In the past week, I have become a great expert on the hydrogen bomb, its effects, and its uses—and the topic bores me completely. Things are quiet on West 42nd Street [where *Newsweek* resided], no one bothers me and I bother no one. Karl Hess has found Lethe on *Freeman*. My novel moves so slowly that its rate of growth can be measured only by a micrometer.... Bill Buckley's book on McCarthy is doing well, which proves that there are some eggheads on our side.

Ralph

April 8, 1954
Dear Nora,

I have the sense of giving you a great deal of unpleasant work. It isn't fair but I am grateful. We have sent the doctor's statement [attesting that Chambers was too ill to appear in court]. Otherwise, I do not quite know where we go next though I think it might be helpful to learn where in Government young P[ogany] works. My first surmise would be the Voice of America. And JB [Matthews], Jack Clements, and Sokolsky, are they of no help? [Clements was working mightily but behind the scenes to ensure that any trial would be non-hostile.]

Esther has recently learned, from a wholly unexpected quarter, what this is all about. It doesn't make her very happy, and though I suppose she thinks a good deal about it, she doesn't say much. We scarcely discuss it. People would never believe, I suppose, that the Hiss case had gone a long way before Esther and I ever compared notes about the past. This case is too gratuitous a trouble. At our age and in our general mood, the mind asks: Are there really enough hours left to make this worthwhile? It is unseemly.

Though I have indulged moods of gloom in the past, I am more baffled than pessimistic at the present. The one person who had really relevant information to give has simply funked. I heard myself saying to him: "To all effects, I am just as friendless in 1954 as I was in 1948." It is true. You and Ralph and I cannot constitute an army. But the enemy is like the sands of the sea for numbers, and his resources are limitless. When Alger fought me, half the power in the nation leaped to his side. The pumps still feed him sustenance.... I cannot claim one public voice to speak for me or, indeed, help me in any way. This is not heartening. But I am not complaining nor am I especially dismayed. It is just interesting to cast up accounts.

I suspect that I shall soon say: One way or another, let's get this over with.

Whittaker

April 8, 1954
Dear Ralph,

A few minutes before your letter came, I had written Arthur Koestler
that I seem to be one of the few among my fellow countrymen who
has not been jellied to neurosis by the H Bomb. Now I am glad to
learn that there are two of us. I added that cataclysm has been an
intuition with us for as long as I can remember. The only real question was how. Now we know. I do not see why this more precise definition should appall our attitude toward a conclusion so long
surmised—as Winston might put it.

The press and the radio have never been so diverting with the
most casual detailed accounts of H Bomb Day plus one—complete
disintegration of law, order and property; hordes of maddened savages hunting, each man for himself, among the radioactive ruins—all
coupled with household hints about keeping a sack of old potatoes
and a jug of water in the cellar. Poor people! Dante's people *"che han
perduto il ben del inteletto"* ["who have lost the benefit of the intellect"]. But I am no longer sure that the Devil is a nice-looking young
man in a brown suit like Master Oppenheimer. I have long suspected
(at least since my *Time* cover story on the A bomb) that he is a sad-
faced, humanitarian, progressive old gentleman who looks like Albert
Einstein. The smell of brimstone is getting stronger, too. We learn
that the smell of brimstone over Chicago is startling. So perhaps
D.H. Lawrence was right: "Delenda est Chicago!" Ain't been such
goings on since young Stoneseifer got drunk at the still over the hill
and drowned in the Pipe Creek.

For me, so far, the high spot has been the voice of our local
AP-UP stringer, Mrs. Gracie Wimert, broadcasting yesterday over
Radio Westminster, on the subject of the American Woman and the
H-bomb. There will, we learned, be no question of washing-machines
or vacuum cleaners in the post-thermonuclear world, if only because
there will be no electric power. Once more the washtub and the

scrubbing board will appear. But the American Woman has always known how to make do, and we can depend on her to see us through though the H-bombs fall. Mrs. Wimert did not say what will happen to the AP and UP. But we are not forbidden to hope…. Only Senator McCarthy, and Cohn and Schine, the goldbrick twins, compete with the H-bomb hereabouts.

I was going to respond in kind with some words about Grace, the Devil, and Karl Hess. But I suddenly feel tired out, so you are spared. If you see Hess, will you tell him I wrote him a long letter in answer to his, but had the good sense to spare him, too. Later, I shall write him another, shorter. I'm glad he is back in the swim, even if in Lethe.

Did you see in the *New Leader*, Granny [Granville] Hicks's attack, along Stalinist amalgam lines, on Max Eastman, John Chamberlain, John Dos Passos, myself and others? A real man-eating squirrel, Granny. Somebody should firmly push in his long front teeth.

Such acute pain yesterday that I had to sit down on the ground. But it does not add up to a new attack and I am not telling anybody else about it. As you see, I have got up (against orders). But our spring is here and worth skipping a heart beat to inspect. You have never seen us in spring with yards of forsythia, the magnolias, plums and peaches in bloom….

What H-bomb?

Whittaker

14 April 1954
Dear Whittaker:

Apropos of nothing, I wish to communicate the following intelligence to you. For some months I suffered as the judge (along with George Sokolsky, Eugene Lyons, and Merrill Root) of an essay contest on academic freedom and Communism—open to college students. In

the course of reading the many entries, I was struck by two things:
(1) Young Americans don't know how to spell, and (2) young
Americans have read Whittaker Chambers very thoroughly and taken
much of what he had to say to heart. I put it in the past tense because
I refer to Witness. The bad spelling we owe to John Dewey; the reading of Chambers to the good sense of these college kids and to something rather hopeful that is taking place among what they bitterly
used to call the younger generation when I was a part of it. The
bright, the enterprising, and the rebellious students today are anti-
Communists and conservatives. The vicious and rigid conformity
which the liberals have imposed on the "intellectual" life of the country is paying off, however slowly for us. Fortunately, the Siberia created by the liberals for counter-revolutionaries is more of the Tsarist,
than the Soviet, kind. We can write our books and tap out messages
to each other on the plumbing. Maybe when Dwight David Kerensky
is banished for life to the Burning Tree golf course, the slave labor
camps will be set up.

But I see another course ahead. The liberals are polarizing the
country and the man who said that he was against all schisms except
American schism may well be having his way. It may be that this
country will divide into two armed camps, one led by [Adlai]
Stevenson with a hole in his shoe and the other by McCarthy with a
hole in his head.... I remember a Jewish refugee boy who trained
with me. He had one idea, to return to his home town in Germany
and walk through the streets, bayonet fixed, settling old scores. [He
ended up in the South Pacific.] The bayonet is a horrible weapon, fit
only for Englishmen and savages. (Let's give them a taste of cold
steel, men!) and much too limited. But I could think of worse ways to
die than spraying the *New York Post* city room or ADA headquarters
with bursts of sanitary Tommy-gun fire. Then there's the dum-dum
bullet—as neat an instrument for ventilating dirty minds as man has
devised—at 6 cents a round, or has inflation brought it up to 8 cents?

This is a long digression from what I started to say: namely that everywhere I turn, I see the tremendous and lasting impact of *Witness*. It sits like a great rock in the middle of the road. The liberals push and tug it or chip off little pieces, but there it sits. You are a fact which they cannot talk out of existence, and so they hate you. And since a rock responds to assault most effectively merely by being, frustration is added to their hate. As for me, I am perched on the rock "like Patience on a monument"—except that, unlike Patience, I occasionally spit in their eye. I suspect that this irritates them.

All this apropos of nothing. For the past ten days I have been confined to home, and sometimes to bed, with a stomach virus. Do you think radioactivity will cure it?

Ralph

April 21, 1954
Dear Ralph,

It was a most sprightly letter, and I have been quoting it freely to the casuals who come down here. I was surprised at what a virus tummy could do for your spirits. People seem to like best the line about the liberal-Tsarist Siberia, the books, and the messages by plumbing. I like the final conflict with Adlai-Hole-In-Shoe and McCarthy-Hole-In-Head.

I wish I could reply in kind. But… I have taken the pledge not to disconcert my friends with subjective letters, which are practically impossible to answer. So this is merely an acknowledgement. I will otherwise note chiefly that spring is here (for a day or two at least) with weekly successions of blossoms. Last week it was the peaches and pears. This week it is the apples, cherries and pea trees, as people here call Flowering Judas. This is open-handed spring, and I itemize it with interest at once casual and intent. We wait all year for this, warming ourselves with the prospect during cold and muddy months—and in four days the blossom-storm sweeps it all away.

We were disappointed that you did not come from Washington (probably you did not get there). I mean to tell you something when next I see you, but not to write it. It is a bit of prescience that... dampened me, on the eve of this year. I am wary about writing it because I mentioned it to one of my friends and I sensed the slight uneasiness of solid souls in the presence of people who feel that they sometimes see around corners. But I think it should be in the record of somebody's memory if only because it is amusing to see how such things prove out in the sequel. [At the time, Chambers's recurrent fear was of a reopening of the Hiss case, which Hiss perpetually attempted, as well as of an assault on his family.]

I hope that, by now, you are better and able to devote your time to that news-magazine [*Newsweek*] which has become my favorite reading by reason of the fact that I can now zip through it in about two minutes flat. I begin with the obits (it's sometimes heartening to see how we are dwindling). Then on to Periscope (less amusing but easier to parse than Edward Lear). Through National Affairs on a breeze that blows me without stopping, more than to glance, until I reach Books. There I make my decision by a system as mechanical as the machine that checks the answers to the College Boards. If the pictures show Indians, Westerns, Confederate generals, McClellan, Lincoln, William Faulkner, I close the book without benefit of [Raymond] Moley [whose column ran on the back page of the magazine]. But if it is an expose (as you make it out) of T.E. Lawrence, I read every word. Not because I have any question that I want to have asked of Colonel Lawrence, or answered—I am a Lawrentian in this dispute—but because I am fascinated, and a little appalled, at what the story has done to its writer. I assume I know who he is [he assumed correctly that it was Robert Cantwell]; indeed I do not see how anybody else could treat it quite so creepily or with such pleasure. I do not know enough about psychoanalytic matters to be sure of my ground. But I find myself wondering: if a quiet little man really wanted, with all his heart and soul, to be, say, Lawrence of Arabia, but failed it in reality—might he not then, by a wrench of the mind, transform himself into an unreality of Lawrence, or his like; and take revenge on the reality because, all the while, he deeply senses that his unreality was unreal? With that confusion I think I had better end.

Whittaker

May 25 [?], 1954
Dear Ralph,

You and Nora have a right to hear from me directly what, no doubt, you already know—that I have a grandson named John Norman Into, after John Chambers and his other grandfather. I keep just behind a new attack, sometimes almost pushing over the line, in ways I once described to you. The birth of the child has simplified a great many things. There is a new focus of life for its mother and for Esther. John must begin to be a man. In three months, he will be 18, and the world is waiting to assist him to mature. The G.I. Bill [?] plus his own ingenuity and industry plus a little help can see him through. So I am free at last.

   2 Soldier: Hark!
   3 Soldier: Music i' the air.
   4 Soldier: Under the earth.
   5 Soldier: It sings well, does it not?
   3 Soldier: Peace, I say. What should this mean?
   2 Soldier: Tis the God Hercules, whom Anthony loved,
                Now leaves him.

Whittaker

11 June 1954
Dear Whittaker:

Nora's call to Westminster was really no answer to your momentous
announcement that you were a grandfather. John was so overcome by
the thought that he was an uncle that he may have forgotten to give
you our message of congratulations and solidarity....

We're preparing for another summer at Fire Island. And this time
we will have a larger place, with a spare bedroom. It is yours and
Esther's, should either of you wish to smell the sea or feel the sand
dunes under your feet—and for as long a time as you might want....
Kismet is small, it respects privacy, and to the west there are miles
inhabited only by gulls....

There is no news except that life has settled into a routine. And I
have learned that writing a novel is much more difficult than I
expected. I was supposed to deliver a completed manuscript on
15 May. If I have one by September, I shall be pleased.

Ralph

July 22, 1954
Dear Ralph,

To catch you before you go to Fire Island—if I have not held off
too long.

First, thank you for the Gouzenko book [*Fall of the Titan*]. I
should like to have liked it. It is a remarkably expert construction job,
making it very difficult to believe that this is a first novel. As you
noted recently, novels are not easily put together. But I stop with
competence. The talk about Tolstoi and Dostoevski—the compar-
isons [by book critics]—I find just the usual draughts blown through
empty heads. This book has no tone, ambience, accent. Then, one
night, when I was about three-quarters through the book, the words

"Mosholu Parkway" [a bourgeois residential street in the old Bronx]
rose out of nowhere into my mind. But I am glad that G. has had so
good a press. He caught the tribe of scribes at a strategic moment,
when they were in a mood to praise a book (fiction) that would
attack Communism in Russia, and thus get them off the hook and on
the record—so long as nothing was said about Communism in the
U.S. May Gouzenko now find some kind of fulfillment, security, and
happiness.

Whittaker

[Igor Gouzenko, a lieutenant in Soviet military intelligence stationed
at the Soviet Embassy in Ottawa and its code clerk, had defected in
1945, taking with him documents which broke open a vast atomic espionage ring operating in Britain, Canada, and the U.S. I was the first
newsman to interview him, years later—an interview granted because,
as Gouzenko said, he had read *Seeds of Treason* and felt that he could
trust its author. I returned to Canada, after his interview was featured
in *Newsweek*, on an intelligence mission. On this second meeting,
Gouzenko opened up completely to me, discussing his personal life,
the difficulties of living under an assumed name and keeping his identity secret even to his own children, and even showed me the manuscript of the novel he was working on. It was an interesting manuscript,
because every time Gouzenko introduced a new character, he did a
drawing of him on the manuscript page. The book was a huge success
and even became a Book of the Month Club selection. I received a
copy of *Fall of the Titan* from Gouzenko and sent it on unread to
Chambers.]

Sept. 3, 1954
Dear Ralph,

You must be back in N.Y. shortly, if you are not there already. I hope
the summer was good. Your long silence suggests that you have been

writing, or, what I find almost as good, not writing. A writer told me recently that he hates to write, but likes to have written. I think most of us would agree, though the values we give to write and having written must be diverse. Hemingway claims that writing is the ultimate satisfaction—in *Green Hills of Africa*, a book that seems to me, chapter by chapter, like repeatedly gutting a fish. Shot a kudu (oh, boy, what horns!); did not shoot a kudu (my world is ruined!); drank two gimlets; poor old Mama's feet hurt etc. etc. Yet one keeps reading—it requires so little effort. Isn't there something I am missing, something very subtle that slips between life and death, opening profound glimpses, atavistic and (like *Blut und Boden*) beyond intellection, only to be glimpsed in Africa? But after each chapter, I merely feel that I have drunk another gimlet.

In the Circumference bashed by the silence to which (in *Vile Bodies*) Mrs. Melrose Ape had reduced the sinful upper classes: "What a damned impertinent woman!" What a damned impertinent man—Mr. Hemingway—with those bullets always "slapping" against kudus' neck bones, and teal pitching out of the hot air of Africa, pinged by a *coup du roi*, which, I should think, requires some pretty un-raw-like squatting to bring it off. Yet the old man must have some vision that sustains him, if only I could get at it. Besides, I am getting too captious about writing. I guess the great difference is that Hemingway feels "quiet" after killing something, while I feel slightly ill and highly expiatory, even if I have been hunting that something with intent to kill for some time. Quiet? Why should anyone feel quiet after killing except in the sense of feeling aghast that he had ventured to break a link in the chain of creation?

Whittaker

4 September 1954
Dear Whittaker:

It has been a long time between letters—but that is what vacation does to me. The typewriter was busy, but only at finishing the novel. And the rest of the time was spent fishing with the boys, lying in what sun we had, and fraternizing with the Kismet folk. It was for the most part a quiet summer, climaxed by the hurricane which shook the house thoroughly and sent Great South Bay swirling around us and up our doorstep. The storm would have been quite enjoyable except for the frightened looks of the boys, when the water began to rise, and the ever present thought that one's capabilities and bravado dwindle to nothing when there are young ones to take care of. When the wind had subsided, however, we waded to the Kismet Inn and watched the raging waters of the usually placid bay. That night we thanked God that the wind had been from the East and North, rather than the South (which would have brought the ocean rolling in and resulted in tragedy). That night, too, just before he went to bed, Jamie said, "Even though we don't go to church like other people, we are just as God-fearing as they are. Maybe more."

None of this is any excuse, of course, for not having written to you before. Even extra-sensory contact seemed to be broken, perhaps because the production of so tawdry a work as my novel taxes the spirit…. We had hoped that you would be able to visit us, for the pound of the sea, like its taste and its smell, is tonic. At night the crash and drag of the surf can be like a great, placid heartbeat, but lonely and eternal.

Now I am back in New York, not yet tensed up by the city, and full of the almost forgotten yearning to write merely for the sake of writing. But there is *Newsweek* and the routine. There is the need to make money and push ahead, so writing what no one may wish to read becomes an expensive luxury. The novel was a kind of compromise—the commercial, garnished here and there by a few quick

touches, a line or a paragraph which pleased me but which will puzzle or annoy the editor at Henry Holt…. I am of many minds about
the whole project, often thinking that you were right when you
advised me not to embark on it. I have been tempted to send it down
to you, but lack-of-confidence and self-esteem say me nay. Suppose,
they whisper, that he returns it bearing it at arms length, between
thumb and forefinger, and with the pained look of one who has
stubbed his toe on a rotten cabbage. What then? So I will wait until it
is, I fondly hope, in print….

Ralph

Sept. 25, 1954
Dear Ralph,

You said the other night that you would not leave the ACCF [the
American Committee for Cultural Freedom] on the McCarthy issue.
I meant to come back to that, but somehow it got lost in the conversation. I take it that your reason is a practical one, and I think you
have a point. The resignations—[James] Burnham's, followed by
[George] Schuyler's and [Max] Yergan's—seem to me to illustrate
much that is wrong with the Right; people popping out like rabbits;
no common consultation; no possibility of getting six Right-wingers
around one table at one time, or, if you could, little possibility of finding common ground. The Left is not really particularly strong or
clever. But the Right is a trampling herd. So the game goes to the
Left by default. And the same goes for the world picture. Is it really
too much to ask that 20 (or even 10) conservative intellectuals should
meet and see, at the very least, whether there would be any point in
their ever meeting again? And who will bell the cat? In any case, it
seems to me that you and I should discuss the ACCF with (or at least
in the hearing of) John Chamberlain. What an absurd comment on
our time that this ridiculous organization—a typewriter and some file

cards somewhere in a cubby-hole—can cause such a flutter, or that anybody should take it seriously....

Whittaker

[The ACCF, an organization which included Right, Left, and Center, served the purpose of bringing together people ranging from Norman Thomas, the Socialist Party leader, and strong conservatives like James Burnham—not to mention black leaders like Schuyler and Yergan—to confront the liberal and Stalinoid intellectuals in control of the book review columns, the media, and academia, and to serve as a wedge with which to penetrate the liberal/left monopoly. The organization foundered in the warfare of the McCarthy Era—and when the ACCF seemed to capitulate to anti-anti-Communist pressure, many of its strongly anti-Communist members resigned. I remained because it provided contact with nonconservatives.]

October 21, 1954
Dear Ralph and Nora,

When I was thanking Mr. McNulty, at the end of Scene 1, Act I, of the Pogany case [in which the suit was thrown out of court], it seemed natural that I should then thank you; and I thought you must expect me to. But I found that I could not do it. I thought that this was just that I could not do it before others. Later, when we were alone together, I found that I could not do it at all. So I went home and wrote you a letter to try to tell you some of what I felt. I found I could not do it then, either.

Part of the difficulty is, of course, in trying to talk in an ordinary tone of voice about matters not suited to that. Somebody mentioned "Providence," and Nora shied away from the word—quite naturally. For that is what this is all about, and why it is so difficult to talk about. It involves a mystery in the religious sense. The whole Hiss case, properly understood, involves this mystery. That, and not what most people suppose, is what sets it apart from other cases, loosely similar, and which shallow people sometimes imagine to be the same; even though such people, I believe, are often puzzled, or even annoyed, at a difference they cannot put their fingers on. This mystery is the mystery, the tremendum, of the case. I do not claim, or even actively seek, to understand it, though it has touched me in ways which are precisely what I find least possible to talk about.

One way in which it has touched me is in the persons of you two. What I was thinking when we were with Mr. McNulty, and later on, was this: Early in this experience, you were given to me—I hope you will not resent the proprietary verb. You two, and you almost alone, were given to me. And now, six years later, in a world turned upside down by this business and its implications, you two, and you almost alone, are still beside me. It is not that there are not, or were not, any others. We know that there were. But this is a special enfoldment. I still have not said it. But it would be a great sin if you were left to suppose that I am not aware of it.

We have not come to the end of the mystery. One aspect of it, which the world should not know, is the degree to which I have foreseen, step by step, what the darker terms would be. So I think that the end will not be what we call "happy." It will not and it cannot be. In this there is a right and inward logic. The test is to be equal to the logic. This I have known from the day it all began, and even before, though I permit myself to put it out of mind and even to act at times as if it were not so. That is almost a human necessity. But it is so, though I myself may be surprised at the form it takes.

Now let me resume our ordinary speaking voices. One thing that distressed me in New York was Ralph's difficulties with Holt [the publisher under contract to publish my novel, *Day of Reckoning*] and the way he subdued them in favor of my own. In this matter, I think David [McDowell's] counsel is most workable: to wait, however hard it is, until Holt [which had the manuscript] gives some sign of life. Meanwhile, there is something else to be done, and that is to get another copy of the novel typed. This is what the check is for.

As one of my Jesuit friends once wrote me: *Omnia cooperantur in bonum etiam peccata*—all things work together for good, even sin. And as I once wrote of this to someone else: "How odd it is, and as trite as the centuries since its truth first arose on the astonishment of the Saint." It is the coldest comfort on the flight deck just before the 4 AM mission. But that is perhaps because always we imagine that we know what good is. It too is a mystery.

Whittaker

[That Whittaker Chambers should have felt the need to apologize for not having "thanked" Nora and me needs no comment. We had worked long and to our full capacity to rally support for Chambers as he faced a suit which would have destroyed him. The nature of those efforts and the extent of the mobilization must not be recounted, but it contributed, along with the good sense of the trial judge—in the dismissal of the suit. And we did not need to be reminded of the mystery which Chambers noted. I had written along this line and had once been admonished by Sidney Hook, professor of philosophy and anti-totalitarian activist, who, subscribing to Hiss's guilt and the justice of the Chambers cause, could still anguish, "But why, Ralph, does he have to bring God into it."]

30 October 1954
Dear Whittaker:

This letter should have been written long ago. Then your letter came and it required a real answer, which at the time I lacked the sitting flesh to write. Here, in broad detail, is the chronology of events since we saw you.

Having waited for what I considered a reasonable length of time
for Holt to stir, I applied my own kind of subtle pressure by "ingenu-
ously" telling my story to Alex Hillman, a friend of Clint Murchison
who owns Holt [he had bought it as a graduation present for his son].
By the sheerest of coincidences, I heard from Holt 48 hours later—a
call from [William F.] Buckley, the V.P., and [Howard] Cady [the
Holt editor], and they—to use some of the elegant language you have
been employing with me—gave me a long *megillah*, telling me why
they did not like the book but ending up with the statement that they
would publish it. "Why?" I asked rudely. They were rather evasive
[not mentioning Clint Murchison], but suggested that I might wish to
place the book with a publisher who would be more enthusiastic. I
took this under advisement—then followed David McDowell's good
advice and wrote them an ominous little note saying that it would do
neither me nor them any good if I tried to peddle the book elsewhere. By return mail, a pleasant letter and a check for the balance
of the advance reached me. So Holt and I are on chummy terms, the
book is in the works, and except for the slightly fearful tone in their
conversations with me, Buckley and Cady are acting in normal editorial fashion.

The balance of the advance took care of the financial problem—if
such it was—of getting copies typed for submission to the magazines
and Hollywood. To make matters better, *Colliers* [at the suggestion
of Herbert Hoover] dropped a nice, lucrative nonpolitical plum in
my lap—an assignment to do a two-part series on the Hoover
Commission, its guiding lights, and its work.

If I had the problems of the book on my mind when you were
here, I certainly did not "subdue them in favor" of yours. God, I
hope, has given me some small sense of the fitness of things. I know
where I stand and I know where you stand; and neither in my mind
nor heart can there be any debate over it. I am trying to maintain
"our ordinary speaking voices" when I say quickly that I received
your check with great joy that it was offered. In the changed circum-

stances and having had that joy, I can return it in exactly the spirit you gave it.... My words are awkward, but I am certain that you will understand the feeling behind them.

I was touched by the quotation from your Jesuit friend, perhaps because it parallels what a character in my novel, a priest, says: "If you were a good little Christian, Paul, you would understand that there is a reason for everything—even evil." Out of the viciousness of recent shuffles at *Newsweek*, to bring it down to the lowest common denominator, has come some good for me. The new National Affairs editor [whose major experience was as a speech writer for Adlai Stevenson] is such a shaky reed that he leans on me and this has given me some freedom of movement for the first time in months. It has also bestirred me to look about. So... if [I] should [find] myself in a rather fancy job at *Colliers*, it should be no surprise. Nor will it be to me if I don't. But the promise is there from Paul Smith [the magazine editor] for whatever it is worth. Even without pinning any hopes on it, the thought is of some comfort. [Paul Smith, who had gotten his job through the good offices of Herbert Hoover, rejected my articles on the Hoover Commission's work as being "too friendly" and gave the assignment to the *Herald Tribune*'s Robert Donovan, who managed to minimize what was a major achievement. And I never got the position that was promised me.]

All this phosphorescence, perhaps, is meant to pretty the seascape and make me forget that under the shimmering water swims the monster. I know with some fatalism that when my book comes out the critics will give it short shrift—or worse still, no shrift at all. The disorganized Right lets a every man shrift for himself, so our works die unshriven.

...One thing only remains to be said, and I have saved it for the end only because I have said it before. You do wrong in thanking us. It is we who must thank you always. But we can all thank God.

Ralph

1955

3 January 1955
Dear Whittaker:

Nora says you're coming up to New York, which is wonderful news
The purpose of your visit is a little cloudy, but we shall at least have
one evening together, I hope. For that space of time, we can communicate. The typewriter sits between us, and ideas do not come right.

On the trivial side, there is not much to report. I have found a
niche at *Newsweek*, and like the Madonna's in Dorothy Parker's
poem about Marion Davies, it is a tiny one.

> [*Upon my honor,*
> *I saw a Madonna*
> *In a tiny little niche,*
> *Over the door*
> *of the popular whore*
> *Of a prominent son of a bitch.*]

Mostly I write about dogs that can do square root, horses that can
handicap races, and virtuous criminals. In part, this is due to a new
system of having the Washington bureau turn out finished copy
[instead of memos]—which means that most of the politics is written
there. In part, this is because Debs Myers [he replaced Kenneth

183

Crawford as National Affairs editor] who brings the great journalistic expertise of having been a Stevenson speechwriter, thinks I do that kind of story better than anyone else in the department. When a story like the Reece committee report on foundations, which is too hot to openly slant by giving it to a liberal, comes up they give it to me with firm instructions as a form of insurance to themselves. If someone like Ray Moley complains, they can always say, "But we gave it to Ralph." I am learning to be quite a juggler.

The novel is in the page proof stage and I have suddenly grown terrified at the thought of what will happen to it. The *Times* will give it one nasty paragraph. The *Herald-Tribune* will not review it. *Newsweek* will damn it with faint praise. *Time* will ignore it or give it a quick sideswipe. The columnists who might go to bat for it will decide that a novel isn't worth their attention. It is not, after all, a great book—and the brains on our side will never understand that just because it is a novel it can do more good than, say, *Spies, Dupes & Diplomats*. So at this late date, I have come to the conclusion that you were right—that I should not have written a novel. But the deed is done.

Ralph

[I was too pessimistic. John Dos Passos, Morrie Ryskind, and Eugene Lyons (who had been sent page proofs) wrote glowing comments which appeared on the jacket. And by and large, it received good reviews and had a good sale. Howard Cady at Holt summed up its greatest drawback. Holding a copy in his hands, he said, "If this book weighed a couple of pounds more, it would make a fortune."]

January 5, 1955
Dear Ralph,

This letter, which should have been written ten days ago, is, in part, to clarify a somewhat cryptic telephone conversation I had with Nora about that time; and also to seek help and counsel.

Background is this. A day or so before Christmas, the vice president picked up a suggestion of mine that he should sit down and talk things over with a group of people like you or me. Question of when was left hanging. Question of where was loosely fixed as NY. Since then, he has written to suggest Sat. eve. or, better, Sun., Jan 10 or 11. Place: here. This latter has some obvious advantages, but, I think, greater disadvantages for most people (inaccessibility, distance, etc.). The time, too, seems too close upon us. But these are minor matter compared with *whom*. For, once I began to consider what people like you and me the gentlemen might sit down with, I was consternated to conclude that there aren't any other people like you and me. Perhaps you know some. I don't. I mean some people with some sense of how the world runs and is run, how it wags: some sense of tact and discretion and a basic loyalty to the man in question.

So the problem now presents itself to me in this set of choices. Either we three sit down together in NY or Wash (or even here if that is possible for you). Either that, or a much broader set-up which would include certain friends of mine, none of whom I think you know. All of them are well-disposed toward our friend, but certainly feel no first allegiance to him. All could be counted on to observe a minimal discretion and decency about things seen, said and heard, such as civilized baboons are accustomed from pre-school up to preserve. Of course, they seldom do preserve it. And that, in general context, is what I do not like. This group is, in effect, my little right-wing cell at Time, Inc. which, for the most part, I have kept out of any public connection with me. They are good, useful, strategically placed people. Pool their brains and experience, and you have a fairly high-powered engine. I should like to swing it to the VP. That is, I have toyed with the idea of bringing them together so that he may swing them to himself. But, ma fren, it wouldn't be easy. All these people are from Missouri. Well, that's one kind of set-up. They can't be got under one roof quickly, either.

The third group is much more miscellaneous. It is a group of the
level: Buckley, Schlamm, John Chamberlain etc. The hazards here
are perfectly obvious. So conspicuous that, perhaps, they stop one
before it starts. These gentlemen have got themselves publicly fixed
in so many contortionate positions, and have been so unselective in
their public associations, that you may feel such a meeting is out. If
you felt it that strongly, I should have to concur. On the other hand, I
see, or think I see, certain advantages. All these boys have been gun-
ning for the VP. All have a case. Ventilation might not hurt at all, and
it might just happen that the VP would win them all or piecemeal.
Besides, a lot of good threshing out might occur; useful.

I myself am much disturbed about a determined bolt of these people from the Administration and from N as a man. They are not just
nobody. They get around to a degree that I think might amaze you.
Pray (as Winston says) let me know what you think…. There is also
the question of prestige, since they might gossip. Should it be possible for anybody to say that the VP sat down with such a group? Or is
that what you call being democratic? I think it cuts two ways; it has
its uses, but it can be used by columnists and enemies within the
Administration to say: "The company he keeps!"

Now comes the next problem: how to communicate these views to
N. I could write, but I do not know through whose hands mail passes:
I could telephone, but I assume that both our telephones are moni-
tored. This may not be true, but, then, it is an elementary assumption; and while we have nothing of any great moment to discuss, one
never knows how such things can be used and by whom when. It is
the VP I am thinking about, of course; it does not bear on me except
as I affect him. This has always been on my mind; and I have been
extremely careful to leave to him any mention that we ever meet. It
is impossible to foresee eventualities. We simply do not know how
any relationship between him and me may be used by what
scoundrels against him at what touchy moment…. All this adds up to

the reason why I simply do not drop by the VP's house or office. Will you take up the matter with him? Will you also let me know your thoughts?

I realize that I may have been too harsh in talking [about gossiping among our friends]. Many things just slip out. I try to keep the controls on simply by marking off areas of activity, or individual people, about whom I do not talk at all. If talked to about them, my mind wanders. It's the best system I have been able to devise.

I am surprised not to have had from you an offer to join the staff of a new magazine, or at least contribute to one. Practically all my other friends have tapped me. Aren't you starting a magazine? You know, you and I are perhaps the only two people who might get a magazine going (Heaven forbid!) and... might co-exist peacefully and effectively. But then, I suppose, neither of us really wants to be an editor. That's a great help. Recent experiences have left me with the impression that, as with conspirators, people who long to do it are rather bad at it. It's those who don't care that bring it off.

I'm sorry that this letter is so loose and diffuse; haste and interruptions. The latter in the form of three Passionist Fathers who tell me that Peter Viereck [a writer who emerged for a while on the speaking fringes of conservatism] has copped my thesis that Senator McCarthy is at heart a revolutionist. I wrote this to Henry Regnery several months ago; Henry would not take me seriously. If the Senator ever finds out, he'll be irresistible—I don't feel that even the Presidency of Harvard University will be beyond his grasp. Comrade McCarthy! McCarthyism is Twentieth Century Schlesingerism! I can hear the shouts from the Yard, and there is wafted to my nostrils, across the astounded Charles, the acrid smoke of burning books—the Watkins report [a Senate report churning up a good deal of dust about McCarthy]. Is it too much to prefigure Jeanie [McCarthy] as a new Goddess of Reason, her Daimler, with engine dismantled, drawn by upperclassmen amidst cries of *Sieg Heil! Sieg Yoe!* and *Slava Stalinu!*

(for when the train of history makes a sharp turn, some are always thrown off). Then the thunder of boots as the Time Inc. contingent marches in to the chant of: Luchay! Luchay! Or do I dream? For, all for the best perhaps, the unhappy Senator will never know his strength or its sources. He doesn't *want* to be a revolutionist and has convinced any number of Taft Republicans that he's one [of them] too. Surely, one of the funniest misunderstanding of our little-understanding age.

Whittaker

[The strategy meetings with the vice president never took place, in part because there could be no agreement on the composition of the group and in part because what Nixon wanted was a politically and/or socially high-powered group to serve as a nucleus when the battles for the 1960 Republican presidential nomination began. Nixon was always uncomfortable and slightly troubled with "intellectuals" or with those he considered were of the social elite. Whittier and Montego Bay did not mix.]

[During the months between the previous and the next letter I was busy keeping my head above water at *Newsweek*, gathering material for a new book, and doing a certain amount of traveling. Chambers had suffered a second thrombosis. Much of the burden of communication fell into Nora's hands—and she was on the phone mostly with Esther.]

July 7, 1955
Dear Ralph,

By now Ahmed Akhmetov Ege has probably written you about his book. I first became aware of him when I read his testimony before the Jenner Comm. [the Senate Internal Security subcommittee, then headed by William Jenner]. Without knowing anything more about

him, I thought: "This, at last, is a man who really knows something."
Later, David McDowell, to whom Ege sent some manuscript and
book plans, connected us. I found Ege a highly likable man. The
adjective is faint, but I always have to fight my way to such people
across a barrier of my inveterate dislike of Soviet nationals. It seems
to me that I know just what every gesture, expression, little silence,
means. Ege is more like Krivitsky, in a pathetic human way, than any
other of the kind I have faced or observed from afar. He says, if I
remember his testimony correctly, that he was chief of the Third
(formerly Fourth) Section, Red Army Intelligence. Krivitsky said
that he was head of the West European office of the Fourth Section.
I incline to think that, de facto, he was. Officially, it seems clear from
[Alexander] Orlov's book, and other sources, that Krivitsky was the
Fourth Section's Resident in Holland. ([Ignace] Reiss, I learn of late,
authoritatively, was the organizer of the Rote Kapelle [the Red
Orchestra, once of the most effective espionage organization's that
the Soviet mounted, operating throughout World War II against
both the Nazis and the Western allies], a very different story to
Krivitsky's). So I will settle modestly for Ege's having been the
Resident in Berlin, which seems to be the chief point. At present,
he seems to be some kind of outrigger for CIA. He told me this
the first time we met, and has repeated it since. Only his frankness
puzzled me.

Ege wants somebody to write his book for him. He tried [Isaac
Don] Levine and they blew up. He tried somebody else and then
me. I wanted to help him because I think he has something pretty
important to say. But I cannot get free from my own writing problems. So he asked me recently about you and I strongly recommended you, of course. I hope you will do the job for him, if you can
fit it in. I think it is time somebody with a mind wrote one of these
books. Levine is an admirable craftsman. But the Rover Boys in the
Underground, and foul play as the meaning of history, doesn't get us
far. Besides, Ege is a Moslem. That, in itself, opens new vistas. I

suspect that he is a Moslem by conversion, and that he began life on the Orenburg steppe (his version) as a member of the Jewish community there. But why haggle over a prepuce since neither Judaism nor Islam does.

[Isaac Don Levine, who had written the Krivitsky series for the *Saturday Evening Post*, and was ghost-in-chief for a series of Soviet defectors and others who broke with Communism, had by this time turned violently against Chambers. In 1939 he had taken Chambers to see Assistant Secretary of State Berle—after trying in vain to arrange an appointment with President Franklin Roosevelt. And he had made very good use of the Chambers disclosures—about which he felt he had a proprietary interest—as well as of his encyclopedic background knowledge of Soviet underground operations. After the Hiss trial Levine had approached Chambers, suggesting that a book should be written. "I can get you a $2,000 advance," Levine told Chambers. "But on two conditions. The first is that you tell all, and the second is that I write your book." Chambers laughed, and Levine never forgave him—even to attacking him in his memoirs. Having helped Levine start *Plain Talk*—designing the format and handling all production as managing editor—I knew the story and found it more than funny that a journeyman stylist should demand that he be the ghost for one of the finest writers of the time.]

I should have been more concerned over your long silence if I were not wholly silent myself by reason of occupation and preoccupation. What I have to say is made more difficult as the nation settles back into drowning in its own complacency [a habit, Chambers would have remarked today, that has extended to the waning years of the century]. More and more it seems clear to me that I smoothed too many rough points in *Witness*, for the sake of sparing Americans the harsh impact of history. The result is that almost nobody knows what I really said in that book. Of course, this was fated to happen anyway. But I am sick of smoothings and gentle descents: I have con-

tinually to fight a desire to dash reality in people's faces, and say,
"Take it or leave it." That is childish since it defeats its purpose. But
this running battle with myself makes me lots of hard work.
Everybody seems agreed that we are back in the 1920s. There is also
a strong feeling fogging up from the grass roots (whipped up, too, to
some extent) that, if only the American farmer could bring his wisdom and his culture to the Russian peasant, we could all troop
together back to Eden. Like Noah, I just hammer away at the Ark,
keeping an eye on the historical weather. It is written: And the Flood
destroyed them all. For even God gets bored, I suppose.

Do not imagine that I do not know what you were saying in *Day of
Reckoning* [my first novel], or what I believe you were saying directly
to me. But don't expect many others to understand it. This is a period
where utter cynicism is perhaps all the wisdom the time allows.
Cynicism and money making (if one has talents). For from him who
hath not, even that little which he hath will be taken away, yea, unto
the last phagocyte. This is why I don't write letters. The bile is better
kept within.

Whittaker

[Chambers was then working on a book whose scope was broad
enough to include the Russian concept of a thousand-year Third
Rome, and the inner drives of the Soviet empire and its leaders. The
hard work consisted of his repeatedly destroying large chunks of
manuscript and beginning over and over, of sharpening his vision and
at the same time making his grim message clear to Americans.
Repeatedly, I tried to convince him that, even if he felt he had to
return to square one, he should not drop past work into his stove.
But after his death, Esther Chambers found so little left of what
Chambers had produced over the years, that she had to call on friends
and those with whom he corresponded to let her have his letters and
theirs to him. Though Chambers had agreed that after his death, his

correspondence with me should be published as a kind of memoir of our thoughts and our friendship, I passed on copies of almost everything in my possession. The book produced from the patchwork of material by Duncan Norton-Taylor was *Cold Friday*, which never grasped what Chambers had in mind or his apocalyptic vision.]

14 July 1955
Dear Whittaker:

I saw the familiar typing on the envelope and felt a pang because you and not I had broken the long silence. Nevertheless, though we do not celebrate *le Quatorze* in this family, a few rockets shot out over Henry Hudson's river. I shall not send off as many when Eisenhower, Bulganin, Eden, and Fauré conclude their meeting at the summit and issue a dynamic, progressive Sermon on the Mount. The country is fat, prosperous, and apathetic—and the only encouraging symbol was the recent slaughter, by mistake, of a Judas goat in some abbatoir.

None of this explains my long absentia from felicity. Though I have known why you did not write, there was no way for you to know the causes of my cramp. The reason, simply, was that I did not feel that I should afflict you with my woes. *Newsweek* has become an unspeakable bore where I am unspeakably underpaid—and I remain because there is no other place to go. I had hoped, for a few misguided weeks, that *Day of Reckoning* would do well enough to give me some leeway. But the Commie-liberal boycott, which I had expected [and which had been planned even before the book was completed by a Communist cell in the book-publishing business], and the equally pervasive and effective silence of the Catholics [there were objections to my use of the word "tawdry" to describe the image of Jesus in a poor Puerto Rican church, considered "offensive"] hurt the book badly. It is a ghost clanking its chains. The only surprise was that it had a certain *succès d'éstime*—and that one of

Hollywood's B picture factories offered first $3,500 and then $5,000 for all the rights. I turned down the offer. I am still somewhat active, in the manner of a fluke which has been caught and tossed to the bottom of the boat where it occasionally flaps its tail. I wrote you some of this, at considerably greater length, but tore up the letter.

The idea of writing *The Ege And I* is intriguing, although I have reservations about Moslems, having lived among them as a small child.... What pride they had, they left with the Spaniards; they have forgotten that Mohammed carried more than a sword, and they express their defiance petulantly.... From what I read of Ege's testimony, I could see that he had something to say of significance. If Levine has stepped out, it means that there was no money. If the prospects remain as tenuous as you indicate, I can't see how I can extract that story from Ege, a long and tedious job, merely to round out my education. And there is the question of my own writing to consider. I am playing with the idea for two novels—one whose hidden hero will be the Devil, the other to be called *The Day the Russians Landed.* If I write either one, it will keep me occupied for some time.

The shortest and best non-fiction account of our times I got today from Frank Conniff [with Bob Considine, William Randolph Hearst, Jr.'s, ghostwriter]. When he was interviewing Marshall Zhukov [leader of the victorious Red Army in World War II and buddy of Dwight D. Eisenhower, for a piece Bill Hearst signed] the question of Soviet intentions came up. Said Zhukov: "If our intentions were to conquer the world, we could have marched to the channel in 1946 when your country had demobilized." Conniff: "But, Marshall, it is generally believed that the reason you didn't march was because we had the atom bomb." Zhukov: "Ah, yes, but you only had five." I wonder what Mrs. Roosevelt, who keeps popping out of the pages of *The Possessed* in the form of Mihailovna, the governor's wife, would say about that? Or, for that matter, J. Robert O.

Ralph

Aug. 1, 1955
Dear Ralph,

Dozens of pressing letters long overdue for answers. Lots of other things I should be doing. So I'll write you, instead, if only to send you the headlines I have just confected for the edification of my son: Ike Pledges Mice Not to Attack Cats. Pussies Nonplussed by Philosopher-Warrior-Statesman's Shrewd Proposal to Let Cats Examine Mice's Claws If Cats Will Let Mice Examine Theirs.

I haven't been able to talk about Geneva. People either know what it means, or they don't. Besides, it's tactless as well as tiresome to keep explaining to the man who has taken all that trouble to seal himself in the barrel, what the dangers are in shooting Niagara Fall. And the Irishman's comment on all that crashing water remains standard: "What's to stop it?" For our time, I am afraid it's final. But I am fascinated at the way the world's illusion can take diametrically opposite forms to sustain a psychosis. At Yalta, the illusion was that the Communists wanted peace if only we'd be kind to them. At Geneva, the illusion is that the Communists want a world war, which they are prepared to launch unless we're kind to them. Wrong on both counts. If you stop to think how many people of extremely limited intelligence see quite clearly what the situation is, and how many people of much greater intelligence can't see it at all. Mr. J.B. Matthews [who had always taken a strong position on the Soviet Union] is obviously not of the same order of intelligence as Mr. C.D. Jackson [a top level *Time-Life* operative who had become a top level Eisenhower Administration operative], not to mention range of worldly experience, interests and contacts. Yet, in these decisive matters of state, J.B. is a Bismarck, compared to whom C.D. is a raving lunatic.

When the asylum is taken over by the incurable inmates, the rest of us might as well get what fun we can out of the experience *pour le sport*. (Irrelevant point of sport: C.D. is immensely credited down below for dreaming up the idea of sending toy balloons, freighted with

commands to hope and await *der Tag*, to the sufferers behind the Iron
Curtain. See: Arthur Koestler's *Invisible Writing* in which is reported
in detail how Willi Muenzenberg [the Soviet equivalent of Joseph
Goebbels] dreamed up that one. Question I: Do great minds move on
the same air currents? Or question II: Who, in C.D.'s entourage, was
close enough to the Muenzenberg mind to remember?)

I like especially Tony's [Anthony Eden] boyish triumph in cheating
a little and not telling [John] Foster [Dulles] that Nikita had
promised to come play with him in London, in the spring. Oh, to be
in England, now that April's here: new theme song of the Politburo.
And that is how I should have titled that little story if it had not been
decided that I, in particular I, am never again to be permitted to title
such little stories. Hard cheese, old man. But, of course, Tony's
cheating is strictly for the birds, that is to say, the press. I do fear
that, like Anne, Foster knew. Ever since you mentioned Syngman
Rhee in our living room last spring, I knew that nothing I could suspect would be too dark, nothing I might conjecture too dire; nothing
that anybody could do of any real use. I see that Mr. Nixon is to go to
the Soviet Union. He should have died hereafter; there would have
been time for such a word.

Whittaker

[The reference to Syngman Rhee: In the course of my journalistic
endeavors, I had discovered that some years back, the CIA had
planned the assassination of Chiang Kai-shek, president of the
Republic of China on Taiwan, appropriating $3 million for the pro-
ject. The information had been conveyed back to Chiang, and his security people began planning a welcome for the CIA murder team the
moment that it landed. "No," said Chiang, "wait till you get their $3
million." The team arrived and began enlisting assistance. When its
money ran out, the CIA agents were arrested, and those Chinese who
had collaborated were executed. No announcements were made. The

story seemed so impossible that I sought confirmation from Vice President Nixon. "Of course it's true," Nixon said angrily. "The CIA tried to do the same thing to Syngman Rhee." The vice president added that a CIA team, stationed near Seoul, Korea, had fired on President Rhee, missing him but wounding some of those with him. A quiet complaint had been made to the U.S. Ambassador who referred it to a State Department, antagonistic to the Korean president, which had said, "So sorry!" and that was that. The story was suppressed and efforts to give it currency have been thwarted, with flat denials from CIA.]

[What follows here intermittently and at considerable length is what Chambers would refer to as "the Stein File"—letters from Nora, and some from me, and responses from Chambers about a play presumably based on *Witness* written by Sol Stein, later to head the publishing house of Stein & Day and to turn on all who had once helped him. Stein, who had interested the Theater Guild and enlisted the help of actor-director Elia Kazan, submitted a first draft to Chambers—which was rejected out of hand. Through the intercession of Nora and me, Chambers had agreed to allow revisions. But most editorial supervision fell on us. Our side of the correspondence has been drastically cut. The Chambers comment, however, offers insights into his view of his book.]

November 28, 1955
Dear Whit and Esther:

…As I told Esther over the phone, this association with Sol Stein has turned out differently from what we expected…. The failings, errors of commission, and all the rest [in his first draft] were based on lack of information primarily [and] on differences of background and experience so great there was almost no intuitive guidance….

Our first meeting must have been a horror for him, and was exceedingly painful for us, as we ripped the play up the back and dismembered it mercilessly. And then he returned with a rewrite of the first act that... far exceeded our expectations.... Over and above the play itself, we made it clear that his first, and if necessary only, interest must be Whittaker Chambers's interest....

Although the Guild has said that there is no chance of bringing [the play] in this season, they intend to proceed as though it were to be done this spring in order to tie up the best possible theater, director, and cast. This means that they have to have Whit's general approval and conditional approval of future changes and emendations, what Sol calls "an understanding for operational purposes."

...We have a script here, ready to send to you whenever you want. Sol, of course, would like your judgment beyond the technical need for it.... Sol said something to us about the original outline which Whit approved, indicating something of astonishment himself at how it came out. If Whit cannot at this time, or prefers not, to deal at first hand, Ralph and I are perfectly willing, etc., etc.... for as long or in whatever capacity Whit wishes, to whatever degree suits him.

I don't recall if Sol wrote to you about this. Elia Kazan... told Sol that he had read *Witness* and that it was only after reading it that he understood much of what had happened to him in relation to the Party and his break. Our great hope is that Kazan may direct the play, but he promised Sol that if he doesn't, he will be available to advise, and to backstop Sol in case of need.... To finish the business—if we could have some answer on this approval matter by the end of the week, it would be very helpful.

Nixon [a biography of the V.P.] is going ahead very well indeed. We created the impression, with the connivance of Holt [the publisher], that they had a finished ms., in order to discourage any other publisher who might like to put out some competition, and so of course Ralph is again writing under familiar pressures. [Nora and I

did not know at that time that Nixon would, after a pro forma bow to
me, encourage James Keogh, a *Time* writer, to proceed with his own
competition, or that he would give his backing to that book rather
than to mine.] But he has more than passed the halfway mark in less
than four weeks of work, so we can hope to have it completed by
Christmas.... I was startled to find, as I read material I had taken for
granted, that this man is considerably bigger, more to be respected,
more of a hope, than I had realized.... As to what his chances are—
barring acts of God—[eventually] to become president, it seems all
to be in the twin zones of rumor and guesswork. We get "reliable"
reports which run all gamuts.... However, the V.P. told Ralph in confidence that Herbert Hoover told him that as his last service to the
Republic he will do everything in his power to stop [Earl] Warren
from ever getting the nomination. The question is, of course, is it in
his power. Another question also: is Warren the man who will have to
be stopped.

We have been more favored than you in that we have seen the first
two issues of *National Review* (though they were not sent to us)....
But I must say that I have one bitter question to put to Willi
Schlamm if the occasion presents itself. A few weeks ago he gave me
a working-over, on the grounds that Ralph had betrayed the Cause by
not Daring All with [William F.] Buckley's baby, it being the "Last
Great Hope" (yes, Willi's words). [I had been offered the managing
editorship but turned it down—first because I had a wife and two
children to support and so could not gamble, and secondly because I
was not sure that Schlamm, Buckley, and I could work together.]

Nora

December 15, 1955
Dear Whit:

Your silence on the play has an ominous premonitory quality, as perhaps you intended it should.... But there are so many immediate reasons to urge you to reconsider any unfavorable position you may be taking... practical reasons of which you may not be aware. And of course there is always the risk that what I may say may further dismay you, if you are dismayed.... We feel that Sol has made a valid synthesis of the most important elements of the case, and that the presentation is forceful and moving....

There has been a truly remarkable reaction among test readers of the play.... Thornton Wilder, Lionel Trilling, Joseph Mankiewitz, several non-intellectual *aficionados* whose theatrical interests are financial, have all described it as "electrifying," among other things. All predict great financial success, which means favorable reactions among the public.... The Guild, whose attitude has been pretty much "wait and see," has been emboldened by these reactions.... [However] without some kind of nod from you we barely mark time.

Once again, it is not only possible but customary, that many changes be made in a script in rehearsal, even if it should be rewritten before then.... Whatever the nature or content of your misgivings, please believe that we need another bold challenge from our side, strongly delivered and soon. Not only do we urge that the play be it out of necessity, but out of conviction that it serves both you and the battle truly and effectively.

Nora

Dec. 27, 1955
Dear Ralph and Nora,

I have just had a letter from Sol Stein. It is terse, but, in the circumstances, should be more properly called restrained. The circumstances are, of course, that he wants to know my reaction to his script....

First, I think he must realize that I am convalescing from the second thrombosis in two years. This leaves me weak. I'm just not up to much putting effort into anything.... If I could have been enthusiastic over Stein's script, I should have no difficulty. As it is, I have been concerned as to how my disapproval can be broken to him in such a way as not to offend and hurt him least.... But I cannot possibly approve this script. I could write a long screed on what Stein should do, but has not done; and what he has done that he should not do. I haven't the strength for it; nor for that matter, the interest.

I know how to dramatize *Witness*, or at least tell somebody else how to. I know its parts and proportions: I organized them in the first place; scored them for certain musical, but also for certain dramatic, effects.... I was willing that Stein should try the job. If he succeeded even passably, I should have been most interested. In my opinion, he hasn't succeeded at all. He doesn't understand the Revolution, Communism, the Hiss case, its characters or their motivation. Therefore, he creates, instead, caricatures, not only of people, but of situations. If this dealt with antique Rome or the Middle Age, or even the Dreyfus case, perhaps no great harm would be done. But it deals with something going on at this instant. So a pastiche becomes impermissible. What Stein does, with a peculiar certainty of touch, is to sentimentalize and vulgarize.... He does not understand the nature of tragedy.

When he was here, I spent some time trying to explain just that point to him because around it swings all the rest. I told him that tragedy is not the conflict of right and wrong, but the conflict of right and right.... I also gave him a reference where he could find the general principle stated in Hegel. It is in the *Vorlesungen Uber der Aesthetik* and goes something like this, quoting from memory: "*Die ursprungenlich Tragische besteht nun darin dass, innerhalb solcher*

*Kollision, beide Teile des Gegensatzes fur sich genommen Berechtigung
haben.*" That sounds like lousy German to me. But that's how I
remember it. And it means (very roughly): "In origin, tragedy consists
in the fact, that, within such (tragic) collision, both sides of the contradiction hold themselves justified." Now this does not mean (repeat,
not mean) that an Alger Hiss figure says to a Whittaker figure (or vice
versa): "Didn't we both want to be king of the hill?" [Stein's line]—or
something to that effect. At that point you burst with frustration or
laughter.

The prime, first, fact about Alger, as well as myself, is that we are
figures of a humility of a kind a Stein is organically incapable of con-
ceiving. The second fact is that our fierce, searing, pride is rooted in
the force of that humility. It is the humility which, "within such tragic
collision," compels one man to go to prison or where have you, forever denying, and enjoins the other to die, if that is necessary,
because *both* are justified. This is a meaning of *askesis*. But there is
involved, too, a dialectic that Stein is not to be blamed for not grasping. Only, he should not fiddle with what he cannot manage. And
dialectic cannot be taught or explained. You are that way, or you're
not; you feel or you don't. It is outrageous (because it is most deeply
false) to make two such characters say: "We wanted to be king of the
hill." Neither of us wanted to be king of any hill. Only socialists and
liberals think in such terms. Each of us wanted to give what he had to
make that quantum leap of humanity and history possible. Each of us
did, too, though in ways neither of us foresaw. So I can say now:
"Alger—that is one of the most extraordinary men of this age."...
And do you think that real Communists, in the secrecy of the lodge,
do not know my inches? They know them better than any man on the
side I stand for: and they say: "We should not have lost him. *Das war
eine dummheit!*" If I seem to be making too much of one phrase of
Stein's, it is because that one phrase sums up, I think, what is basically wrong with this script. I could take errors of detail and correct

them in passing. But Stein does not understand his matter *au fond*, and that is irreparable. It infects everything.

But let me take just one detail. It is the very funny scene in which I am "chasing" (Stein's word) my wife in what I can only take as incipient amorousness. If the personal aspect is excluded, the initial shock overborne, and the passage read straight, it is seen to be terribly funny. I suggest that it must seem so to others too. But that is not my point here. There is an episode, not told in *Witness*, "because there are kinds of music the world should not hear," because, at bottom, the world is not matured through suffering to the point of understanding them. It occurred during the first Hiss trial, when it looked as if we should be borne down and destroyed, and could not dream of leaving our children in a world where such things were possible. We used to get up before dawn, in those days, to milk. One morning, my wife and I sat together, drinking coffee in the pre-dawn, and, somehow, I explained to her that it might be necessary for us soon to kill, first our children, and then ourselves. Somehow, she told me that she had reached the same conclusion. Then she placed on my hand her own hand which was as cold as if she were already dead. That is the kind of woman I am married to. That is the kind of people we are: we plan to kill our children, but not to let them fall to the mercy of the enemy world. Tell Stein to keep away from the artillery fire. He does not know what war this is. But this is not said harshly. How should he know? But let him not write *bétises* about my wife.

...The problem is exactly the one Aeschylus had to solve in opening the *Agamemnon*. It is all in *Witness*, as a matter of fact. But Stein will not find it. He doesn't know what he is looking for. He shows this, in one way, by personalizing the characters.... These are not people, these are forces. A Greek tragedy is not written to celebrate personal tragedy but to explain why certain rites are yearly repeated to perpetuate something that was done by someone for a reason that affected the lives of those who come together to perpetuate the memory. The question to be answered in dramatic terms is a well-known one: "Wherein is this night different from all other nights?" [Question asked by the youngest child in the Hagaddah on Passover eve.] There are no people (in our sense) in Greek drama, any more than there are people in a Bertoldt Brecht drama. For the same reason. Brecht is the only literary genius Communism has produced. Let Stein ponder Brecht, if not Aeschylus. But part of Brecht's genius consists in the fact that he grasped that the problem is essentially the same—the problem of the Aeschylian and Communist theater—philosophic, religious....

Whittaker

Will you try to explain to Stein that writing is an area where I am almost merciless, beginning with myself. There is nothing personal in it. Something just is or isn't. When my own integrity is not involved, I am a loose constructionist. Where it is, I have no choice: writing is truth—at least the effort to reach truth, understanding that truth and reality are not necessarily the same thing. I suspect that Stein does not grasp the distinction. Perhaps his mind knows it as a fact. Creatively, he disregards or violates it. In dramatizing *Witness*, I should guess that his means in distilling truth would almost be in ratio to his rejection of realism. It is his lapses to realism that are so disastrous to him. No doubt he senses something of the truth of which *Witness* seeks to give one expression. But Stein cannot throw off the realistic ritual. I venture to say that, if the Hiss case could be set out realistically, it could not have occurred in the first place. Any attempt to reduce it to realism is self-defeating because the values (on both sides of the... tradition); which *Witness* tries to fix—whose values occur beyond the order of realism, and are testimony to the degree in which our world has left behind the reality of 2000 years of Western civilization.... In terms of realism, neither Alger nor I can exist, because, in terms of the real world (Communism with capitalist

deformations, or capitalism with socialist deformations), people do
not die for their beliefs. People clip coupons, or try to apply the general line correctly, or pass production norms. Hiss and I are asserting
something beyond this reality (in different personal ways, with different rationales, for different ends—or so it must seem to Alger).

Dec. 31, 1955
Dear Ralph and Nora,

Several days ago, I wrote the attached. It has lain here because I
could not bring myself to send it. I simply cannot bear to disappoint
Stein. And I know the attached letter is not simply inadequate in
itself. Worse, Stein will not understand what I am driving at. He
thinks, I believe, in terms of Broadway theater. That is good enough
in its way. It won't work here. It seems to me that the quickest way to
get at the point is to note this: If the credit line "Based on *Witness*,"
were cut, Stein's play would simply fall apart. It does not stand on its
own legs. I am afraid, in fact, that stretches of it would cause laughs.
Not very hopeful theater. It would be shocking if, from the line of
experience I stand on, I should approve such a play. People would be
perfectly justified in asking, How could you? So would my children.
I am sorry, one does not traffic in the Holy Ghost....

For two years, I have been trying to write a book which, in some
kind of simple, graspable way, may tell people where we are. Its legend is the opening line of *Prometheus Unbound*: "*Force* (to his com-
panion, *Power*, and to their prisoner, Prometheus): 'We have come to
the last path of the world, in the Scythian country, in the untrodden
solitude.'" The Hiss case, including *Witness*, was the effort of a man
to hurl himself against the rationalism which must destroy the world,
and seems to be on the point of doing so. It was a lunge against
Communism *chiefly as the logical, the inevitable epitome of that*

rationalism. It is rationalism that has brought us to the last path of the world and the untrodden solitude—(the Scythian country is just the most curious of literary coincidences).

Whittaker

1956

Jan. 2, 1956

Jan. 2, 1956
Dear Ralph and Nora,

This is rapidly becoming the Stein file. I send it along, all together, to show my rambling reactions.... I have read through all of Stein's script by now. I am of the same opinion still.... Here I will venture only two points. The ms. should be sent to Brandt & Brandt for Miss Baumgarten's perusal. This will assure Stein, or should, that I am not just an unpleasant old man. B & B are my agents. Stein can deal with them much more impersonally than he could with me. I, on the other hand, am attentive to whatever they have to say to me....

Point Two (this music crept past me as I read the whole script) is the question: Who cares? Nobody really wants to see the Hiss case re-done (even if it were much better done). The reason: the technical guilt of Alger Hiss has been settled to a point where it is quite impossible to respect the good sense of those for whom it is a burning issue. There are a lot of them, of course, but that's not the point. Interest now centers on getting beyond that side of the Hiss case, in trying to grasp and fix the meanings of the post-Hiss case, which are, inevitably, the end of capitalism. The people who still believe Alger innocent are (with the usual passel of exceptions) the people for whom he can never be guilty. Not because the facts do not prove him guilty. But because Guilt is Innocence. It is a function of Double Think.... Alger is Innocent *because* he is Guilty. This is not a matter of blind partisanship or ignorance or what have you. This is the mind of a dying age, screaming because someone has touched the aching neurosis; and the war-whoops of a triumphing age, one of whose effective symbols has been imperilled, even if only a little. I might put it another way, which may seem wild enough. The horror of the age isn't that H-bombs may vaporize us all: the horror of the age is that people think they want to reach the moon. The first is an effect, however vast. The second is on the main line of dementia; it tells us what the matter is. So does Alger's guilt: that is why he has to be innocent, why he has to be believed innocent, the more fiercely, the more incontrovertibly, [when] in terms of proof he is manifestly guilty. With Alger the justification of the entire age stands or falls—technology, votes for women, UN, noble experiment, food made from plastics; it's all of a piece, and Alger is one with it; gives it, in fact, precisely the physiognomic form such a one-way trip to Hell must have. That is all that Alger's "innocence" means. If he is guilty, not the New Deal, but the whole Age of Reason is guilty. And Chambers? He is chaos and old night.... A dramatization of *Witness* must be at least as good as *Witness*, and preferably better. I can't agree that this is; or short of that, there is any reason, beyond box office, for producing it. Box office would be wonderful, that is, most helpful to a man without a job. I scarcely need explain why that cannot be a consideration here.

Whittaker

I note with some amusement, after completing Stein's script, that he has already read Brecht. You will see from another section of the file why this strikes me. There is a clear echo of Brecht's *Die Massnahme*.

[Chambers was correct; Stein had read it at the urging of Eric Bentley, theater critic for the *New Republic*.] Before Stein began Version II, I suggested that he read *Blindness At Noon* and *The Possessed*. I have since thought that I was wrong. I should have urged him to read [Stalin's] *Leftism, An Infantile Sickness* (a brilliant thing, if ever I read one!) and a brief work by an eminent lecturer on finance at Ralph's alma mater and mine. It notes that weakening issues may be worked off "on less alert or intelligent investors. The convenient impersonality of the securities market removes the ethical taint." The real dynamite is not to be found in the great propagandists, who, to a surprising extent, never knew the real nature of the capitalism they were condemning, chiefly on moral grounds. The real dynamite is to be found in those eminent conservatives who explain, with unblinking knowingness, how it all works. "The convenient impersonality of the securities market removes the ethical taint."

The intellectuals never get to the point of grasping that such a formulation can be made without raising voice or eyebrows. Millions live and die without the dimmest notion that they are flies clinging to the walls of a cyclotron; no notion at all of what a cyclotron might be or how it works. The intellectuals! Poor damned souls! Some of the best are among the worst, which gets us briefly back to Double-Think.

2 January 1956
Dear Whittaker:

For some time I've had the feeling that coping with one more version of the Hiss case has been a trying experience for you and is the main factor behind your silence. I felt that this might outweigh everything else in your evaluation of Sol Stein's play. But for obvious reasons, I have hesitated to suggest that you relieve yourself, at least temporarily, of the immediate burden by authorizing me to act in your behalf. The play, after all, is about Whittaker Chambers, not Hecuba.... The play will have impact, at a time when such impact is desperately needed. Further delay will give those who oppose the project a chance to kill it. Approval of the script, even with great reservations, must come now; literally nothing of all that must be done immediately can be done without your authorization to move ahead as stipulated in the contract you signed last summer. Once that approval has been granted, the complex job of preparing for production can begin. Before the play goes into rehearsal, it can be revised at leisure following your suggestions, Sol's second thoughts—and Nora's and mine. Were I not so completely convinced of the play's importance, I would never have the brashness to nominate myself for this office. I am aware of precisely what you will be entrusting. If I have correctly interpreted your silence, and if you are willing to let me be your representative, let me know.... I say nothing of how you are and how you have been. But a symbolic candle has been burning at the shrine.

Ralph

Jan. 5, 1956
Dear Ralph,

No, the silence didn't come from that. It came from ill health, from awkwardness in not wanting to disappoint and hurt Stein when I do not approve of his script. After a couple of months in bed, too, you get to living outside time; and, since they keep me doped a lot, I mean lightly doped, at the knock on the door or the voice below the window, I just fall asleep. I was wondering last night after I got to bed how to make this health thing real to you when I found myself lying on my left side, and noticed that I cannot do that even yet without a slight discomfort. And I think that says all I need to. President [Eisenhower] is setting a shocking precedent, and will kill off half the coronaries in the country, keeping up with him. I must say, he doesn't

look, or sound, very good to me at that. I look as usual, like a horse.
So that's that part of it.

I hope you and Nora have been able to piece something out of the
rambling Stein file, which, of course, crossed your letter. In no more
than one hour, I could write out both the first and the last scenes of
Mr. Stein's script, simply by lifting, not snippets poorly spliced and
veneered and out of place, but whole passages out of *Witness*. But I
have the whole dialogue, in fact, in my head, plus—what?—half a
dozen questions and answers, some six or seven words long apiece.
Stein could not know what they would say. The last scene would be
perhaps six lines long, perhaps only four. Then you would hear off-
stage another line, repeated as a whole, then in part, then even less,
overlapping like a whispered sound. But it wouldn't be the Solovetsky
Prison Song. It would be a line from *Witness*. I would lay you a small
bet that even the men would leave the theater blubbering. But I am
not writing Mr. Stein's play for him. If I had wanted to write it, I
should have done it. I have other fish to fry. But when I said Stein's
problem was Aeschylus's in opening the *Atreidae*, I wasn't being
smart-alec or fancy. Stein's problem is to set his drama against physical space: the watchman on the tower, the tower against the night, the
signal torch…. Don't you see, Ralph, what's inherently wrong?… I
mean a style, that is to say, the outward propriety for the inward force
and meaning. There is no style now; because there is no grasp: there
is only clutching.

I have myself moved on to something else, as I tried to suggest
confusedly in my letters. I haven't the time, I haven't the strength
(they interlace) to do Stein's script for him. Not now, not now. It
might have been earlier: it might just conceivably be possible later. I
scarcely think so. I don't like going back to something. I suppose this
is where your generous offer to act for me comes in. Do not think
me ungrateful. The very opposite is true. No one can act for me
here, even if I were heartless enough to let you do what you should

not be doing, since you, too, must move forward, not turn back. Stein must write his own play: and it must be a better one than Versions I & II. You see why I am so widely loved as an editor. But you know, you are an artist: it is right or it isn't—and I'm not talking about gingerbread which can always be scrapped off: I'm talking about an inwardness, which partakes both of mind, force and grace (in the theological sense).

The basic difficulty is that Stein, and certain of his friends, kind hearts and loving people, have decided that the Hiss case must be adopted and the heathen redeemed *theremit*. But Stein is not himself converted. He is only converted to an attitude towards the case and against Communism; he is not converted to what made the case possible. I think that, brought face to face with all that, he would be shocked in a quite schoolboy way; rather decently, perhaps. He is a bourgeois. I was once praising somebody to a ranking Communist who heard me out and then asked: *"Hat er je verschwort*—Has he ever conspired?" Stein has never conspired. There have been times, there may be places even yet (Winston likes to talk about the "sunny uplands"), where never to have conspired is to be happy. I have a dreadful, unredeemed sense that, not to have gone to the heart of an environing experience of scope and range, it is not quite to have grown up. So I used to amuse Esther by describing a certain kind of young American to her as "Motherless at 33."... Forgive me for writing this way.... I wish I could see and talk with you and Nora. Typewriting letters, too, is like lying on my left side.

Whittaker

...Why should I be a tease? The last line of that play, spoken out of the darkness, should be: "Voices of beloved children, calling to me from the garnered field at dusk." But Stein is completely wrong. The Man would not be sitting somewhere. He could be walking, back to the audience, into the dark. At that line, he would turn and stop and,

for a moment listen. Blackout. Where did that ending come from? I
will tell you: it came from the garnered fields at dusk. Would you like
to hear another line that came to me from the same place yesterday:
"You know what age this is—this is the age when Lazarus must raise
himself from the dead."

[Excerpts from a four-and-one-half page single-space letter from Nora
about the Sol Stein play.]

January 9, 1956
Dear Whittaker:

...Unlike you, Ralph and I do not believe the failures of the play or
of Stein's understanding are irremediable, and also unlike you, we do
believe... that it is important to have it and to have it produced. If it
were not for the last, and overwhelming reason, we would not trouble you or ourselves with any further discussion. As a matter of fact,
at a minimum we would let the matter rest for a time, if you yourself
had not left a small door open by the suggestion that Miss
Baumgarten see the manuscript.... It goes against every instinct to
press you at this time—at any time, really—when you must be barely
convalescent from the attack....

In many ways the gap between [Stein] and us is as great as the gap
between him and you. The remarkable thing is that he has [some-
times] been able to leap across.... That is what has given us encour-
agement to keep working with him. This boy is 29 years old, from a
completely bourgeois background, without any experience whatso-
ever of the Communist Party, of forms of self-immolation or exalta-
tion, of the depths and heights of daring and courage and horror and
despair and challenge and submission.... He is still in the process of
assimilating ingredients with which you and Ralph were born....

Ralph and I have been put to the curious task of pre-digesting some of the components of his current experience and force-feeding them to him....

There will never be a play, unless you write it—and perhaps the physical limitations of the form are such that not even you can write it—which will be as good as *Witness*.... That is an impossible condition for you to impose and one which I hope you will withdraw.... If you are willing to withdraw that condition, we can return to the basic question of whether the trouble with Stein's play is organic....

Ralph's letter, which crossed yours, was as explicit as he can ever be in such a situation.... Ralph is prepared, now that *Nixon* is off his hands, to move in on Stein to a degree and in a manner that was not physically possible until he finished his book. He is ready to rewrite for Stein, if that proves necessary. At a minimum, he can now work with him, rather than on him....

When the final script is done, you can still say no. But it would give us time to work on the script with the assurance that if it is satisfactory the Theater Guild will be committed to the hilt, and it will give us at least six months in which to work with Stein... and to see in a degree of tranquility whether the trouble is really organic.... And if the revised manuscript should meet your approval, you can further delegate to Ralph the authority to assume the responsibilities actual production will entail.

(We don't know how much you may or may not know of the mechanics of a theatrical production. Through Ralph's and my experience—of which you may not be aware—we know very well that a play can be, and very often is, entirely different in production from its original conception or draft. You would have to have someone present to exercise supervision of it all through rehearsal even if you approved the original script.... Such a proviso should therefore be contained in any contracts.)...

Nora

23 January 1956
Dear Whittaker:

Such a failure of communication. And after the ominous correspondence, I am tempted to stay thoroughly and completely out of it. But
the Nixon book is finished—we okayed page proofs this week—and I
am at loose ends. So I will repeat what I said perhaps too briefly in
my last letter. Then I will move on to other things.

I once began writing a play [a rewrite of Euripides' *The Trojan
Women*]. The first scene takes place at dawn, outside the burning
Troy. The curtain rises on a dark stage, lit only by the reflection of
flickering fires. A Greek sentry stands motionless. An old woman, her
head covered by a shawl, enters.

Sentry: Who goes there?
Hecuba: A woman.
Sentry: That's hard to deny.
           What woman, then?
Hecuba: A woman too full of years.
Sentry: But not too old to sneak about a question.
           (*He steps up close to her.*)
           Well, I don't blame you. (*He laughs.*)
           Pass, Queen of Troy, Hecuba, majesty of ashes.
Hecuba: Your mouth is full of bravery.
Sentry: (*Laughs again*) But not of dust.

This is bravura. But it's a good way to start a play. And I think the
manner of it would be right for Sol Stein's play. I quote the passage to
lay my cards on the table. Because I would like a crack at Sol's
play.... The main trouble now with the play is not only its lack of
understanding of the case and its import. That is a matter of education and could be achieved more easily than you imagine. The
rhythms are wrong. I feel I could supply both the understanding and

the rhythms. I am sure I could whip the play into a form which you
would find reasonably acceptable....

I must sound very eager about this. And I am, for all the reasons I
have given you—plus one. It will give me a chance to work at something I believe in, to do the kind of writing I have not done in years,
and to get out from under the terrible hand of boredom which by
decree is my workaday lot. I have been placed in a limbo, told I will
neither be fired nor promoted, and given the pettiest kind of routine
stories to handle. If you've noticed the masthead, Time Inc. has
moved in with a vengeance—with more to come.... I have a feeling
that if I offered myself up to *Time*'s editors, they would hire me just
to do *Newsweek* in the eye. Nora is convinced that they would hire
me, for purposes of revenge, and then drop me quickly. This, more
than anything else, has stayed my hand....

How much of the shenanigans in Washington have reached you?
They have been lovely to behold. The writhing agonies of the [anti-
Nixon] palace guard over Nixon seem to have subsided, at least for
the time being. The first two-headed President in history—James
Milton Eisenhower Hagerty—has decided that Nixon can't be
dropped from the ticket. Uke has just about decided to run—or so I
am reliably informed—and it is generally realized at the White
House that to drop Nixon would be a damaging admission *in re*
health and longevity [that the president would not be able to last out
a second term]. The palace guard has also realized that Nixon is the
only man it has. [Chief Justice Earl] Warren has turned down all private overtures. He's much too happy destroying our jurisprudence.
So that leaves Harold Stassen, the idiot boy of peace. Ergo, it must
be Nixon, even if Uke doesn't run.... I'm still betting 6-to-5 that
[Averell] Harriman will get the Democratic nomination. Which is a
pity. Stevenson would be so much easier to beat. [And was.]

What else goes on?... the opinions of *National Review* seem to
carry just about as far as Bill Buckley's voice. I am not on the mailing

list but I have seen most of its issues and have a view of its *weltan-schauung*. One of my agents informs me that between issues Willi Schlamm shakes his head sadly and asks, "What's the matter with Ralph? Why is he behaving so strangely? Why isn't he with us in the thick of the fight?"...

Dear Whittaker. All this chatter and so little said. And nothing about you, about your illness. If this were the better of all possible, or even probable, worlds, I would be able to visit you if only for an hour or so. Get better quickly, for we love you and need you. Other than that, I cannot say directly. But what I have been feeling I have put into a small verse recently. Perhaps, if I type it out below, it will tell you what has been happening for the last few months.

> *In these my private devotions*
> *there are no roads, no signs,*
> *no thin horizons smudged by use or time,*
> *only a skeleton to rattle in the light,*
> *and the taste of salt on my tongue,*
> *the honk and hoot of my desires.*
> *In the private moment that is all—*
> *all as a function of some,*
> *as a constant of nothing.*
> *Who then can speak to God—*
> *the tangible nail in the vanishing skin?*
> *Who knows the syllables of recompense,*
> *the torpid epithet,*
> *the burbling sigh and gasp?*
> *The single mind returns to its single station.*
> *The private moment leaps forward.*
> *But the rattle on stone is no hallelujah*
> *to the God within.*
> *The silence of the measuring pulse*
> *gauges the irremedial span.*
> *the visible hope divides*
> *the gesture at the door,*
> *the tender murder at the gates of Hell.*
> *In this my private devotion*
> *there is only the adequacy of not enough,*
> *as when the mind returns*
> *to the overt scrutiny of the public square.*

Or more succinctly:

> *Go to the thicket:*
> *in a hollow tree*
> *the face is hidden, its mouth*
> *bloody as a pomegranate.*
> *The thicket and the tree*
> *mean nothing,*
> *but in the face lurks more*
> *than the secret eyes.*
> *Lift up the face:*
> *there is no bone behind it,*
> *only the terrible accoutrement of shape*
> *depthless as water.*

Ralph

Jan. 24 [?], 1956
Dear Ralph,

I should say that those two poems that close your letter are very good poems; very moving, too, especially to someone who knows you…. I hear in them your way of saying: "This is the age when Lazarus must raise himself from the dead." But they are not poems I could ever have written. To me it is *la musique dodecaphonique.* What troubles me is that I am not sure whether it is sounding from a point in the landscape ahead of me or in back of me. You do not, I think, have to ask this question: you have only to sing; it is your voice. I, as a listener, must ask the question because to answer it involves not only locating the source of the music, but that raises another question: what does this idiom, apart from the meaning, disclose?

Around Christmas, there arrived in my mail a small quarterly, styling itself: *i.e.,* the *Cambridge Review,* which seems to appear to have some undefined relation with Harvard University. In this issue was an essay, called *To the End of Thought,* by someone identified as

John Hurkan. I know nothing about him and had never before heard
mention of the *Cambridge Review*.... The central [theme], at least
the most important, it seems to me, is Hurkan's perception of Marx's
psychological profundity. Marx's economics, Hurkan notes quite correctly, citing the record, were an afterthought. It is Marx's psychology
that is all-engrossing and all-justifying and all-explanatory. This was
the theme of the third part of *Witness*, of which only the bare bones,
not even the whole skeleton, found print; and its lack is one of the
howling failures of the book. But there is much more in Hurkan than
this; and I hope that (perhaps through *Newsweek*) you will get hold
of, i.e., last quarter of 1955, and read the piece. I should like to have
your judgment on it. Offhand, I can't think of anybody else whose
judgment in the matter interests me, except perhaps Willi. But Willi,
of course, was a Right Winger, if, indeed, he was politically classifiable even to that extent; and, of course, to me, Right Wing
Communists are simply Social Democrats *manqués*. To this must be
added the puzzling fact that they became Communists. I think, only
the academic mind could have much interest in unscrambling that.

About a year ago, I found myself chatting with a West European
former Communist, a member of his country's Central Committee,
and a friend of Bukharin's. I'll call this gentleman Teddy, since the
only name I know him by is a similar pseudonym. Teddy told me that
he himself, even when a member of his Central Committee, had
never believed in the dialectic, and further, that Bukharin had told
him that he (Bukharin) did not believe in the dialectic, either. It was
like hearing somebody say, "Of course, His Holiness has always
remained a Presbyterian." Yet I have no reason whatever to disbe-
lieve Teddy: he is obviously a highly intelligent man, even if undialec-
tic (and there is, as they say, more than one road to Heaven).
Besides, we have Lenin's corroboration in his Testament in which he
says, like a wise Reverend Father, who sniffs the truth but deems it
improper to have it set forth too barrenly: "I am sure that Bukharin

has ever really understood the dialectic." Even when I first read this (as a child of 28 or 29), it seemed to me a mind-staggering statement, though I could not see that it affected my comrades as having more than political implications.

Well, I dragged in Teddy to make a point about Willi. But, at the risk of telling you again what I may have told you before, I think I will tell you that story, or a bit of it. For it seems to me most wonderful. Friends arranged my meeting with [Teddy]. He had long been aware of me. But I did not know he existed until shortly before he walked into the room. The experience is always the same. The two men look at each other with a glance, half smile, half challenge, in which each says: "You old pteraspis, how did you survive from the pre-Cambrian seas?" Then we sat at opposite ends of a couch (just as it had been with Krivitsky) and, in five minutes, we were locked in a conversation that seemed to have been going on all our lives. It went on for about an hour. Then Teddy asked me: "Is there no hope?" I said: "There is no hope." He repeated his question and I repeated my answer. We had been speaking in English. He said in German, tears coming to his eyes: "*Ich zittere in der Nacht*—I tremble in the night." I saw that he had not understood exactly what I meant, and also that he never would. But I thought that I must add something. I said: "You see, there are no *political* solutions left. There are only martyrdoms. And martyrdom does not speak to the present. It speaks to the future and to posterity." He answered: "*Dann bin ich am Ende meines Lateins*—Then I am at the end of my Latin"—which is German for "Then, for me, school is out."

I tell this story for its own worth which to me, at least, seems great. For me, it gained something by the fact that, as I may have told you before, I spoke the next day with a Russian Anarchist, who had spent part of his youth in Siberian exile. He was dying (may have died since) of a heart condition. He got up from his couch to talk with me and to bring me a snapshot of himself as a young man, sit-

ting beside a window of a Siberian *isba*. He was a typically dreamy
young revolutionist and the window was filled with potted plants. He
pointed to them and said: "The Siberians are not so mellow as the
Great Russians. But there are the flowers. So, you see, there is something gentle in these people, too." There is no spoke of formal logic
that conjoins these two stories. The link is different, and, I think,
larger than logic; or it is of a larger logic than usual. I do not know
any ready way to try to include it all other than a well-known phrase
of Nietzsche's: "We are all Hyperboreans." Do you know how *The
Trojan Women* ends:

Wrath in the earth, and quaking, and a flood that sweepeth all....
And passeth on.

(Incidentally, we are not only the Hyperboreans, we are the
Nietzscheans to a degree most of us do not understand, and which
would have horrified the master.)

Now I shall put the question to which all this wordiness has been
leading: Do you still want to work with Stein on that script? If your
answer is still yes, I guess I may not say that I shall be surprised; I
shall simply talk with you about it, and about the Hyperboreans.
Meanwhile, other things are happening in this connection. B & B
sustains Stein to some extent: certainly a much larger extent than I
had expected. As I promised, this forces me to a basic re-examination
of my position, not so much of the script (B & B, in the main, sustains my objections about a lot of that) as of other angles. I will act as
quickly as I can. For one thing, I must not be outdone by the speed
of my president in announcing his availability. Is there anybody
(except *National Review*) who doesn't know that he is going to run? I
will keep you informed soonest of what goes on *in re* Stein's script.

Now I want to reply to a couple of points in your letter that seem
important to me. Second things first. I am not sure that you are
deprived of *National Review* due to petulance (see this week's editorial on fulfillment woes). I am sure that the counsel I gave you about

going with NR was, with respect to the grounds involved and your prospects, right counsel. I would give it again; now with greater assurance…. But I am not sure that the voice is not carrying a little farther. It seems to be paying to carry; some kind of deal must underlie the iterations on the air that NR is the voice of our common humanity….

Much more important is the question of your going to *Time*…. In the past, I have said to you about *Time*: Better not. This is the first time that I have thought: Think carefully. It all lies in the timing and its implications; in the competition between the weeklies; the new arrivals in your shop and your stagnation there…. Would it harm if you went now and talked to someone at *Time*, Roy Alexander presumably, about a switch? The great risk, it seems to me offhand, is that intelligence of your action would fly back to 42nd St. For it seems to me that *Newsweek* has its friends inside the *Time* structure. I could tell you something about Alexander, but [orally]…. He and I were never friends. It would never surprise me to catch his knife sinking (if the room were dark enough) into my kidney. Yet I rather like Roy myself and do not count him among my active enemies. There are people with whom it is possible to have such curious relationships—the kind of relationships that intellectuals do not understand because they do not conform to book reason. Besides, Roy is a Catholic, and, with respect to me, that often counts for much. One of Roy's brothers is a Jesuit. The other, Jack, foreshortened *Witness* for the *SEP* [*Saturday Evening Post*] (and, curiously, the mail that brought your letter brought one from Jack).

What I am saying is *not*: Act! I am saying: Think carefully, to try to determine whether this is not the time to act. If I can give you further information that may help you to act, ask. If I thought that recommendation from me could help you at *Time*, you could write your own ticket. I would probably raise your ante. But I am so poor a thing, that I believe a recommendation from me might positively hurt you; and that the less you say about me in that quarter, the better it might be for you....

Whittaker

7 February 1956
Dear Whittaker:

Que veut dire "dodecaphonique"? I have looked it up in all dictionaries to no avail. I can only assume that it alludes to the twelve-tone scale. Or am I crying out in the cacophony of the Twelve Tribes? My poems are much too private, both in their voice and their distribution, for that. A wilderness crying out for a voice....

I was somewhat startled by your reaction to my veronica about *Time.* I was sure you would oppose it, so I was merely doing pyrotechnics with the cape. But I was to a great extent serious. I agree with you, however, that the timing is all important—and there I am at a loss. The basic problem is this: I don't care if *Newsweek* finds out that I have been flirting with Time Inc. However, I don't want to make the approach and then be rebuffed. Tactically, this would be bad. Some kind of tentative gesture must come from *Time,* and I haven't the slightest idea how to bring it about.... The only possibility I can think of is to join the Church and then have Bishop Sheen confess me onto the magazine. But about and beyond questions of dogma, I am too irritated by the treatment accorded me since the publication of [my novel] *Day of Reckoning.* The brethren have dropped me cold. No more invitations to speak at Communion Breakfasts, no more friendly hints about conversion, no more conspiratorial chattiness....

...And now to Sol Stein's play. First a report. I met with Harold Freedman of Brandt & Brandt [their chief dramatic agent and], Bill Fitelson [a lawyer for the Theater Guild], and Sol. We plighted our

troth over coffee (I had scotch) at the Gotham—and Freedman's performance was a wonder to behold.... I know Freedman of old; he
used to be my brother's agent [in the days when, as Edward Trevor,
he was a Broadway leading man]. The purpose of the meeting was to
find out what he thought of Sol's play, but for fifteen minutes he
ducked all questions and attempted to cross-examine us. Finally, he
began to give us his account of a letter written by one Whittaker
Chambers to one Bernice Baumgarten. You may be interested to
learn that as interpreted by the Prophet Freedman, this is what you
said or implied: Times have changed. The Hiss case educated people
on the subject of Communism. Then McCarthy came along and they
were faced with the fascist enemy. Now McCarthy is demolished and
the people can think about Communism again. But they must think
of it in terms of the Spirit of Geneva and the hydrogen bomb.

From that point on, we all went ice-skating on the tablecloth.
Freedman talked more and more, said less and less. Sol listened in
horrified amazement. I made one statement in which I summarized
what were your objections. Fitelson made a small oration in praise of
Whittaker Chambers: "He was a great man when he was in the
underground, he was a great man when he broke, he has shown
tremendous courage in spite of what was done to him during the
case." Freedman looked slightly sick at this point but said that for
dramatic purposes you should be slightly less saintly. I said that of
course you should be less saintly, that you were a tough boy.
Freedman didn't know just what I meant by that, but there was a
flicker in Fitelson's eye. (After Freedman had left, Fitelson said,
"Sure times have changed—for the worse.") If you want my summary
of what Freedman's real views are, he believes that Sol's play can be
molded into a first class script—and that's precisely what he's afraid
of. I kept thinking as he spoke that, of course, he was Clifford Odets's
agent, Robert Sherwood's agent, and (I'm reasonably sure) Lilian
Hellman's agent. This kind of bridge between the two worlds should
be carefully mined.

Anyhow, I didn't have to pay for my two drinks of scotch. That is my normal fee. But the play still lies between us. Yes, I want to work with Sol. From your letters, I think I know what you have in mind. I am going to go over the play speech by speech with Sol, taking notes. If you want to write me about it, that would be fine. If you can bear the strain, I'll go down to Westminster. Or we could do that at a later date. I assume that in your last letter you were saying, "Be thou my exequatur," and I will proceed on that assumption. I suspect that this will make it tough for Sol, because I too can be tough as an editor. I rejoice, however, that you have reconsidered enough to let us take a whack at it. For the time being, the Guild is holding off the pressure.

Right now I am seized by the pre-publication jitters. We won't have books until late in the month, there is the impending competition of Jim Keogh's book, and I sit and wonder whether I have done the right kind of job. This is a very carefully calculated book, designed to do a very specific job—and there is always the possibility that my calculations were all wrong. Moley saw the manuscript and rose up in arms over the second sentence: "Conscience is the luxury of kings and newspaper columnists." The McCarthy people will be furious and so will the troglodyte Right, for different reasons. My sole consolation to date is that Murray Chotiner—the shrewdest politician I know and Dick's campaign manager—is very pleased. Heigh ho.

Ralph

PS: This may be of interest to you. I've just returned from Canada where I had a talk with one Captain Mikhail Tulin, courtesy of an MI-6 friend who introduced us. He's a Soviet product—born in 1927, Komsomol, CP, Smersh, and then *zampolits* in the Red Air Force. One of the things which made him defect were the NTS leaflets, dropped by balloon, which explains the present clamor [among many administration people] against cooperating with the organization.

[Nationalniy Trudovoy Soyoz (NTS) was a clandestine organization, working in and out of the USSR with considerable effectiveness— and roundly denounced by American liberals.] I asked Tulin if the Russians were afraid of the H bomb. He said, "Yes, very worried." Didn't they feel reassured by the fact that they, too, had the bomb? "No," he said. "The Russian people don't believe they have it. They think it's all propaganda. When I was a political officer, I was ordered to tell the troops about the great weapons we had. But whenever I asked to see any descriptive material, they told me that I couldn't see it, that it was too secret. There is a joke among the troops in East Germany. They say, 'Of course we have the atom bomb. When I was in Leningrad, I saw the factory.'" The implications of this, I think, are tremendous.

At one point in the conversation, the Brit who arranged the meeting asked Tulin, "Do you attend the Greek Orthodox services?" Tulin's wife broke the silence that followed. "That's not a question you ask someone who was brought up a Communist." (She's Russian, but British-educated.) Tulin said, "In Russia, it was dangerous for a Communist to attend services, and more than dangerous for a political officer." There was silence, and then I changed the subject. He is anti-Communist, but not for the reasons you and I are anti-Communist. He hates the regime because he loves Russia. There must be millions like him.

Feb. 8, 1956
Dear Ralph,

Dodecaphonique? Ca veut dire: 12-tone. I picked it up from Randall Jarrell.... I think I was boorish about your poems; I mean, all thumbs in saying what I meant to say. I meant to say that they moved me and that that "wondered me" (a localism) because it takes a good deal to wonder me these days, and because the idiom was not my native idiom, and I do not believe that it will remain yours. Yet it may; and that set me spinning ineptly. I was reached in another way: I know how intimate an honor it is when somebody (somebody grown and sensible) lets you see his verse.

We could spend a good part of the day, talking out points in your letter.... First *Time*. So far as I can recall, I never asked H.R. Luce a favor for myself. Never at any time. Twice I asked favors for other people. One was shortly after Pearl Harbor. A year or so before, I had been given an office boy to train as a writer. He was from Harvard and wore low white tennis shoes, winter and summer, to work.... I greatly dislike to train writers, and the ME promised me that this one would be the last one he would ever inflict on me. All the youth had to recommend him (so far as I could see) was the curious history that had moved *Time* to try him as a writer. As an office boy, he was horribly bored, but also observant. *Time* was in one of its episodic thrift campaigns; and memos were going out... to urge writers not to waste paper, ink, and pencils. They were signed Winestock, or whatever was the name of the economizing genius behind them. One morning, everybody found on his desk a memo that went like this, but better: "In the interests of economy, *Time*'s management urges you not to throw away your Lily cups after using them. In future, used Lily cups will be left at the water coolers so that others may take advantage of them. (Signed) Winestock."... All the office boys were taken into Authority and made to sign: Winestock; and of course, the lot fell where it belonged, on Jonah, who said with utmost frankness (he was a devout Catholic as well as a Harvard man) that, certainly, he had got up the memo as a lark because he thought *Time* was being peculiarly stuffy. So they decided to try him out as a writer.

In those days, *Time* did things like that; maybe it still does. But I doubt it. Anyway, Jonah was passed on to me. His first book review was horrid; all the worst. He re-wrote it. There was nothing left to edit. He became one of *Time*'s really good writers. He also became

one of my really good friends. Then the War came. Jonah had not the
least desire to go up unto Nineveh. He was married; a child was on
the way. I do not think he was afraid, no more, I mean, than 160 million other people. Everything subsequent seems to prove that he
wasn't. He just thought that it was peculiarly stuffy. He asked me to
help. I saw War Correspondents Teddy White and John Hersey
(superb in uniform) and that awful Yugoslav, Stoyan Pribitchevitch
(sp?) also splendid in an officer's uniform. I thought, "Why not
Jonah?" So I wrote H.R. Luce a memo and said: "Why send writers
who can write to shoot machine guns about which they know nothing. Why not send Jonah as a war correspondent?" There was no
reply. At the time, I thought that was the proper reply, and I guess
(from the mists of some peculiarly stuffy Olympus) I still do. That
was Solicitation No. 1. At the price of digression, I must go on a little
about Jonah. I have a sad feeling that I've told you all this before.
But, at my age, one repeats because there is so little time left to tell
all the wonderful things that happened: so one crowds. Anyway,
Jonah's last hope was being turned down at his physical. He found
himself, during the physical, far down a line of New York youth. The
doctor, progressing slowly down that line had been tapping hollow
chests, looking into liverish eyes and at the fine sum of malnutrition
and bad living. The doctor stopped in front of him and stepped back
to admire. "Well," he said, "it's a pleasure to find one healthy speci-
men at last." They made Jonah the man with the walkie-talkie who
goes in advance of the wave [the point man]. On D-Day, or D-Day-
Plus-1, he went into Normandy. He was an NCO and a tough a soldier by then. From his experiences, he wrote me some of the best
stories of the war, the kind that never get into history books, the kind
that seem so untelling that even censors let them through.

Here I will remember only a night after the fall of Paris, when all
of Jonah's troop piled into a brothel; piled upstairs. But Jonah sat
downstairs (Catholic, wife in America, and, by then, a baby son)....

The madame sat studying him, incredulous, asking, from time to time, if he did not mean to go up. She was deeply puzzled, and probably a little affronted, as tradespeople get. Clearly, she considered the usual possibility. But, no, in this case, it was simply not thinkable. At last the truth dawned on her, with one of those prolonged Latin expletives, "*Aaaaaaah!*" she said, in wonder and comprehension, "*un serieux!*" How right she was. And how rare to meet one, and how refreshing at times. This *serieux* walked unsolicited into my room last December and sat down beside my bed, where I was feeling fairly low. "I think you need help," he said. "Here's how I propose to give it to you." It was extremely interesting to listen to because he has since become someone most amusingly able in the world of finance. Something about bread on the waters.

[Chambers had another account of how he succeeded in the stock market, at a time when his finances were low. "When Bill Buckley buys, I sell; and when he sells, I buy," he said.]

That was the first of my two personal appeals to Mr. Luce. As I said, it raised a nice point of ethics, provided one could see it over all the lapses that had been raised first. Still, I could say that Luce had behaved with perfect propriety, and that his silence was perhaps a sterner rebuke to my own lapse than the most shocked rejoinder. Besides, the gentleman is shrewd; he knew that I would have no regrets and no apologies; had not then, have not now. My second intervention came a year or so ago. No point of higher ethics was involved. The man I was pleading for had served Luce well, with volunteer intelligence and faith, when a good part of the crew was mutinous or disloyal. Luce wrote me that he was taking personal command, would himself talk with my client. What happened next is too recent to write about. Besides, I become apoplectic, just as in a Victorian novel. It is why I did not send Mr. Luce a Christmas card last year; and no doubt, why, for the first time in a decade, he did not send me one. I am rarely righteous, I hope. I am unsparingly

righteous in this case. But it tells me, past peradventure, that my intervention for you at *Time* would ruin you quickly.... But, Lord, I don't
know how to proceed from here. Yes, I know a way, but I would have to
go to New York to initiate it; and it is no guarantee. At most, I could say,
"He's mine!"—meaning you. I am told that in those fraternities where a
unanimous vote is still required for acceptance, if a brother feels that
his brothers are less enthusiastic than he is about a pledge, then the
brother says glacially: "He's mine!"... It means that, if the brothers
blackball his man, he will blackball all the other pledges when the box
goes around. Obviously, I am not in quite so good a position.

Whittaker

If Chotiner likes your book, I should think you might feel: "That's it."
I thought I heard the president say distinctly, yesterday, that he
meant to run again. But Fulton Lewis [a right-wing radio commenta-
tor] and a great many other minds seem to have heard him in just the
opposite sense. I still think he means to. But I am proverbially wrong
about U.S. politics (Americans never do what I expect them to do—
at least, that's one way to phrase it).... My rule of thumb is: the man
never willingly relinquishes power. Most people do not know how
potent a brew power is. So, in my experience, most people tend to
miss out on central motives. This may be the thrice wondrous exception to the rule. But I still think I heard right....

I note on page 3 [of this letter], I credit our age with disbelief as
an article of Orthodoxy. An Irish bull, I do believe. Do you know Ld.
Rothschild's mother's definition of an Irish bull? "Of twenty cows,
lying down in the field, the one standing is the Irish Bull."

14 February 1956
Dear Whittaker: ,

We have just had a long session with Sol Stein, going over the play in
great detail. I'm afraid I gave him a rough time—I in my small way

can be a merciless editor—and he took it very well. I ripped apart
the scene between Chambers and Hiss—the attempt to get Hiss to
break. I told him that he missed the whole point…. Hiss as the figure
of the Communist. He understood what I meant when Nora quoted
at him what you had written us—that tragedy is the conflict of right
and right. But guidance is needed in the re-writing…. If you have the
energy to write one or two paragraphs, that would light the light. I
am grateful that you have gone this far along the way with us—but
gratitude always demands more to be grateful for.

When I wrote you about *Time*, I was more or less thinking aloud,
with perhaps the hope that you might know of some crevice in the
armor through which I could poke a spear. But even if I were dead
certain that your intercession would do the trick I would be inalter-
ably opposed to it, simply because it would not be right. Your position *vis-à-vis Time* is on another plane. There is also the question of
leaving *Newsweek*. At this particular time it would be wiser to
remain.

I am sure you that you heard Eisenhower saying he was going to
run again. (The best demonstration of this came last night, at the
National Republican Club dinner, at which Leonard Hall
[Republican National chairman] and Thomas Edmund Dewey
rubbed up against Nixon as if he were drenched with catnip.)
Incidentally, if you have been hearing stories that Uke would resign if
the doctors made an adverse report, the source was La Luce [Clare
Boothe] via Herbert Hoover. This is off-the-record, but I know as
fact that she did say this to HH. *Et rose, elle a vécu ce que vivent les
roses*…. With a Nixon victory, I may bloom again.

Ralph

[There were two questions being voiced at the time. The first was
whether Eisenhower would run. The second was whether Nixon
would be his running mate. There was strong pressure on Eisenhower
to dump Nixon as being "too political"—the role which the president

had assigned to Nixon, allowing him, Eisenhower, to play the father figure. Eisenhower, moreover, was ambivalent about Nixon. He had not once invited his vice president to the Eisenhower farm in Gettysburg, a calculated slight. And there were times when I would find Nixon literally close to tears after a session at the White House during which Eisenhower humiliated Nixon, as he had done regularly to some of his generals at SHAEF.]

Feb. 17 [?], 1956
Dear Ralph,

I've been supposing that you had my letter. But when yours came this AM, I realized that I had burned mine to you.... I had written you to say that I had sent B & B some script. But that was the day the stock market went up one to six points on the rumor that the Prez will run. I had so much fun wishing that I had been one of the soft-faced men who did well out of the president's coronary, or the hard-faced men out of copper wire to Russia (most when we had been warned by the knowing ones that "coppers are wearing thin") that I got ashamed of myself, and dropped the mess in the fire....

In [a] letter to B & B, I made several points, of which No. 1 was: "I do not (repeat *not*) want to write this play." I wrote that because it did not take much wit to foresee that this is just what I might end up doing. But I am writing a book, and, finding that all I can handle; and perhaps a little more. The book is much more important to me than a re-tread of *Witness*. *Ahora quisiera un vaso de vino blanco muy seco* [Now I would like a glass of very dry white wine]. Poor Stein, 'e probably needs Scawtch. But why did he ever want to tangle with me in the first place? Didn't he know? Didn't anybody warn him?

It does look as if the Prex means to run. This was the strategy *qua* strategy that I had supposed the strategy to be. It was Esther who managed, within the last fortnight, to give me pause by reminding me of something that, in my vast adding up of infinite details, I had,

not so much overlooked, as given, in my wife's opinion, a wrong value
to. By God, I said, for I am very shy and modest about such matters
as in so much else (humor), I said: I believe you're right. And, by
God, I was. So that made me wrong. At least it tempered my specula-
tions. If you want speculation in all its horrid humor, you should have
listened the other evening to Felix Morley [a libertarian writer and
broadcaster] explaining to the millions what Khrushchev means to
say when Khrushchev said what he meant.

Foster Dulles's chief sin is that he seems not to know that we've
always been on the brink; but only when the enemy wants to push
does it have much hazard, or high hazard; and so far, they've generally
wanted not to. Still, I think history will show that there was a fierce
division in the Politburo circa 1946-48 for and against war in Europe.
But not, I think, since. Perhaps the ICBM does go (shooting from east
to west, of course) about 1500 miles. Still—well, it should be most
interesting in the rather near future. That is, whatever happens. A
play about *Witness*, however, will change nothing at all. I didn't even
handle the thing right in *Witness* because I left out the step by step
progression whereby events (bouncing off me like atoms) moved me
to act—seizure of Czechoslovakia, Berlin blockade—when I was out-
voted, all the rest to one, to make *Time's* policy one for crashing the
Blockade with a tank division and air cover). Until that moment, when
the case had begun, and Dick Cleveland and Macmillan and I got
down to Light Street, after a busy day upstairs, and saw the big headlines that the Chink Reds were in Harbin or Mukden; and I pointed
to the headline in appalled silence. They looked dutifully, and I realized that they did not know what it meant. I knew at that moment that
I was falling right down 29 flights of the Baltimore Trust Bldg. It was
all over that day. History is so untidy, takes so long to mop up. But the
world's lost now. So you can understand perhaps a certain dragginess
on my part when it comes to dramatizing *Witness*.

Whittaker

...I wonder where you heard that "Uke" thing. There is no Uke. So long, that is, as long as our boy [Nixon] is protected. I pay off. I try to, anyhow.

21 February 1956
Dear Whittaker:

Just a brief note [about the play].... My own creation has been limited to the construction of some 46 feet of bookshelves which, frankly, I find a more satisfying way of passing the time than in writing books. Carpentry has both therapeutic and theological uses.

Ralph

Mar. 2,3,4 [?], 1956
Dear Ralph,

So deep a silence lies over both flanks of Operation Stein that I suspect that my script offerings have embarrassed everybody, and that, to spare me, silence has seemed best. But it doesn't matter at all. All have my blessing in saying, "To a trash basket, go!" The only usable script is usable script. Do what seems best for now. I have no notion whatever, at this point, how the battle goes, or, indeed, whether there is any battle. I am convinced that there is only one way to get all straight, namely, to talk with everybody, eye to eye. This I cannot do. So you must do what you find best insofar as you are interested.

Your book must be almost out. Despite the clamor, I have not, at this point, the slightest doubt that the vice president will be re-nominated. Whether he and the president can be re-elected—well, I have been a little bearish. But the great bonze, who advises me in such matters, says: "Yes, the Republicans will make it, though the results may be much closer than anybody would like to think about. And the

Republicans are likely to lose heavily in Senate and House, thus can-
celing a good part of winning the executive." I am sure I do not
know. So many rumors trickle through these hills, a body simply can't
be sure. There's talk of a great battle at a village called Gettysburg,
not far off. But, Lord, others say it's just that this president has a farm
there. Some talk about Stonewall Jackson, but you can't be sure is it
him or another fellow named C.D. Jackson. Only one thing us here is
clear about—this writer fellow named Autherine Lucy has a piece
wrote in *Life* magazine this week. And once they give him the Noble
Prize? Well, he talks right mad. But he hasn't got a feather up on his
neck to what folks are saying from here to Pascagoula. And, if it is
Secesh again, like they say, I mean Carroll County, the way they talk,
I mean Carroll County is going with the South. I don't believe they
understand up North, the way they feel, folks feel, down below.
Colored? We haven't got much Colored. But the Supreme Court,
they hadn't ought to have done that. And if they try to send the soldiers with those guns? I'm telling you, friend, I don't believe they
should do that. What I mean is, I mean, I just don't think they'd be
just the smartest to do that—and the voice gets so soft, so soft. It's
that quiet voice that the noisy folks pushing desegregation might do
well to listen to—just to the tone of that voice. They need not even
take note of the quiet look in the watchful eye, that is, not unless
they're connoisseurs of physiognomy. But what Liberal ever was?

Whittaker

7 March 1956
Dear Whittaker:

…I have not written because life has been too hectic, too gruesome,
and too scatological. For the past week I have been sitting on a vol-
cano, praying that the seat of my pants (applied to the crater) would

keep it from erupting. By the time you get this, it may be that you will know that my efforts [to put some backbone in Nixon] resulted in failure. Or it may be that my very careful and point-by-point explanation to Nixon of what the liberals [in the Republican Party] were trying to do to him had its effect. Meanwhile, I spend my days in terror, watching the news wire and my evenings listening to the broadcasts. And the most terrible thing about it is that the booby-trap they have set up is so obvious that [Nixon] may not see it. You want to know who the Lady Macbeth of the Eisenhower Administration is. I'll tell you: Herbert Brownell Junior [President Eisenhower's attorney general].

[The strategy of the liberals was to get rid of Nixon by offering him a cabinet post, thereby blunting the anger of Republican conservatives. The air was thick with trial balloons, and pressure was being placed on Nixon to step down in order to assure a Republican victory in November. In response, Nixon was going through one of his bouts of masochism, saying privately that, if Eisenhower asked him, he would step down for the good of the party. The opposite was true, for Eisenhower badly needed those elements in the GOP which supported Nixon. It fell to me to tell Nixon in very strong terms that he would not only be terminating his political career by taking a cabinet post, but also delivering the November election to the Democrats—and to tell the president to go to hell. All I could get from Nixon, after listening to a stating and restating of the case, was a promise that he would not commit himself either way, thereby forcing Brownell and others who wished to get rid of him, to move overtly—which of course they could not do. Eisenhower, as usual, played the benign father, saying that it was up to Nixon. I was the only member of the press who helped convince Nixon not to play into the hands of his enemies.]

Now and then I leave my cosmic rescue operations for long enough to pat my book on its two heads and say, "You poor child."...

Your analysis of the Uke situation—you asked me recently where I got the "Uke" designation; it was from John via you—may well be true. One factor, however, is left out: The complete, though perhaps temporary, demoralization of the Democratic Party. Northern and Southern Democrats are at sword's point over desegregation, some of the New Dealers are loudly declaiming that Uke stole their whole program. And so he did, and so he did…. If Eisenhower were still alive, this would be a wonderful opportunity to put the Democrats back in their pre-New Deal stage…. I am buying myself some burnt cork and joining the Master Race. How about it, Mistuh Craw-zley?

Ralph

[undated]
Dear Whittaker:

…These events have duly marched since Ralph's last note to you: Stein had a six-hour conference with Elia Kazan, one which in almost every detail he underscored your specific objections and ours (he called some of the scenes "soap opera" and insisted they go out in toto) and at the same time affirmed our, not your, belief that it is basically a good play…. Eric Bentley, our neighbor across the hall, a liberal who is rapidly learning the facts of life, has translated [Bertolt Brecht's] *Die Massnahme* so we who refuse to know German have access to it. Ralph has not had the time, but I read it the other night. And of course the points you made in relation to it are very clear. The only misleading aspect of using it as a kind of criterion, is that it is agit-prop and not really a play in terms of a theater-going public which has not been conditioned quite that far yet….

As for the book, you should have it by now. Poor Ralph has been in a fog since he spoke with the vice president last week and learned that he *was* considering taking that cabinet post, not because he wants it

but because he suspected that he was being finessed into having to
take it…. Our simple little prayer has been that Nixon say nothing at
all for a few weeks, to give the book a chance to bolster him up if a
book can do anything…. At this point I heard what the Prez had said
at his press conference—and got too depressed to continue….

Nora

[My almost brutally stated counsel to Nixon—to tell Brownell and
James Hagerty, Eisenhower's press secretary and assistant-president,
to perform an anatomical impossibility and to insist that he would
remain on the ticket—saved Nixon from the tumbril, and for it, I was
not forgotten by anyone except Nixon. After I had been transferred
by *Newsweek* to Washington, a request was made by Kenneth
Crawford, now bureau chief, to Hagerty to issue me a White House
pass at the time that Eisenhower had again been stricken, and Nixon
was quietly and apologetically taking over the reins of government.
"If *Newsweek* wants another White House pass," Hagerty wrote to
Crawford, "ask for one, but leave Nixon out of it."]

[Undated, postmarked 1 April 1956]
Dear Ralph,

It is Easter morning. It also happens to be the day I turn 55. But,
most of all, it is the first free moment when I could write you the letter that has been on my mind to write. Until now, I have been doing
a Life piece, which I wrote rather with my finger-nails. Now it's in,
and I can say, as one always does: "However poor a thing it is, at least
I gave it all I had; I can't think about it further." But it is your Nixon
book I want to write about. I find it a difficult job excellently done. I
should think the subject would find it a god-send. [If Nixon so felt,
he never communicated it to me.] Of course the inscription moved
me above all. Esther and I happened to glance at it at the same

moment; we took care not to glance at each other then; we don't like
to show each other what we know too well—that we're human. The
inscription, and what lies behind it, wipes out the memory of many
sad years. I take it that the vice president's troubles are pretty well
over—from that side. I said nothing to him through this crisis. I was
busy, ill, and I felt that it would be a gratuitous intrusion since there
was no specific help I could offer him. You and New Hampshire
brought that.

Fifty-five is a great age. I hope you have my obit ready. What fun
the little yappy dogs will have then. I don't even begrudge it them,
rest seems so welcome.

I hope the opening movement of the *Life* piece will not scandalize
you. It is a new way to score the *Internationale*. I have a feeling that
Buckley will find his worst fears confirmed. I think he suspects me of
a secret drift toward Communism. This is funny, of course; and this
fun, too, I do not begrudge. Either for Pantepec Oil or forth to chaos
and old night. There is no Sweden, no middle way—to which I
largely agree, claiming only that there is sometimes a middle tactic. A
couple of Sundays ago—or was it longer; time blurs so—Esther came
tearing up to my bedside with the portable radio, and I listened to
you do brilliantly on Sokolsky's hour. [The columnist George
Sokolsky was ill and for several weeks turned over his radio broadcasts to me, who mightily enjoyed doing them.] "The president is an
honorable man," "Brownies at the *Herald-Tribune*." I enjoyed it
mightily, and maybe that's enough. I fear it was caviar for the general.
Most caviar is.

John is at Mass. He is becoming a fearful Papist; and, when I said
something last night about the beauty of the Orthodox Easter rites,
he remarked: "Schismatic," but added in fairness after a moment's
thought, "though not heretical." I find myself, 55 on Easter morn, too
much in the graceless state of our First parents, glancing back at the
Garden:

Some natural tears they shed; then, hand in hand,
From Eden took their solitary way.
(I think this is misquoted, but I can't remember how Milton did it.)

Whittaker

Say, how's Stein? I learn from Mrs. Diana Trilling (to quote Bill) that Stein is leaving the NAACP, or whatever that group is called [the American Committee for Cultural Freedom]. That we all belong to, but not really. Since I hear nothing on his score from B & B, I infer: stalemate, armed truce, or what R. Jarrell calls "a war of the future in which the inhabitants of the enemy country wake up one morning to find that they have all been dead for a week."

I was alarmed that our friend [Nixon] has been reading Tolstoi. Who knows what lies let around that corner?

10 April 1956
Dear Whittaker:

Do not twitch your nostrils. I am surrounded by dead cats, tossed at me by the liberal brethren [in their reviews of *Nixon*]. It may be that some day I will become accustomed to the fury which I seem to inspire in them, or even learn to ignore their *billets doux*. I doubt it. My reaction is emotional, for it is hard to be a writer and know that whatever you write will be rejected out of hand and without examination. It is even harder to know that this hostility limits me in subject matter to subjects which carry their own impetus.... So the question arises, *A quoi bon écrire* [To what good is writing]? Which is precisely what the brethren want me to ask.

There's no point, however, in maudling. Instead, I will answer your questions about Sol Stein. We have been working with him. Or, more accurately, Nora has been working on him. I have been some-

thing of a voice from the wings—after one long, brutal session of vivi-
section. It would have been easier for me to take the play and run it
through the typewriter, but this was impossible. But the project has
moved and improved. What you will see in the near future will not
be perfect, but certainly within the realm of measurable good. You
will then be able to say whether Nora and I, acting *in loco parentis*,
have adequately fulfilled our function.

I'm afraid the bit about our friend [Nixon] and Tolstoi is not very
accurate. At one point in his life, he told me, he did read all of
Tolstoi—"even the non-fiction"—and I could not help being just a little malicious to the eggheads by making it present tense. I toss it out
now and then just to watch their reaction, and they are visibly
impressed—just as they are when I casually quote Ronsard or Verlaine
or Corneille. (I have a small stock of quotations which I save for such
occasions.) The amusing thing is how uneggheady the eggheads really
are. Someone who visited Adlai Stevenson's home in Libertyville told
me, in a shocked voice, that she had inspected his library and discovered it was all "journalism" of the John Gunther school. "No primary
sources," she said. I expect that by now Stevenson has bought himself
a Bible, which should be primary enough for him, until he discovers
some Dead Lake Michigan Scrolls....

I'm glad you liked the broadcast. I did four in all, and they were
fun to do. It gave me a sense of communication, of being able to say
things I want to say—a feeling that has departed from my work for
Newsweek. As I grow older, the need for such expression grows
rather than diminishes. Perhaps that is why I have gone back to the
writing of verse, but there again I am talking into a vacuum.

I make no mention of your "great age." But that your birthday
should come on Easter has its interesting points. My view of the Holy
Day is completely heretical. For it is the day on which the world was
suddenly presented with a *fait accompli*. The Son of Man was
entombed but the Son of God emerged from the sepulchre. If you

read the Apostles closely, I think you will see that no one was more surprised than they were. They discovered that after all there was a God. They hadn't been following another rabbi like, let us say, Karl Marx. Someday the Protestant clergy will discover this too. I suspect that Saint Peter was quite disappointed that Jesus was not the Messiah who would bring the classless society to the world. Please don't tell John about this. He may be able to tolerate schismatics, but not fugitives from an *auto da fé*.

I did not know that he had turned his face toward Rome. I applaud, even though Rome has turned its face away from me since *Day of Reckoning*. Did you know that I sent a copy of *Nixon* to Bishop Sheen inscribed, "From a Catholic fellow traveler." He did not acknowledge the book. Is he a Democrat or did he misread the inscription? I should have written instead, *Culpa rubet vultus meus* [Shame makes me flush], my favorite quotation from the Requiem, so he would surely understand.

One last piece of news. I saw Henry Regnery at a Dutch Treat Club luncheon. I came upon him unawares so that he could not flee.... But I was gentle. I did not ask him why he had published a glorification of Kathe Kollwitz [the great German Communist artist].

Ralph

April 13, 1956
Dear Ralph,

This is a scrambled day on which your letter came. I woke feeling tired. So I lay some time with my eyes closed, and, in that unrestful state, I decided that this was the day to have my hair cut. It hasn't been cut since that day I unloaded the hay bales with you last fall. I've just hacked at it with one of those comb-razor-do-it-yourself trimmers. At least, that has kept me from looking like Nature Boy.

So, I thought, this is the hour of decision, which means a trip to Hanover, Pa.—far, far, for me these days. While I was shaving, I heard a sheep note that meant trouble. (You get to know the meaning of most of these sounds, just as you do with a baby.) Sure enough, there were sheep in the yard, breakfasting on the spring flowers. I called to Esther, who was still abed, and, without wiping the suds from Sweeney's face, went down, and by opening a side gate and making some whisper sounds (luckily, they know my noises, too), I got them easily on to their pasture. But they were only a scrap of the flock. I climbed up in front of the barn, and there they were, over eating my neighbor, Victor Bixler's, springing wheat. The Bixlers are wonderful neighbors, but they are extremely touchy about straying stock. I started after the sheep with a hail from Esther in my ears, something about don't move another inch, I'm bringing the jeep. I ploughed on—my first venture of this kind since last fall.

I was very pleased to feel the familiar swelling pain around the heart before I was half way to the sheep. You understand, I don't want an attack; I just like to know the gun is loaded since they are many, I am few; and, in a situation of that kind, with our enemies as unscrupulous as they undeniably are, it is a comfort to a man to know that his last shot—why, it is within. So it was a kindness the sheep did me. I soon reached them. I am a famous shepherd, which consists chiefly in knowing that if one sheep moves, the others follow, and in being quiet enough yourself so that the sheep move in the direction you wish. The sheep were in two bands. I got a little way between, made the familiar whispering command. A yoe and two lambs started for home, and both bands followed in stampede up the lane just as Esther blocked the other end with the jeep. The flock swirled around. But, by then, I had them in the bottleneck.

Next I learned that *Life* had bought, and, in fact, paid for, the 20th Congress [of the CPSU] piece. I suggested that if they do not run it soon, I could whip together, as a stop-gap, something lively on, say,

the Battle of Cannae; each would soon be about as topical as the
other.

I decided, tired or not, to go to Hanover and get my hair sheared.
We did. We also went to Doubleday's and I saw your book well dis-
played and bought something I have long wanted: Czeslaw Milosz's
Captive Mind in paper covers. Also: Prof. Kitto on Greek Tragedy
(John has been reading it *in partibus infidelium*, i.e., Kenyon);
Gilbert Murray on Greek something or other; some Strindberg plays
(I used—as a youth—to gobble Strindberg by the megaton "including the non-fiction"); Lawrence's *The Plumed Serpent*, etc.—all in
paper. Then I said to Esther, for I began to feel that if I could not sit
down, I would fall down: "Let's go home." But Esther, who is otherwise almost pathologic about my state of health, is, when unloosed in
Hanover, like a stalking tigress. It is a modest and amusing vagary
and asks to be pampered. So I let her take me to the hardware store
where we loaded up on seeds. Then disaster struck. She wanted to go
to McGrory's, a dime store.

While she pawed inconclusively at jerseys for her grandson, I wandered off, and that was fatal. For around the end of a counter and the
end of a Hanoverian such as we only in Hanover build such women, I
came upon what you would least expect to come upon in Hanover—a
big cage full of the little birds called Javanese Temple finches. They
are little birds with pink slender feet and pink fat bills, and lovely
contrasting tones of grey and white. I watched them quite a while
and listened. They have no language but a squeak. They cost: $1.69.
There are, of course, lots of better things to do with $1.69. I found
Esther and said: "Let me show you what *I* want from the *Life* piece."
Esther is very understanding; she understands that your friend is the
kind of man who will buy a Temple finch. I asked the shop girl:
"What is their life expectancy—two days?" She laughed, partly·
because she didn't quite know what "life expectancy" meant, though
she guessed; partly because your friend seldom has no trouble talking

to shop girls—only to intellectuals.... Anyway, I thought, the bird will have two days after all the horror of its untraceable journey, being taken care of by people who will humor it a bit. So now the Templefink is squeaking in the living room. Don't tell anybody. Then we went home.

Meanwhile, we had telephoned B & B, and an idea I have had for a book lifted Miss Baumgarten out of her chair, or so she said. I, too, now that she has approved, think it is somewhat of an idea. So somewhat that I am going to try to go to NY next week to discuss it further—also, if you are available, with you. The trip is secret, the book is a secret. Please brace yourself for the unexpected: I am a quantum jumper; just call me Max Planck.

I am not going to say more about your letter than: Yes. Of course, you feel that way and so do I. I don't think anybody claimed that Sebastian liked the arrows. I don't. Write all the verses you can; if I could envy, I would envy you. You see: *Perdidi musam tacendo, nec me Apollo resicit; sic Amyclae, dum tacerent, perdidit silentium* [I have destoyed (my) muse by being silent, nor does Apollo cut me back. Thus Amyclae, when they were silent, destroyed its silence]. Prose is men's work, men's hard labor. But for poetry and music, an angel must sing through us. And as my beloved (but also vaguely abhorred) Rilke says: *"Ein jeder Engel is schrecklich."* That, since you refuse to know German, means: "Every single angel is terrible—terrifying."

Whittaker

This keeps going on and on, so I had better spare you the script. There is this private angle on the 20th Congress—my last great argument with the Hisses in the Volta Place house was about the purge, Stalin, etc. Now history (and the Presidium) has ruled: You were both right. Like flies to wanton boys are we to the gods: they kill us for their sport.

That damned finch is squeaking again. I must go.

I almost never repeat to anybody any verse I have ever written, so it is unlikely that I have ever quoted to you this stanza, one of the last I wrote, before *perdidi musam tacendo*—at my brother's grave:

> Either being gone,
> Or struggling, deciding, resolving to decide;
> Life once befell
> From which you have withdrawn:
> The earth affords the quarry space to hide.

By that, at least, you will know how much you are my friend. You will also see why I turned to prose.

Here is a little of what I meant by the first movement of the *Life* piece which something tells me, *Life* means to bury in its heaped files. It begins with the last scene of *Boris Godounov*, after the murders, the madness, the treachery etc. "It is all gone; it was all for nothing. Even the darkly muttering peasants have gone. All that is left is the village idiot, lying alone in rags, with the snow falling. He lifts his face to that snow, and then his throat utters those animal sounds that have not their like in tragedy: 'Aooh! Aooh! Aooh! Aooh!' You may have thought that the words of the enslaved women that close Euripides' *Trojan Women*, utter as much about defeat and suffering as speech or mind can bear: 'Wrath is the earth, and quaking, and a flood that sweeps all and passeth on.' But they are words and they have rational meaning. The idiot utters the sound for the immeasurable, irrational evil and suffering that lies at the heart of life itself. First of all, and last of all, that sound is the utmost that can be said about the meanings of those words which stand for: Great Purge, Reverse Purge, Communist Revolution, Communist Party, the Communist Experience as it has tempted or tormented millions of mankind. They are the lucky ones who died." That is what I meant. I think that is chiefly another way of saying what you say in… your letter to me.

There is a remarkable book which I am reading in French: Manes
Sperber's *Et le buisson devint cendre.* Unqualifiedly recommended.
Sperber is a friend of Koestler's, his closest friend I believe. *Et le
buisson* often suggests *La condition humaine* which I re-read
recently in English—great book. I don't think Alger liked it when I
gave him the French version before it was translated—or perhaps he
had less French than I supposed.

April 26, 1956
Dear Whittaker:

I have just come from another brainwashing session with poor Stein
and my thoughts are a trifle discombobulated as a result. Poor Sol,
these have been terrible months for him—and he doesn't know yet
how terrible. Last night I thought we had gone as far as he could go,
and it was not far enough by a long shot. Tonight I am withholding
final judgment for yet a time more.... If he doesn't approximate it a
lot closer this time, I think in all decency we will have to deliver the
coup de grace.

Some of us suspect that *Life* decided to run your piece because
Alger was speaking at Princeton. At any rate, we are grateful, whatever their reason. It's as effective and moving as anything you've
done.... I don't see why you should have had misgivings about the
opening. I suspect even the idiots will sense its meaning. Or is it the
intellectuals you mistrust.... Incidentally, *U.S. News* reprints [Alger's]
speech and the Q. & A., such as it was, in full. He has not lost his skill
in the particular technique of not answering, which Ralph likes to
illustrate by a Groucho Marx exchange: "Where do you live?" "I
moved." But then he has had time to improve himself and his
technique....

Ralph was going to write to you tonight, also, but his poor stum-
mick is stummicking because of some of the things he was going to

write about. We are in a little more than our ordinary state of bewil-
derment as a result of the latest *Newsweek* gambit, which may not be
a gambit but common bad manners. At any rate, last week, Ken
Crawford, in NY for a visit, telephoned to say, "I'm so glad you're
coming to Washington"—to which Ralph could only say, "Huh?" It
seems that Ken had just been told by the ineffable Mac Muir, Jr., that
Ralph was being transferred. This was Tuesday. We thought, of
course, that on Wednesday morning R would be called in and told, in
some form. Nothing, then or since....

[Ralph] was in Washington Friday, to see Nixon for *Newsweek*, to
get a story that only he could get from Nixon for *Newsweek*, and for
the first time in many months has a by-line coming up and a story he
went out for actually appearing in the book.... It will be pleasant to
see the story running, and he had a good session with Nixon. The
association of by-line and subject may also be a little booster for the
[Nixon] book. The announcement [that Nixon will be on the
Eisenhower ticket] also seems to have persuaded the Hearst organization that a serialization of the book can run in the near future.
(They had taken a "bold" option to publish *if* Nixon got the nomination.) [Despite much support within the Hearst organization for syn-
dication, the project was, as usual, vetoed by William Randolph
Hearst, Jr.]

And that is our week's work. Except that Jamie is 12, and that is
even harder to believe than that we will be forty.

Nora

May 3, 1956
Dear Ralph and Nora,

...About David [McDowell]. He wrote [asking if the book would be
ready for fall publication]: I haven't answered yet. But [Bennett] Cerf
had written earlier, and I answered that to say: no book yet. If this

makes many happy at Random House, I don't mind. I have no interest in election year in this connection. I have no writing interest in
politics of the partisan kind. I have moved much closer to the
Administration's practical purposes, and hence farther than ever
away from the die-hard Right. The extreme Right seems to me to act
with a minimum of sense, and I greatly doubt that they even understand what all the shooting's about. I also suppose that, if Senator
Taft were living, his position and mine would be about the same. It
has to do with plain realities. I have done one of my notorious back-
flips too. This mail takes a letter to B & B, saying that I have split my
book into two books. Much better that way, I think. If everybody
agrees, and, I am afraid, even if everybody doesn't, that is the way it
must be…. I feel much relieved. More, I feel invigorated. If I live to
do it, I shall have done a triptych, of which *Witness* is panel I, and
the other two books a logical middle and end. This, I think, reflects a
general change and a personal one, which has taken much time and
flue-smoke.

…Nothing is really worth the labor of writing, the ordeal, unless
you issue it for time to test, to assay. Reckless? I can't be but what I
am. Somebody asked a paratrooper, why he liked to do anything so
crazy as make jumps. He said: "I don't like to. I just like to be around
the kind of people who make jumps." I think it possible that, within a
year or three, Alger will have "rehabilitated" himself. I suspect
Americans will begin to love him. It's really what they want to do.
He's their baby, not mine. "Are Americans stupid?" Czeslaw Milosz
asks somewhere. I forget his answer….

Now to the main point—Ralph to Washington. The possible hazards are perfectly obvious. On brief balance it looks better to me
than worse. I think it might do Ralph much good to be in the capital.
I think it might do all of you good to get out of New York; especially
the boys. (Is Jamie really 12; are you really 40?) Needless to say, your
being closer is a selfish interest of mine, so that doesn't count. But
the deal, on the face of it, looks pretty good to me. If nothing serious

happens to Nixon before or during the election, I should think Ralph
would be fairly well entrenched. You shouldn't get so upset. That
kind of behind-the-arras dealing is old hat at *Time.* And suppose
Ralph had gone with *National Review*? My advice would be: Don't
bargain, at least not much. Better to say blandly: Dee-lighted!

If this seems an abrupt ending, I'm falling out of my chair—
fatigue.

Whittaker

May 5, 1956
Dear Ralph,

This must be a letter for your eyes only. I have been horrified by the
news that Victor Riesel will be permanently blind. He was once kind
to me, but that is scarcely at all the point.

The man, who meant goodness, must not be left to believe that
the world would simply leave him in darkness. He must not be left to
grow bitter with the thought that, of the millions he can hear moving
around him, not one will give him what alone he really needs: light. I
propose, if an operation can be effected, to give him one of my eyes.
I mean now, in a living cornea, if that is what you call it. I came to
this because I found that, when I tried to write him, there was nothing truthful to say unless one was prepared to help in the only way
that matters.

This depends on two sets of factors which only doctors can determine approximately. The first concerns the condition of his eyes,
whether the damage is so deep-going that an operation, a transplant,
is impossible. Only medicine can give an answer. The other depends
on the condition of my own eyes, which are not as strong as they
once were: and, also, on my general condition. That is, whether due
to the heart, surgeons would be willing to venture a shock to the sys-

tem, even though it is localized. I incline to believe that this is the least important factor.

It is clear that the utmost secrecy is required. First, Victor must not know, since if the doctors say no, the disappointment might set him back. Second, if the doctors say no, I must be protected against those who would cry publicity seeker. The best would be if it could be kept absolutely secret but that is very difficult in a world of so many key-holes and key-hole listeners. Let the proper surgeons, who must pronounce for or against this, be told simply that there is some- one anonymous who will give an eye provided they agree. If they can be bound in any Hippocratic way so much the better. I don't have much faith in such things.

Do not try to dissuade me. I have thought about this for 24 hours, which, for something so serious, is a short time. I have the peculiarly liberating sense, which is unmistakable when you know it, that this is the one absolutely right thing to do. I have considered the fact that this operation, even if approved, might not prove successful. I have considered it and discounted it. It is the common risk of action. Also, I loathe hospitals, medicine, and, I am afraid, I am highly sceptical of the medical mind, *qua* mind. So, at the point of performance I might be expected to appear nervous or even shaken. That would be physi- cal. My will is firm and fixed. This is an offering for Victor, as a man; and against the evil that maimed him, not in the hope of exposing it, or in the hope of moving it to expose itself, but in the hope of moving some part of it to convert itself to goodness (which perhaps will never be known). For only in such conversion is there ever any hope. Otherwise, the Manichaeans are right; and it is simply the pointless war of the children of light and the children of darkness, in which everyone is at last destroyed and no one ever wins. Do you under- stand my intention? Therefore, do not try to argue with me.

I foresee that, in dealing with the surgeons, you may need some authority. I presume that the power behind Victor is [David] Dubinsky [head of the International Garment Workers Union, and a leading anti-Communist]. I have met him only once briefly years ago. He struck me as a man who knows his way around this world, and could be counted on to keep a secret (he must keep some howlers). Perhaps you must work through Dubinsky, and I think he will keep quiet once he grasps why, for Victor's sake, if not mine, secrecy is imperative.

I incline to suppose, on most imperfect evidence, mere wisps and guesses, that the Washington assignment might not be the worst thing for you. But we shall talk more about that as it develops.

For now, please do what I have asked—as quickly as you can for many reasons.

Whittaker

[Victor Riesel had been managing editor of the *New Leader*, a full-size newspaper then, when I went to work for it. He had moved on to the *New York Post* as labor editor, and then had become a syndicated columnist. He was blinded when a labor goon threw acid in his eyes as he walked out one night from Lindy's in New York. Several days before it happened, I had tried to reach Riesel on the phone, only to get repeated busy signals. When he finally got through, I said to Riesel, "That was some long phone call." Riesel answered: "If my phone is tapped, I'll be a dead man in a few days." The Chambers assessment of Dubinsky was a sound one. Dubinsky had driven both the labor racketeers and the Communists out of the ILGWU, and also ran his union not only to benefit his members but to help employers to run better and more profitable shops. Among the secrets that Dubinsky kept was a personal one—that he had voted for Thomas E. Dewey and against Harry S. Truman in 1948.]

Dear Whittaker:

I will make no comment about what you have proposed to do. Instead, I'll give you the facts. The damage to Vic Riesel's eyes is beyond mending. It is not merely a question of the cornea. Ironically, one cornea is relatively sound. The acid ate right into the eyes, the lids, the nerves, and the blood vessels. Sulfuric acid keeps on eating away, and not until it had stopped could the doctors determine the full extent of the damage. Now they know. There is still light and dark perception in one eye, but the doctors say that will go in about a week.

Nora and I visited Vic last night. I had to drag myself to the hospital—hospitals and illness and death have that effect on me. But he was bright and chipper, spoke freely of the fact that he would no longer see, and said that knowing this had no traumatic effect on him. The real emotional crisis will come when he's on his feet and coping once more with the world. But he has incredible courage, and I'm sure he will make his way. We can, and will, help in small things, but the big fight will be his own.

If you have the strength to write him a brief note, I know it will mean a great deal to him.

Please forgive the cut-and-dried tone of this note. I've been a friend of Vic since 1940. This is the only way to write about what has happened to him.

Ralph

May 11 [?], 1956
Dear Ralph,

Yes, that was the way to answer. I was afraid that, clinically, that might be the reality. But, if that reality changes, I shall not have changed my mind. My offer is the same. I shall write to Victor, though I am sure I do not know what there is to say. I have come to have a horror, almost an obsession, against the pieties of inaction, the smug evasions that kind words are used for. It makes the brief obscenities of Army speech a justifiable eloquence.

I have forgotten whether I told you—when we were scheduled to go to N.Y. some weeks back, we got into our City disguises and were on the point of leaving, only to find that there was not enough energy. I wanted particularly to talk with you; I wanted your advice. As you know, I almost never seek advice, holding that a man must take his own responsibilities; so you see, this seems fairly important to me. It is nothing dramatic or instant. But I feel that I have reached a point where roads fork. I want your opinion about the fork I pro-pose to follow, or, should you convince me to the contrary, the one I shall not follow. But I want to talk, not write about it. You will be able to speak with specific authority in this, even if, in my dogged way, I go against.

The form of the decision I must make was clearly set several months ago; and certain practical steps were taken. But I must say that Alger at Princeton was a powerful catalyst. I am not particularly interested in that event except to the extent that circumstances may force me to be. It is the long range implications which interest me in an absolute way. It makes a nonsense of effort, and a man would have to be a fool to suppose that anything is worthwhile in a community where this could occur. It is not my wife or myself that I am thinking about. What difference does it make to us? *Somos viejos; hay siempre una frontera que podemos atraversar si seria necessario; y en todo caso, esta frontera no se queda tan lejos de cada dia. De hecho para nosotros no importa. Pero nuestro hijo—es de el que me pienso. En realidad, siempre hemos vivido en forastero dentro de esta gente. No esta bien. No deseo la misma suerte para el* [We are old; there is always a frontier that we can cross, should it be necessary; and in any case, that frontier is no further away than a day. For us the move does not count. But our son—it is of him that I think. In reality, we have always lived as strangers among these people. It is not good. I do not wish the same for him]. Stendhal says somewhere that a man's country is where there are the most people like him. *Es de eso que*

*quiero hablar con ti. Es aqui la verdadera significacion del suceso de
Princeton* [It is of this that I wish to talk to you. The true significance
of the events at Princeton lies here]. Dispense the lousy language (as
used by me); *sin embargo, inegablemente, me falta practica*
[Nevertheless, ineffably, I lack practice].

Whittaker

[The great decision on which Whittaker Chambers sought advice was
this: He had decided that remaining in the United States, no matter
where, posed a serious danger to his life, and to his wife's. There had
been threats by mail and phone—threats which he did not wish to con-
fide to the FBI, which he felt was an instrument of state power, however well it had stood by him in the past. He was thinking very
seriously of Spain which, at the time, was as free of Communist pene-
tration as any country in Europe and would remain so as long as
Franco was alive. There was nothing hysterical or overblown about
his sense of danger. And the possibility that there might be a
Republican defeat in November, which would terminate the protec-
tion which he felt Nixon afforded, was very much on his mind.]

18 May 1956
Dear Whittaker:

I have been in bed for the past days with some kind of respiratory ail-
ment, which accounts for my silence. In a way, it was good that I did
not write because now I have something concrete and definite to say
in re the Stein opus.

    This evening, we finally got a copy of the current version. And
frankly, it came as something of a shock. It also explained why we
were not favored with a copy the moment it came back from the typ-
ist. The opening scene had been carefully worked out among the

three of us. It may not have been perfect, and perhaps you would not
have liked it. But it had both dramatic and Chambersian validity. The
scene as you read it has only a casual relation to what we had thought
it would be. The Hiss-Chambers scene, which Nora and I think is
crucial, had been a bone of some contention. Finally, Nora and I sat
down and wrote it out as we thought it should be—borrowing liber-
ally from *Witness* but filling in some of the understood lacunae. We
made no determined attempt to write polished dialogue, but we were
offering content, structure, and mood. It obviously needed paring
down and heightening; it was a draft. The present scene, if you read
that far [in Stein's version], makes neither logical nor ideological
sense. It is meaningless and dramatically dead. There were other
parts further along, not as important but important enough, which
Stein agreed to change. They were not changed. In short, we were
editors without editorial authority. If you ever read the play through,
you will see that we had some successes in improving the script and
making it, from our viewpoint, more acceptable.

And so, to more practical matters. In your letter to Stein, you say
that if B & B turns thumbs down, there is no need to discuss the
matter further. If they hold for the play's possibilities, then the subject is open to a point. I still think the play should be done. I agree
with you… that the play must be right. I am also convinced that
B & B will not turn thumbs down, though balancing approval with
disapproval. If I am right in this assumption, it raises the question:
What is to be done? Just to give Stein another crack at the first
twenty pages would be futile, mainly because he has gotten himself
enmeshed in *amour propre*. If the play is to be revised, there must
be a heavy editorial hand over Stein's. That cannot and should not be
your hand. That leaves ours. And to put it undiplomatically, we will
not participate further unless it is clearly understood that no new version of the play will be submitted to you until we have said, "This is
it." In earlier letters over earlier drafts, I wrote around this point—

out of a kind of diffidence and also because I dread exposing what might well be shortcomings on my own part. At the moment, I feel committed enough to take the risk.

...For the time being, [my current difficulties at *Newsweek*] seem to be in abeyance. It has become a question of sitting tight, of out-staring one another. And since they don't quite know what reserves I can throw into the battle, they are worried. They know that Moley is on my side, but not how vigorously he will fight. They don't know who else will come to my support. They wonder if they will lose any advertising [they were aware that my brother was an executive at National Steel, whose ads frequently occupied the centerspread in the magazine, and that both the chairman of the board and the presi-dent of the company were Toledano fans] and since *Newsweek* is so greedy it takes ads for rupture cures, this is a very important factor. What's more, they have heard that I have a pumpkin stuffed with papers—memos to myself of certain conversations I have had with a number of people of consequence on the staff. I suspect that if those memos fell into Malcolm Muir, Sr.'s, hands, two other editors would join me in the exodus. All of which has its elements of humor but butters few parsnips. I am of two minds about Washington. So I sit like patience on a monument.

I remember a play I saw many years ago done by high school kids. It was about the French Revolution, and there was one highly dra-matic scene in which Citizen Something, who has been kept out of Countess Somewhat's chambers, bursts in and says (ironically), "My compliments on the celerity with which Madame has finished her terlet." And the Countess answers, "Vanish, obesity! Flit, whale." This is the level of the battle I am fighting.

Ralph

21 May 1956
Dear Whittaker:

We have reached a moment of definition. Harold Freedman has read the play and, subject to minor reservations, thinks it is a worthwhile property. You will hear from him, through Bernice Baumgarten, shortly. For this reason, Nora and I are of a mind that we should state our position clearly and fully.

1. We think the first fifteen pages are impossible.
2. With emendations, we feel that the rest of the play is good.
3. We still feel strongly that the play should be done.
4. We have labored long and mightily to get Stein to make the first fifteen pages acceptable to you. We have failed, in part because our position is anomalous. We are editors without editorial authority.
5. We have therefore sat ourselves down and written what we consider a compromise version of those fifteen pages. They are not exactly as we would want them, but they are written in the context of the limitations placed upon us.

Point 5 is the hinge. If you can read what we have written—and if you find it sufficiently close to what you will tolerate, then we can move on. If we have failed, then the rest of this letter is academic. Proceeding on the debatable basis that these pages are tolerable:

6. From this point on, Stein must be handled with a very firm hand. Using our copy as the model, he can be held in line. He must also be bludgeoned into deleting certain vulgarism and false concepts from the rest of the play.
7. We are asking for explicit authority from you to do exactly this. We realize that this is a tremendous order—for you to give and for us to carry out.

Our enclosed re-write may convince you that we are perhaps very bad compromisers.

Ralph

Like the mouse, "I been *sick...*" but a personal letter will follow.

May 23, 1956
Dear Ralph,

Thank you and Nora. When the great day comes, and B & B makes
known to me Mr. Freedman's great joy, I shall hold out for your
version.... I had no stomach for Stein's most recent try, and did not
get far enough into it to come to that part where it is said to be great
theater. But, like your mouse, though I do not know what mouse this
is, I have been sick too. Nothing organic, I think, just some miserable
unidentifiable bug, but wretched-making.... Beyond that, I find
myself opposed to the idea as a whole. To take fiction, Koestler's
Blindness At Noon, for example, and freely translate it for the stage,
is not quite the same thing as taking fact and treating it so freely....
Moreover, the moment, it seems to me, could scarcely be worse for
the effort.

Worldwise, we are at the point where the lump of sugar melts in
the tea, falls apart and disappears. Anyone who doubted the analysis
in the *Life* piece should read the current *New Statesman & Nation* to
see just what is happening and what (I can't see any effective counterforce) is about to happen. The triumph of Communism-Socialism
could only be checked provided that there evolved, in the contest
with it, a counterforce of great strength. To that counterforce, I
sought to contribute some action, some legend, some eloquence and
clear thinking. I always knew that it couldn't be done, but history
(there must be a better word) requires these efforts of us. I claim to
have known long before most others that the effort was defeated.
Everybody knows that now, though not everybody knows the depth
or the scale of the defeat, chiefly, I think, because people tend to
divide it into separate problems or areas of experience. The Russian
problem is one. The [Liberal-Left] is another. The Administration
etc. etc. All are approaching the condition of one problem—the same
problem. What almost nobody seems to see is that the U.S. and the
USSR at this moment of tension begin more and more to resemble

each other—I mean, of course, in basic matters, not specific Soviet peculiarities like the secret police. Mr. Eisenhower, Mr. [Joseph] Rauh [head of Americans for Democratic Action], Mr. [Walter] Reuther [president of the United Auto Workers union and V.P. of the AFL-CIO] and Mr. Khrushchev are, for example, on one line in wanting a chicken in every pot. If some are more equal than others in wanting this, it is chiefly because Mr. Khrushchev has to solve the question of which comes first, the chicken or the pot. But the expression of the philosophy of materialism is the same. As they move toward mutual good will and embrace, what must happen? It isn't necessary to think in political terms, which are perhaps a handicap at this point. The inclusive reality is the common materialism inter-beamed in a melting goodwill....

Anyway, what I chiefly want to know is how it stands with you. I keep hearing bits and snippets of worrisome whisper. If you are not telling me how it goes with you to spare me worry, why, I worry more this way. (You incidentally are Exhibit 1 to the above thesis.) Tell me how it goes. What do you think I can do for you? I will try.

Whittaker

24 May 1956
Dear Whittaker:

I'm sorry that whispers have been reaching you about my troubles at *Newsweek*. Ever since February, the "fire Toledano" project has been brewing. The three weird sisters were Frank Gibney [ex of *Time*], Debs Myers [National Affairs editor and former Stevenson speech-writer], and Mack Muir, Jr. [executive editor and professional incompetent].... The obstacles have been two: Ray Moley and the fact that firing me out of hand might cost them a couple of advertising accounts. This latter was, of course, based on a highly exaggerated idea of anti-Communist solidarity and the support I would get from National Steel. Moley's opposition is more tangible, but also over-rated. I think I have written all of this to you.

In the course of this campaign against me, Myers has had several "heart to heart" talks with me, to soften me up. But he talked a little too much and too indiscreetly about Muir Sr. and other related topics. I made memos of these conversations and stuffed them in that pumpkin I borrowed from you, and then let the word filter out that I had a secret weapon. Moley also discussed my status with some of the very top brass, and they told him that they knew nothing about any plan to ditch me.

What did the trick, I don't know. But the cabal decided that I would not be fired—at least for now. They substituted instead "the treatment"—giving me ridiculous assignments which end up in the round file. The Washington move, suggested I am told by Moley (on his theory that I am surrounded by fanatics in New York, i.e., George Sokolsky whom he hates) became the substitute. Everybody knows about it except, presumably, me.... And I have sat tight.

Perhaps by the time you receive this, I will have been told. Whether it will be an either/or proposition, I do not know. Just how anxious Muir Jr. is to get me to Washington is another question. I have school contracts for the kids, involving large sums of money, which *Newsweek* must be ready to pay off. Will I be downgraded on the masthead? What specific assignments do they have in mind? Will I be allowed to play the field or will I be given one of the dead beats, like the Justice Department? In any case, I will be left high and dry, during which freelance sources will no longer exist. Until I find new ones, living on my *Newsweek* salary will be hard. Four years ago, I was the second-highest paid writer on the magazine. No longer.

The good points? We'll be within reasonable distance of Westminster and have a car to get us there. That has great appeal.... Washington is the center of political news, so that other things may open up for me—including radio and TV. But does this balance against the sterility of Washington, the in-breeding of the National

Press Club? And most important, will I be investing more years in a bad venture? Almost nine years have gone down the drain at *Newsweek*. And time means a great deal to me. I'll be 40 this summer. Looking back, I can see only a row of dried cornstalks....

I have a couple of books which may be of interest and of value to you. The first, by Sir David Kelly, an old and astute British diplomat, is full of good material. It was published in England, and because of its leisurely British pace can find no takers here. The second, *From Vienna to Versailles*, says some very wise things about the Congress of Vienna, the diplomacy of Metternich and allied subjects. I also have some leads to the "Third Rome."

This is a dull and nasty letter. My trouble, I guess, is that I'm standing in the need of prayer. But I try not to bother God with my petty problems.

Ralph

11 June 1956
Dear Whittaker:

If this letter is not lucid, it may be because it is now 4:30 AM, with another 4 1/2 to go before I am relieved. *Newsweek* is taking Ike's refractory ileum big and I am keeping the death watch, ready to press the button to notify the printers that they should shove in the already written obit, adding hour and day. But [Senator William] Jenner is more astute than *Newsweek*; Ike is "indestructible," saith he, and the four doctors who passed around his intestine (as if it were a string of pearls to be admired) should have nibbled at it slightly to partake of his eternal youth.

So I have been reading and dozing and thinking. If I could maintain the thought without the doze I might arrive at a counter-revolutionary Messianism and become an American Herzen. Barring that, I will write to you of my human, or unhuman, condition.

As you know, *Newsweek* has spoken. I asked for a few days to think over the Washington proposition. During that time, Nora went down to Washington to look for a house. She returned three days later bubbling with enthusiasm over what she had found—a five bedroom, 3 1/2 bathroom "mansion" in Cleveland Park (Porter Street, where we shall bathe our feet in soda water) with a little grass around it and three trees. There is a fireplace in the living room and another in the master bedroom. The significance of the multiple bedrooms is that we shall have a guest room. Sooner or later, there will be a car to put in the garage—which leaves us a skip and a jump from Westminster—if we can afford the gasoline.

Last Wednesday, I marched into Mac Muir's office and told him that I was ready, willing, and able to go to Washington.... The result of my acceptance was palpable relief on his face and large compliments as to how smart I was and how well I would do there. I also got my first word of praise from Debs Myers & Co. for some rather piddling copy I turned out. The die is cast, the Rubicon is crossed, it is morning, Senlin says. Onward and upward to the nation's capital to be nice to liberals. Oh to be in Oujda now that spring is here. Having made the decision, I feel rather relieved and almost gay about it. Life is not pain; it is relief—which may account for Dr. Paul Dudley White's insistence on notifying the American people and the historians of Ike's every bowel movement. (There are no sounding bells from the wire room; Ike must be sleeping well.)

So I have moved from the sublime to the pediculous, or vice versa. I did not stand before the Muirs *et al* shouting, *"Qu'importe les vagues humanités, si le geste est beau"* ["What matter vague humanity, if the gesture is beautiful"] or other such anarchist statements. I did not stand in Gaza, grasping the pillars, maybe because I am not eyeless.... I was practical, and I guess it's about time. Not everyone can be an Arthur Koestler or a Sol Stein.

If this sounds bitter or maudlin or childish, it's just the fatigue talking. I look forward to the new assignment with some trepidation, because I am really not a very good reporter in the *Front Page* sense, with some anticipation because it will be a challenge of sorts.

The dawn is slowly filtering through the haze and I'm too tired to think consecutively. I will go back to my book and my dozing. For a death watch, this has not been too lively.

Ralph

June 12, 1956
Dear Ralph,

Last week, I had a strong feeling that one or another of you was nearby—a prescience, in the circumstances, not very strange; and abetted by a gnawing conscience that I should have written you. I am delighted that Nora found a house. Porter St. sounds like the second alphabet. If so, that makes it fairly handy in and out of Wash. to the northeast.... The beauty of the Washington move, from one viewpoint, is that it is so right because necessity, blessed Hegelian necessity, left no choice. What you are feeling is the blessed relief experienced by the middle stage of a triad when it has uncontradicted itself into the first phase of a new contradiction. Aren't we all. This playfulness may seem untimely. I predict success in Wash. I think you should be a good reporter. I think it will slide floors under your feet and put confidence in your pocket, and a variety of other goods. I mean a *good* reporter. My fierce detestation of the breed is that most of them are so bad: ignorant oafs, or when they are a little more, biased and unscrupulous. My skunner on newsmen is not anti-journalism, quite contrary. It is like my detestation of intellectuals, not because they are, but because most of them aren't. They aren't anything classifiable, so they are intellectuals. Be a good reporter, and if you must learn slowly and humbly (that is what I should have to do), why, do it with grace. I don't think you should go into it,

thinking of having to play with Liberals. In plain truth, the Right is so
soddenly stupid, that the Liberals would be a relief if they weren't so
implacably, so viciously shallow. Some days, I think: the Liberals are a
true, conscious Fifth Column. Other days, I think: "It's got nothing to
do with politics at bottom; it's just a lot of American collegiate, academic nonsense mixed with the snobbery that flourishes rank whenever
a society is rankless." No doubt I am both right and wrong on alter-
native Thursdays. But, I beg you, as far as you are let (no, much farther than that), treat every barstid in Wash. as if he were just another
Dawn Man, issued without a Harriman button from the womb of
Time.

Anyway, the time had come for you to get out of New York City.
New York, supposing itself the hub of the universe, is actually the
capital of the entertainment industry (I mean no discourtesy to Wall
St., but I think it is possible to blanket it in). Washington thinks it is
the capital of creation, and there is enough reality in this to make it
bearable. I suppose there must be some people in Wash. who know
the facts and are able to read them for their awful portent (as con-
trasted with the hundreds, perhaps thousands, who know the facts
but might as well not). I mean the schools of "Russians are not 12
feet tall," and "the Russians are being forced by our foreign policy to
draw in their horns"—and, of course, all the swamps in between,
including the great Serbonian bog, the Right, where—but it wouldn't
be true to say: Where armies whole have sunk. Perhaps: Where
colonies whole of mud-hens roost. Besides, Wash. is a place, unlike
N.Y., which is merely a clot. Wash. is not, as a woman denizen of
Hannover [Germany] said to me on leaving our compartment in the
middle of the night, regretting in her good German way, that I was to
be deprived of the glories she knew, and must travel on to the so ugly
Rhine: "Hannover," she said, *"ist eine wunderschone, luxe Stadt."* For
you, inveterate non-Teuton, that means: "a wonderbeautiful luxury
city." Nor is Washington a *ville lumière.* It is just what Henry Adams

said it was: a village of the Southern border, where (whoever thought Henry was spinsterish?) the Maryland spring and autumn come and linger with a pang that is pagan. All that marble, all those New Deal facades, that is just the poor orphan American spirit, bucking itself up, swelling its biceps, giving itself one for the road, against the awful prospect that it might, one day, have to whisper: I am the captain of my fate. For, suppose my fate turned out to be different from every-body else's fate? How embarrassing, undemocratic. But never mind the marbled halls. Wash. is still beautiful and I hope it will be so to you. There is something else. I am so slender a reed (no, no, not lit-erally, of course), that any commitment I make in any field is per-force a disservice. So if worst comes to worst for you in Wash., you will not be stranded in a great foreign city; we shall find some way to help, extemporize something.

I wish very much to see you since some matters might be dis-cussed that writing lends itself less thriftily to. No doubt, we shall meet soon. Now I've used up my days draft of energy. I have been writing hard (hence my silence). The material keeps running away with me. No one who has not had to write alone really knows the value of a good editor. I thought to have this stuff in a good two weeks ago. Now it looks like another week at best. But, by slogging, I seem to move by inches. I hope soon, by slashing, to cut my way out of my own copy. I am sorry about Stein, but I don't see why he should be let to make mud pies out of *Witness*. I hear that Alger is readying a book for fall publication. Hm.

Whittaker

Kismet, 3 July 1956
Dear Whittaker:

The single word with the dateline does not mean that I have suc-cumbed to Oriental fatalism. It means only that we are back at the

beach for the annual respite. We have given up the New York apartment, our things have not yet been moved to the Porter Street house,
and we are without even the temporary roots that cave dwellers grow.
(That "Porter Street house" sounds like something out of the Hiss
case testimony.)

For reasons too long and dull to recite, your 12 June letter didn't
reach me until the 28th. The delay in answering stems from the
uneasy laziness which strikes me at the beach. I love the sea and the
bay, the sun and the rain and the mists which blow in so lightly, but
as I enjoy them I continue to feel that I must be at the typewriter. So
here I am.

You misunderstand my doubts about my reportorial abilities. I
know how to be a good reporter. I have been one, on many occasions.
But unless a story really interests me, I tend to shy away from the
indefatigable pursuit of all the little facts and small men which makes
for "good"—though not real—reporting. I always feel that getting at
the guts and the motives is more important than telling the reader
the color of the president's necktie. (I am always appalled at the mail
we get: "You said Mr. Truman wore a striped tie, but *Time* says he
wore a figured tie. Who is correct?") The good reporters I know
really enjoy that chase. So I will have to drive myself to find an abid-
ing fascination in the minutiae of such things as farm bills and tariff
legislation. Fortunately I'll be teamed with Sam Shaffer—one of the
best on the Hill—who pack-rats sources and facts and pours over the
Congressional Record each evening. I would rather be in Poznan.
There, at least, people have chosen sides. In Washington, there are
only split infinitives… and nary a cloven hoof.

Meanwhile, there is the sun and the sea. I have been lying here
reading Souvarine's book on Stalin, taking a refresher course in
Soviet history, and re-interpreting. It makes all the nonsense appearing in the press, including *Time*, seem doubly compounded. All this
talk about Leninism, and from Harrison Salisbury yet, by people who
don't have the vaguest notion of what Lenin did, much less what he

thought or how he functioned. All this prattle about the "new" line, so ungenerously exploded by the workers of Poznan ("We are from Kronstadt!"). Doesn't anyone except thee and me remember the N[ew] E[conomic] P[olicy], Lenin's "shifting" tactics on war and peace, on the farm problem, on the Constituent Assembly?—or how he swallowed the Social Revolutionaries as Krush and Bulge are swallowing the Socialists? Doesn't anybody read a book?

Of course, what makes me so mad at the pundits is that though I can spot their idiocies, I have no real answers of my own. That is, I can see why K & B are acting as they are; I can guess at the interplay of forces within the Soviet Union, and wonder how Mikoyan is spending his evenings. But I have always held that communism is a dynamism which must move forward (the backing and filling can also be forward motion as Lenin knew) and I just wonder what the consequences of the current line may be…. Have we, as the Old Bolsheviks were warning in 1923, reached Thermidor? The radio is reporting that the Budapest stations have been broadcasting their independence from Moscow (but with continued loyalty to Marxism-Leninism?). The theory that the turmoil in the satellites is window dressing arranged by the Russians, which *Time* seems to hold, is not strong enough to include that one. Was Tito led down the garden path in Moscow, again *Time*'s theory, or did he sell a gold brick of his own? Mistuh Crawz-ley, maybe you have the answers. I sure as hell don't. The only rational theory is that this is all part of the incredible Eisenhower luck. Until we can sit face to face and talk, I will ponder, even as I ask myself what Chou [En-lai] and Mao [Tse-tung] are doing.

The questions will keep until we are in Washington and when we can drive up to Westminster. One thing you write, however, puzzles me. You indicate some deadline in the near future, a deadline toward which you are working. Are you doing another piece for *Life*, *Look*, or one of the other capitalist magazines? Or do you refer to your book? I hope it is the latter. It's been a long time since I have been able to read a book I really liked, mine own included. But I wish you'd take time out and do a life of Stalin. I mean a real book, not just *With Rod & Gun Through the Cellars of the Lubianka*.

O slender reed, have you forgotten that one good reed deserves another?

Ralph

July 9, 1956 [absent-mindedly misdated "June" by W.C.]
Dear Ralph,

I intended, as soon as I got back from class, to get back to the writing I had done before going off to college. (Your surmise is right: the deadline refers to a book; the "class" and "college" are teasers that I will get to presently.) But your letter was here. It comes first, all the more so because it has been much on my mind that I have been so silent with you during this disruptive time. I was much pleased to having mistaken your reporting abilities. I was puzzled that you yourself seemed to discount them, since I always supposed you were a good reporter. But I decided that you know best. It is both relieving and saddening to learn the real disability.... Yes, the chase of the packrats after "fact." And it is the chase they revel in. The fact is just the dead deer that some imbecile brings home on his automobile guards. As if fact had any relevance except as a clue to meaning, to truth; and as if these huntsmen had any notion that there is meaning and truth apart from fact. Yet, I can see that a discipline is involved here that has its compensations and victories. I suppose that Trappists, too, have their rewards, though no doubt, it would verge on the sin of pride to think about it.

I grow firmer and firmer in the faith that Washington is going to be a rich experience for you. I may even echo the words (the sense is a

bit different) which Valentine Markin [one of Chambers's colleagues
in the underground; he was murdered by his fellow agents on a New
York street when he was charged with deviation] once said to me one
rainy night: *"Du hast eine grosse Karriere dort*—Thou hast a great
career down yonder." In this connection, you do not know how right
you are about that little vibration which the phrase, "the Porter Street
house," sets up in your inward ear. Let us know as soon as you are
about to claim the squatters' rights, and we shall see what can be
done, mauger your driving an automobile.

About B & K and all the Bunkum and Kommotion. You know, my
friend, I do not know. For the moment, I remain just where I was
in re the 20th Congress. Frank Meyer seems to me to have said it
tersely and conclusively in *National Review*, a fortnight past. He
makes, in other words, the same points I had tried make, and which
anybody "who has read a book" must come close to. The point: the
encirclement of the USSR is over; the socialist encirclement of the
rest of the world has begun. The decisive event was the fall of
China…. This is, in Frank Meyer's words, "the objective situation"
(spoken like a Bolshevik!). It is this which it is necessary to keep in
mind through all the wreathings and writhings and fainting in coils.
The objective situation, the balance of real power in the world. Not
SU *v.* U.S. Not communism *v.* the West. But the SU *v.* a West
divided not merely on the socialist issue, but one in which the consequences of its own technological dynamics are socializing it faster
than the eye can follow. Eisenhower, the Fund for the Republic [the
Liberal-Left], whoever you like—these are parrots. The significant
socializing force in the U.S. is science and technology; the rest is
wind.

I guess this is the point to unfurl class and college. I am taking a
summer session course in Intermediate Spanish at Western
Maryland. I am more serious than you could imagine about what I
once wrote you. I am not only the only grandfather in a little class of

children who have a good deal of difficulty with English, let alone
Spanish. I appear to be the only one who has ever perforce had to
speak Spanish, however shamelessly. Surrounded by this wave of the
future with its faltering but insistent Castilian lithpth, I race along
(reading, not conversing) fearlessly with my unfashionable Latin *ssss*
and my near-Argentine *ll*. Whenever this occurs, some of them turn
and stare at me in wonder and dense distrust. But this is not my
point. My point is that all these young futurists are socialists. Of
course, they do not say it; they do not, most of them at any rate, know
it. We have got beyond opinions; we have got to what simply is.
These little people cannot remember a time when there was not
social security. They do not know the Marxist catch-phrase that who
says A must also say B. They do not need to know; like Wordsworth,
they lisped in numbers for the numbers came. This is also the objective situation. I do not know how Mikoyan spends his nights. I do not
know whether Vyacheslav and Lazar and Georgi spend the nights
with him. Will they win out in the Kremlin Kilkenny? Does it matter? In detail, yes, of course it does. In the round, I think not, not
much. And do B & K, or the Ms and the other K, care much if the
foreign CPs talk sassy? Rome is worth a mess. What foreign CP is an
agent of what foreign government? Everyone wears the hammer and
sickle, but no one is a Communist because everyone is a socialist. If
you would like to see the inwards of all this, read the *New Statesman*
and *Nation* regularly. Not *Time*. I haven't read *Time*, but from something I have heard from one of the Oracles, I gather that *Time* supposes J.F. Dulles is the greatest political mind since—since
Eisenhower. I think there is much less collusion than they seem to
read into events, but that there is some collusion. Above all, there is
the foreknowledge of what must happen given the objective situation, and let the chips fall where they may.

I have heard at one remove from the horse's mouth what the
horse's head at *Time* thinks about Tito's blooper. But there is no

blooper. These are the same folk who yet a few months agone, were talking about B & K's blooper in Belgrade. Let us set apart arbitrarily, for the moment, the question of internal Russian conditions, and ponder upon something else. The Communist super-state is a reality. This power-reality has not yet been reflected in an administrative reality. Perhaps administrative is too pale and thin a word. The super-state has not yet found the form to govern it. I suggest (and I may prove wrong, of course) that, among other things, this is where Tito comes in. The Comintern was a subversive organization fitted (crudely) to the inter-World Wars. What must now evolve is a governing reality which will reflect the power-reality of Russia and the People's Republics, plus the satellites, plus China, plus Yugoslavia. Not only Stalin is being down-graded precisely in Leninist terms. My surmise is that what is being considered is a form loose enough to include not only all the aforementioned pieces, but also India; and hence capable of offering a loose federative hand to any socialist (social democratic) government in the West or the East that wants in; and the big game is West Germany.

I fancy that the great question before the house is how to make this formulation sincerely loose enough to be attractive, and yet tight enough to safeguard and give weight to the reality of Great Russian power. For if you ask yourself: What else can they come to? I think you will find yourself answering: They must come to something like this. Why risk a blitz when it is all going your way without blitzing? A European asked me the other day: "How do you read the world situation as of now?" Answer: "In detail, it presents difficulties. Overall, the two balls of tallow seem to me to be melting into each other." He said: "It is an interesting formulation." How easy it is to talk to Europeans.

Now, about Posen (I grew up with a Silesian city named Posen; I am too old to shift to Poznan). I listened half-heartedly to the newscasts about that matter and read a bit, chiefly in your weekly. But I

depend much more on news photographs than on written copy. The
copy is almost always hopelessly slanted when not densely cock-eyed.
News photos can be slanted by selection, yet it is very hard to pervert
their inherent meaning; at least, in the case of group and action
shots. My eyelids grow a little weary, trying to follow the game of
musical chairs, varied with leap-frog and mayhem, wherewith our
better Mensheviks report the power struggle in the Kremlin. My own
rewarding comes from looking at the facial and bodily expression of
the Presidium members during Khrushchev's speech, in the official
photograph. Mikoyan's face is a study in Armenian frustration.
Molotov's face says that he knows that suns set. Voroshilov's face is
that of a man who has seen too much too long, and far more he is too
old, too old. So I studied carefully the news photos of Posen.

This is the insurgent youth. The youth! This is what the CP stands
to lose, and this too must heavily underlie the great turn. So I said in
the next line, but one, I think, of the *Life* piece. I have long watched
with great interest the True Word of Lenin movement, which is
heavily a youth movement. Two highly secret agents dropped by
recently to seek guidance about such matters. I mentioned the True
Word of Lenin. They had never heard of it. I told them that I knew
the name of one of its leaders and named the slave camp where I last
heard of her in residence. They did not ask her name, I sensed that
they supposed that I was fancying things. I am not. Her name is
Maya Ulanovsky, Ulrich's daughter, born on the same rainy night in
New York on which Valentine Markin said to me, "You have a great
career before you down there." Maya Ulanovsky was one of the leaders of the student strike in Moscow, 1953.

The Posen business looks to me like authentic insurrection. It is
thickly laced with Polish nationalism, no doubt. It was also, I am
sure, rigged by the West; all the signs are there. But it is the youth
angle that impresses me most deeply. If the youth stirs things up
enough to overthrow the Soviet state… a reaction against socialism

will be only but a lull comparable to that between Waterloo and 1848. Kronstadt? As yet I do not think so. Thermidor? Many meanings can be read into that word, and we must remember, too, that Trotsky's use of it was historically mistaken. I also suspect, on a much lower level, that the secret police in Posen and elsewhere are proving how indispensable they are after all. Police have a habit of doing this whenever they are downgraded. They let things get a little out of hand. The dodge is known to police other than the NKVD. Hungary, where the next outburst may well come, offers another set of special circumstances....

I should like nothing better than to write a life of Stalin unless it were to write a life of Ivan the Terrible, one of the most fascinating characters in history. But, like Voroshilov, I am too old. I know now: I shall never write a life of Stalin or Ivan or read *Prometheus Bound* in the original Greek. But, as Ilyitch said, it is more pleasant and profitable to live through a revolution than to write about one. Besides, I am doing something much more shocking: I seem to be discovering that Lenin was a Great Russian peasant *et rien de plus, mais r-r-rien de plus.* Oh, yes, he was a dialectician, the only true one among them. But most of all he was a Russian, and that is to be a peasant. The other kind run (if titled) dress shops; if untitled, they write for the *New Leader.* The characteristic of the Russian peasant is that he is without cynicism. When he learns cynicism, he comes to power, like Lenin, like the False Dmitri (of whom, did you know, there were two—both recognized as her son by the legitimate Tsarina, who was filed away in a nunnery. (Tsarina? Perhaps not, but anyway, the dead Tsarevitch's mama.) No wonder people find current Russian affairs a puzzle.

Next AM. In re-reading, I believe the most heartening thing in your letter is that you, too, are reading a book. If I had to raise a slogan for the Right, it would be: Study. We must go to school; we do not know enough, beginning with myself. The Liberal-Left puts up a wondrous facade of knowledge. An informed Right should be able to cut it to shreds, but to do so, it is necessary to know. I am more and more impressed by Frank Meyer, who, if he does not know as much as he seems to, makes a wonderful fist of it.

I have been downgraded, too. About a month ago, the NAACP [the Chambers name for the American Committee for Cultural Freedom] wrote me with creepy courtesy to say that, due to absence, I was no longer a member of its Supreme Soviet. It was news to me that I still was. But the business annoyed me because, as I told you, I meant to resign from that guild; now I have to leave a decent interval so that they cannot claim, the dogs, that I resigned from pique. You can write in my obit: He was never a Menshevik. The NAACP's action intrigues me, too. I sense that it reflects a profound divergence on the meaning of the 20th Congress, et seq. But I don't know just what the divergence seems to them to be. Recently, *Commentary* sent me tear-sheets of a piece by Bert Wolfe on the Soviet situation; for my edification, I suppose; but, as I did not read it, and have now misplaced it, I shall, no doubt, never know.

Whittaker

[Chambers took up the formal study of Spanish, a language which he handled quite well already, as preparation for pulling up stakes and settling in Spain, though the determination to do so lessened as the Eisenhower-Nixon reelection became more certain. His analysis of events now went far beyond his belief, when he broke with Communism, that he was leaving the winning side for the losing side. The problem went much deeper—to the corruption of Western civilization. The collapse of the Soviet Union and its satellites—had he lived to see them—would not have changed his thinking. For this collapse did not demonstrate the strength of the West but a viral infection which the sapping of the world's immune system could not fight.]

Kismet, 12 July 1956
Dear Whittaker:

Jamie caught a fish hook in the fleshy part of his leg this morning
when I was teaching him to cast, and the doctor extracted it with the
aid of novocaine and a pair of pliers. Your letter arrived not long
after. It was the icing on the sense of relief which follows these minor
domestic crises. A whopping fat letter it was, too, giving me a twinge
of conscience that it had kept you that long away from more important work.

   I sat down to answer it in Spanish, but the product seemed
slightly fatuous and forced, so I discarded it. But I was quite
intrigued at the thought of you being downright about zees and *lls*,
to the "dense distrust" of the young fry. What do they read in
Intermediate Spanish? Pio Baroja or Perez Galdos? Or do they use
the same kind of manufactured language which goes into French
textbooks? As I remember it, the literature of Spain is thin, once you
get past *Quijote* and the *Novelas ejemplares*. For some reason, Spain
has produced little in the way of literature—though my father could
roll out the endless quatrains of Campoamor—perhaps because the
very mellifluousness of the language is defeating to a writer. Painting
is the Spanish *metier*, confining as it does the extravagance of the
spirit which is endemic to the country. And even this leads to the
surrealism of Dali—or in verse the later Lorca. The measure of
Spain's literary inadequacies can be seen in the fact that I am probably the greatest living Spanish poet—on the strength of a few poems
which have startled those critics who have read them. This sounds
like more Spanish extravagance, but it might even be true. Except
for the anonymous poets whose songs fill the *romanceros* and the
devotional poems of St. John of the Cross, Spanish verse is too often
drowned in the sheer viscosity of language and the ease of rhymes
that impose themselves—though to the list of the good, I should add
the verse of Miguel de Unamuno, who once wrote a poem about my

grandmother, Estrella. [My aunt, Zarita Nahon, visited Unamuno in his exile in Hendaye—he was driven from Spain by Alfonso XIII—and was deeply moved when he recited some of the poems he was working on for his book, *Romancero.*]

So you have been eased out of your position in the Duma (never, never, the Supreme Soviet) of the ACCF. This, I assume, was the first act of the new regime. But I am amused and irritated that Sol Stein, who must have been privy to the move, never mentioned it to me. For now it can be told that Master Stein traded very heavily on our goodwill and our time, and the least he might have done was to let us know what was going on in the committee. He is now, incidentally, a full-fledged expert on the "Communist conspiracy" for [Leo Cherne's] Research Institute of America. He is also making a fat salary, which should give him a sense of responsibility and improve his prose style.

While I wait for your book to come out, I have been reading one on my own. I think I told you about something called *From Vienna To Versailles* by a British school teacher named Seaman. It is less history than an essay on history, but it makes the interesting point: that in modern history no revolution has succeeded unless there was no will to resist on the part of the regime in power. And/or foreign intervention. The Russian revolution is, of course, the prime example, but it applies equally well to 1776, 1789, the collapse of the Austro-Hungarian empire, and even the Spanish Civil War, although there are special problems there. Marx glimpsed this, Lenin understood it, and Dulles exemplifies it. This, too, is what makes Eisenhower the significant singer of the era of co-existence, and Adlai Stevenson his guitar player. There are clumps of resistance throughout the country, but the state power is held by reluctant men who have little faith in the system they are presumably there to defend. And the intellectuals who should bolster the system seem to feel that since rape is inevitable, they may as well drop their *culottes* and glorify the rapist.

In the case of the Soviet Union and communism in general, the intellectuals are fascinated by the power of the knout and sustained by the sordid belief that comes the revolution, they will all occupy endowed chairs at Harvard and Yale—or even whisper advice in the ears of the commissars. And as you have increasingly made explicit, it is not the Soviet power but the ideology which fuels the dynamo and is the threat—and that ideology will, again as you have warned, first destroy Western civilization as we like to see it, substituting a culture of its own after sin and decadence have brought us down. That is the message implicit in *Witness*, though how many understood it. We are anti-Communists, but the sickness is far more widespread and insidious—and it will bring blood on the street.

I suggested that you write a life of Stalin, but more important would be a history of Russia, beginning, say, in 1913 and moving through the period in which the Prince Lvovs and the Alexander Kerenskys were out-maneuvered though never out-gunned by Lenin's *anschluss* with the Imperial German General staff and the Reichsbank, both of which shared Lenin's Bismarckian dream of a super-state going from the Rhine to the Pacific, dominated by a Great Russia steeled by the strictures and scriptures of Nechayev and Ivan the Terrible. You hint at that, but it is there in the suppressed record, which Ruth Fischer almost stumbles on. I confess that I, too, have never heard of the True Word of Lenin movement, but I would venture that the word was spoken in German—the language of the Comintern.

We shall be in Washington on the 30th of August or thereabouts and in the Porter Street house thereafter. You will hear from us once the telephone is installed. And once the furniture is in place, the books on the shelves, and the rugs on the floor, we hope to have a sufficiently comfortable room for you should you decide to visit Washington. If you don't, we will visit you. This is a happy-making thought.

Ralph

Oct. 17, 1956
Dear Ralph,

Is there some defect of my eyesight that makes it impossible for me to see things right? I ask because I have just been engaged in a lively controversy with [Bill] Buckley about Frank Meyer's review of *The Outsider.* I hold that the review missed the point completely or deliberately dismissed it, thereby selling Colin Wilson to the Liberals or shutting another window on that stifling little room where conservatives huddle together and hear each other moan. By now, it is less a room than an air-raid shelter. With space and provisions so short, only the elect can beg entry. Once in, you are condemned to lifelong residence because, outside, the air is unbreathable to us whose lungs are pure, while the wells are contaminated and all ordinary food is death to touch because of the fall-out.

[Here Chambers was touching on a repeated theme—the demand for orthodoxy and unanimity of thought by many conservatives, of which Frank Meyer was a leader. For them, excommunication was certain and quick, to the detriment of the Right as a political and intellectual force. In Meyer's case, there were some who paraphrased an old saying that you can get the man out of the Party—or Party ways— but you cannot get the Party—or its ways—out of the man.]

Now I shall be at odds again. I have been reading Dr. Ludwig von Mises's book as condensed in this week's *U. S. News.* By way of advance caution: I have not finished it, and the book may be importantly amplified by much that the condensation omits. Yet what appears is too simply, singlemindedly, argued to make that seem likely. As it stands, I should consider it one of the most pernicious pieces of writing that the Right has produced. Pernicious here is not an epithet. By pernicious I mean the effect that follows when a mind, which speaks with authority in a special field (economics), uses that authority (but not the field it is based in), to offer a false study of our dilemma. The result of this (insofar as its silliness is not self-evident) must be to mislead thousands about the nature of that dilemma.

Therefore, it must inhibit thousands in coming to grips with reality; and, by setting the seal of complacency on our wits, must set us back critically in getting at the truth, which alone is worth seeking, with which alone any battle, worth winning, can be fought. This grossly shallow man has left the field of economics for the field of mass psychology. He has proclaimed, rather than deduced, that the anticapitalist mood of our time is the result of "envy and ignorance." I, for one, have never envied a capitalist in my life. Quite the contrary.

They, their minds, their notions, and ways of life, fill me with nothing so much as an irrepressible desire to keep as far away from anything like that as possible. They fill me not with envy, but with abhorrence tempered by compassion. I do not want to liquidate them; I want to get away from them. They seem to me the death of the mind and the spirit. If these are the ends to which the whole creation moves, somebody has made a mistake. The kind of life into which my daughter, for example, is settling, is one I certainly should not wish to deprive her of, or anybody else who wants it. Yet it seems to me so inherently frightful that I freely predict that, by the time she is forty, she must abdicate her intelligence, void her soul, go mad or shoot out of that orbit of wild revolt. [Whittaker's daughter had married one of the heirs to an important industrial family.]

I began with myself to stress what you know, that my reaction to von Mises is not personal. I am well aware that envy seeps like a rancid poison through the masses. I am also aware why. If you create a market which stands or falls by selling material products to the masses, and deliberately creates in them an engrossing market for more and more of the same, envy will set in whenever the gross product exceeds the ability to sate the hunger easily. Mass production, and the mass hunger for goods it deliberately breeds, is its own nemesis. Marx himself pointed out that poverty is never aware of its condition until wealth builds a house next door. In this sense, von Mises's capitalists are all Marxists; they have erected the unsettling contrast into the operating principle of the mass market. I'll cut this short with one comment further: von Mises must be a sound sleeper. He seems never to have had a waking moment from 1929 onwards; never to have heard of economic crises. Alas, the envious masses have. I should be happy indeed if Dr. von Mises would shed kindly light on this matter, which, as a conservative, I hold to be the troubling crux of much.

I myself am one of those economic illiterates whom von Mises calls "babblers." But this is not because I never lent an ear to economics. As a youth, I used to "audit" economics at Columbia. I listened attentively for one point to which I wanted an answer: the cause and cure of crises. I was struck by the agility with which economics circled, without closing with, this point. Then, one day, Professor Whoever He Was moved in on that subject. He said that the sainted British economist, Jevons, held that business cycles may be caused by sun spots. Even a college man sometimes knows a hawk from a handsaw. I dropped out of economics; and I think it is only fair to Dr. Jevons to say that his sun-spotted finger, though tremulous, pointed me toward the Left. Sun spots have been replaced by envy and ignorance, and this is in keeping with the psychology of the times. I see now that, to paraphrase Clausewitz, socialism is simply capitalism continued in other forms. I see why Lenin said (and, presumptuously, I doubt that von Mises sees) that capitalism at the peak of development is the absolute precondition for socialism. I don't like socialism. But I have never known a man to blink at important reality without becoming a hypocrite or a fool (and there are such things as sincere hypocrites)....

Whittaker

[In conversation, referring to the Chambers remarks about capitalists, I quoted a popular comedian who, commenting on the postwar debate as to whether enlisted men should be required to salute officers off military posts, said: "I don't mind saluting them; it's talking to them that I object to." I also pointed out that God so abhorred envy that he made "Thou shalt not covet" one of the more important of the Ten Commandments. Later, Chambers would arrive at a defense of capitalism as a system which provided some material and spiritual comfort, if bound by what Chambers had aphoristically formulated: "Political freedom is a political reading of the Bible."]

19 October 1956
Mon ami, mon semblable, mon frère:
We are a party of two, I'm afraid. For I read Mises with horror—appalled first by its sheer German stupidity and vulgarity and second by the utter ignorance it exhibited. His blithe disregard of economic crises did not bother me too much, for I suspect that the "people's capitalism"—socialism with handbrakes—and the theory of perpetual inflation may have flattened the economic cycle. I don't know, not being an economist—though I have dined out on the claim that I know more about it because I flunked the subject at Columbia. The regular birth and death of the economy which Western Europe and America have known may be a thing of the past, at least in degree. But the bad politics, the shoddy history, and the watery regurgitation of Irvington-on-Hudson philosophy—forgive me, but oy vey.

"*Il y a, au siècle ou nous sommes, tant de manières de croire et de ne pas croire, que les historiens future auront peine à s'y reconnaitre*" ["There are, in our century, many ways to believe and not to believe, which future historians ill have trouble in recognizing"], Anatole France wrote in *La Revolte des Anges*. To which we might add: *Mais parmi toutes les manières de croire, la manière la plus incroyable est celle des "conservateurs" actuels. Quand l'aube monte dans les cieux, ils chantent, "Vieux jeu." Et la beauté désésperée s'obnubile* [But among all the ways of believing, the most unbelievable is that of today's "intellectuals." When dawn rises in the heavens, they sing, "old stuff." And despairing beauty wanes].

So I shall read Gibbon instead of von Mises and France instead of Willi Schlamm. When civilization goes, its death rattle should sound less like a gargle. And if suicide is the only way, certainly there are methods more dignified than plunging head in toilet bowl. Willi may enjoy the posture, but it ain't for me.

I drag Willi into this because I was thoroughly repelled by his performance in *National Review*. Let him dislike Ike, but as Dick Nixon, in his incomparable innocence said to me in another context, "Sometimes our people go too far." I never considered Willi a real ex-Communist (you have to be a Communist first), and this goes back to the early 1940s when he was writing a column for the *New Leader*; but now I'm beginning to doubt that he was ever *in* the Party at all. Surely he must have learned something about politics in the Rockefeller Plaza jungle [when he was working for Henry Luce]....

I have a new project afoot—or rather an old one revived. I am looking for a publisher who is willing to lose money on a small book which will contain the good pieces I wrote for the *Freeman*, the *American Mercury*, even some going back to my *New Leader* days. If the deal goes through, and I have P.J. Kenedy & Sons (an old and respectable, but small Catholic firm) interested, I will revise and expand and add some unpublished (and as yet unwritten chapters) and make it something of a philosophical and ideological autobiography. The title piece will be *Lament for a Generation*. I want to complete what I began in a long book review for *Commonweal*—a discussion of the *Quijote*. And I hope to be able to get down on paper what has been seething in me for a long time—an experience of God. If I can work it out, it will be a semi-connected work—and the first by me of more than transient interest. Or so, devoutly, I tell myself. In the best of all possible worlds, Random House would be interested. Of course, in the best of all possible worlds there would be no need for the book.

God save us from the New Pelagians.

Ralph

[Tom Kenedy, one of the "Sons" of P.J. Kenedy, contracted for the book. He showed the finished manuscript to an intellectual priest who knew and corresponded with Whittaker Chambers. "This is an important book and should be published," he advised, "but not by a Catholic publisher." It was subsequently submitted to Robert Giroux, who as editor of *Columbia Review* had published me in our undergraduate days at Columbia. Giroux called for more autobiographical detail and for a fully connected book, and it appeared as *Lament for A Generation*, establishing me as a "conservative thinker."]

1957–60

[NORA'S AND MY move to Washington meant that we were in relatively close proximity to Westminster and Pipe Creek Farm—and actual visits as well as frequent phone calls took the place of the letters from New York to Maryland and from Maryland to New York. The visits to the Chambers farm, because they were more frequent, became more relaxed. Whittaker had moved his family from the old homeplace to the backfarm, from a house which had once been a log cabin to one built of brick brought to the New World as ballast on British ships, and the gaps in the walls, which had admitted flying and crawling things during the summer weeks when we had occupied it, were mortared over. During our visits, when the weather was good, Whittaker and I would sit on the back porch, overlooking a pond, watching the kingfishers flying overhead and talking of the world and of ourselves in the shorthand of close friendship. I had a good deal to tell because as assistant bureau chief to Kenneth Crawford, I was in on much that the *Newsweek* staff gathered but which was frequently "killed for space" or for reasons of policy—a process which often kept the most significant news dangling.

Working out of the *Newsweek* offices in the National Press Building, I had greater access to the vice president, and vice versa.

Nixon not only expected me to prevail on *Newsweek* to report all of his activities, he was unsparing in his pressures to prevent the appearance in the magazine of stories which, he believed, distorted his actions, thoughts, and general travail. There were times when, if *Newsweek*'s New York editors wanted a pithy or significant quote from the vice president—and the vice president was not available—they considered it somewhat treasonous on my part. Nixon solved the problem by telling me: "Look, you know what my positions are and how I express myself. If they want a quote, make it up, just so you respect where I stand."

As for Chambers, he was not standing still. During that period he went back to college; he worked on what might have been a major historical work on Russia's dream of a Third Rome and on his version of the decline of the West; he traveled to Europe with Esther, returning loaded down with books and ideas—and a nostalgia for a world which could not be his, for all his insistence to me that "you and I, we are Europeans"; he commuted for a while on a biweekly schedule to New York to collaborate with Bill Buckley on the *National Review*; and he harbored increasingly strong fears that the defeat of Richard Nixon in the 1960 elections would mean the beginning of a new persecution by Alger Hiss's friends in and out of the government. He was not an old man, by contemporary standards, but he was a very tired man—yet driven by the need to explain man's hope and man's fate to an America which seemed determined to take the downward path.]

7 January 1957
Dear Whittaker:

Well. I am working on my book [*Lament for a Generation*] and hating every minute of it. For one thing, the more I go along, the more I see what has to be read and synthesized and written—and the more I see what has to be re-written of such earlier writings as are included.

What I would like, of course, would be several weeks of intensive work—day to night, or night to morning. This would require a sizable grant from some foundation. And I am having difficulties trying to get the Volker fund to give me enough of a grant so that I don't have to fret about free-lance assignments to supplement my *Newsweek* salary, so much lower than *Time* magazine's beneficences, while I am at work. Frank Meyer submitted an outline of my book to the Volker people. He showed me the answer he got, and I was very tempted to tell them to shove it. The outline, it seemed, was very interesting. But, the Volker people wondered, wouldn't it be "journalistic" if I wrote it? And wasn't I, after all, basically an anti-Communist? The implication being: and not much else. They weren't quite sure that I was not sufficiently anti-collectivist. However, I calmed myself down and swallowed my pride—quite a swallow—and wrote Frank a "letter" for Volker's eyes, further explaining my book. But nothing will come of it. In my experience, you either get it or you don't. Once you begin to "explain" the iron cools off.

The purpose of this letter is not to complain or to report. It is, primarily, to suggest a slogan for thee or me or Willi Schlamm or anyone who wants it. I came across it trying to find something amusing in the Oxford Book of Quotations—a wonderful time-killer when you are sick and a-bed and too tired for Parrington or Rousseau or even Dwight Macdonald. The line comes from an anonymous British matron of Victoria's reign. She had just seen Sarah Bernhardt, the Divine Sarah, ripping scenery and emotions to shreds as she played Cleopatra, finally tumbling dead in a quivering heap, wooden leg and all. Curtain. Said the matron: "How different, how very different, from the home life of our own dear Queen."

It reminded me of another great old actress, Alla Nazimova, who in her advanced years could play in a Bernard Shaw pot-boiler, lying on her stomach before the footlights and kicking her heels. Back in the very late 1930s, she revived *Hedda Gabler*, with my brother (then

a Broadway leading man under the unlikely stage name of Edward
Trevor) playing Lovborg, her lover. He was 28, she in her 60s, but
looking on stage like his contemporary. On opening night, my mother
went backstage and was introduced to Madame Nazimova—who
gave off an effulgence. "When I saw you doing those scenes with
Edward," my mother said sweetly, and no one could ever tell
whether she was being ingenuous or otherwise, "I remembered seeing you playing Hedda in Paris, before he was born." At that point,
the temperature in Nazimova's dressing room fell to about 40 below,
but it became warm again when my mother added: "I have seen
them all—Bernhardt, Duse—but you are the greatest, Mme.
Nazimova."

My mother was like that. One Saturday, my brother took her to a
matinee. As they were walking on Times Square, a group of twitter-
ing and limp-wristed young men went by. "What's the matter with
them?" my mother asked. "They're pansies," my brother said. "And
what's that?" My brother explained. "I don't believe it!" my mother
said. At dinner that night, she said to my father, "I was downtown on
Times Square this afternoon with Edward, and what do you think I
saw?" A tolerant smile on his face, my father asked: "All right. What
did you see?" "A bunch of chrysanthemums," my mother said....

Ralph

Jan. 11 [?] 1957
Dear Ralph,

How curious and how very funny. My Grandfather Whittaker, who
like most of the line was shabbily polylingual, and who enormously
disliked the Great Bernhardt, used to outrage his generation whenever they raved about her as Cleopatra. In a caterwaul he would say:
"Aaanntwan est moort! Meeow! Meeow! Meeow!" You see where I
get it from.

About you and your book I have been thinking a good deal. I think I know most of the twistings and turnings involved. I know all (anyway, much) about what must be read and assimilated, and the flight of time. I sit in the shadow of that great rock and often wonder how to climb it. With you it is more pressing because time has longer to run with you; your children are younger; you are younger. These Funds, what good are these Funds? Their minds are calcified with anti-collectivism or pro-collectivism, whichever one you come up against. And this has little to do with thee or me. Whatever our lapses, you and I mean to act as artists. "He is an Outsider because he stands for truth." To those folk (or Volker—a German pun), we must therefore, remain outsiders; and to most others. For we have, by chance, been tossed up on a shore and in a climate, the least preoccupied with truth. The Belgian Congo is not less preoccupied with the problem. So I have nothing to hand you but the bone already well gnawed down by me, in such hours—the recollection that whatever has been greatest in the mind's effort (*The Possessed, The Brothers Karamazov*) was written in circumstances so outrageously defeating that we may hope not to know the like.

It is only, as I say, a bone; no nourishment at all. Cannot you so arrange things that you do not have to do extra-curricular writing? I'm sure I couldn't. But Nora is an uncommonly clever head. Can't she do for you what I have never been able to do for me? It is so much easier to suggest ways for others than for ourselves. But you must write this book and I am convinced that this is the moment, the necessary moment. Of course, what enrages me is that I cannot say: "Here is $5,000; go to work."… It enrages me because, echoing what R[andall] Jarrell calls Augustine's greatest line: "I want you to be." Of course, you are what you are, and, therefore, I never doubt that you will *be*. And, of course, that is no more helpful, in a practical way, than all the rest. So here we are, up against that great rock, which has more than one aspect as the light of day changes.

In the end, nothing matters but that truth, of which the glimpse may only be true for ourselves. It is hard to face this; especially since we cannot, in reason, say why it should be so. Yet we must face it, and even cling to it; for that is what Wordsworth meant by saying: "We feel that we are greater than we know." Rimbaud on the Somali Coast (syphilis, to boot); Villon in jail; Dostoevski fleeing his creditors. The tale is something musty, which changes nothing: we are the protagonists. Nothing else matters in the show-down; and never more so than in the age where the heroes and the saints must be at one, since the real saints are all outside the Church.

I am uneasily conscious of overtones of a coach's pep talk between halves in the locker room. Yet I am right, not because I wish it to be so, but because that is all reality leaves us. America always destroys its men because it makes truth so expensive and half-truth so profitable: bottled gas. Only two, so far as I can recall, ever beat the game: Thoreau; *el echo una carcajada y murio* [he burst into laughter and died]; Whitman with a barbaric yawn which came to much the same thing, the more ironically because its meaning is so widely transgressed. I have no comfort but the blade of the knife, which we can grasp only in our most meaningful hours, because we cannot hold to it without cutting our fingers. It cannot be at any less price. I think what, in the end, we say is: I was one of those who had it in them to pay the price. It is our anger, but also our strength. Yes, it is different, very different, from the home life of our dear Queen, who makes Eisenhower seem so very anachronistic. Like, as R. Jarrell also says, "a wooden leg of the old school."

Whittaker

Re-reading your letter, I note that you say you are hating every writing moment. That seems to me the best of signs; a sense of taxing is the promise of worth. That sounds so much like something the president might have had said for him in one of his speeches, that I hastily add, switching to the Norman Mailer tone-scale: "Sweat, you

barstids." Of course, he more favors another noun. I have been reading a remarkably sharp book, *The Psychology and Sociology of
Communism*, by a Frenchman, Jules Monnerot. He sniffs mighty
close to the thesis of the Third Rome; and, good Lord, he even
touches on it (luckily in a footnote). He even mentions Filofei of
Pskov, whom I spoke of when you were last here. Of course, he calls
him Theophilus, according to the convention that in English good
Russians get their names translated into Greek.

I think I like best the Volker Fund's fear that you are insufficiently
anti-collectivist. What will these people do when they wake up to discover that the satellite revolution has opened the socialist phase of
history.

19 January 1957
Dear Whittaker:

The public reports [of a fire at the farm] said that the second floor
and the attic were seriously damaged. But the details Nora got from
Esther were much worse. So we can only wonder and wait to hear
from you, hoping for the best. I think of the destruction and wonder
particularly how much of your manuscript and your material were
burned. This has eaten away at me, for I know the strain and the
heartbreak it would be to reconstruct what you had so painstakingly
written, and what it must mean to lose personal possessions, not to
mention the financial loss. But a manuscript is a living thing, and I
recall what Jim Farrell [James T. Farrell, the novelist] said and felt
when a fire years ago destroyed much of his work in progress.

...Is there anything at all we can do? Can we give or lend anything
to carry you past this period of pressure? Are there any books which
need replacing and which I can get for you in New York? It has
struck me that your typewriter may have been damaged. We have an
extra standard and a portable which are at your disposal.

There's an old song sung by Italian soldiers, and it echoed during the Battle of the Ebro in the Spanish civil war. I was humming it last night and it struck me with its aptness:

Solo si sentano gli	Only devouring birds
uccelli rapaci,	can be heard,
E giorno e notte il colpo	And night and day the
del cannon…	pounding of cannons…

And so it has been for you—the hovering birds of prey and the endless cannon fire. But we have drowned them out before.

Ralph

Feb. 14, 15 [?], 1957
Dear Ralph,

I was much struck by *Newsweek*'s review of the Petrovs' book [the Petrovs were two prominent Soviet defectors], which seemed to me to sum up in little many of the peculiarities of the West face to face with its favorite sphinx. I take it that the line: "They are not American Communists, recanting in sackcloth and eloquence," is a shot across my bows. For while there is some question about the sackcloth, I cannot recall any other American ex who has been charged with eloquence; and that is clearly a charge so vile as to bring American writers in swarms, thrusting out their plates for seconds if only they could have firsts. The Petrovs, says your reviewer, are not eloquent. How unerringly the West homes in on whatever is second-rate and undisturbing.

The point is not that the Petrovs are not eloquent and not American Communists, but that they are not Communists at all. They are the purest fruition of the bureaucracy that has writ itself large for all to read. This was the high meaning of their experience

that the reviewer had his finger on, but muffed. These are not revo-
lutionists. They are the little people of Ozone Park or Washington,
N.W., clamping leechlike to that little job in Government, which,
with the instinct of field mice and rabbits, they seek to keep obscure,
unnoticed. So they have no opinions about anything. They take care
not even to have loyalties to anyone whose impredictable fall might
one day take them down with him. They are at their desks when the
bell rings, do not abuse the coffee break; do not, perhaps, even venture to keep a cat or an aspidistra. And when, in the course of normal
office hours ("We just want the facts, ma'am"), they are obliged to
spy on Alexandra Kollontai, their reaction is precisely that of the
delivery boy, asked by mutual friends of ours, to keep tabs on Mrs.
Harrington Ousterhouser III—a blend of awe and knavery.

It made me think of a story of Harold Nicholson's about a moujik
whose glory was that he had served in 1812 and seen Napoleon face
to face. Every anniversary, he was fetched out and lionized until, one
year, a Tsar (let us say Alexander III) deigned to address the peasant
and ask: "Tell me, what was Napoleon like?" The hero answered:
"Sire, he was a tall man with a long white beard." It does not mean,
of course, that the peasant had not seen Napoleon, just as Petrov saw
Kollontai. Perhaps to a field mouse even a chicken appears as a
mountainous object with a long white beard. And the pathos of the
Petrovs begins just at the point where their little tunnel in the grass-
stems leads inevitably out into the sunny uplands where, by day, the
hawk gyres, and, by night, the owl swoops softly.

Then, for the first time, they prove they can act; and our sympathy
goes out to them. But the feeling gains no great altitude because the
equation never gets beyond the proposition: "Communism bad;
Australia good." You expect them to appear, like the Papuan chief,
bedizened with small parts of a crashed plane, who greeted the visiting
Duke of Kent with the words, "You, me, brothers. Same father. Same
mother." *Newsweek*'s reviewer was caught up in the same fraternity.

What does he (or the Petrovs) know of the moment when Antonov-Avseenko, at the head of the Red Guard, rushed the steps of the Winter Palace, and the president of the Petrograd Soviet [Lenin] rose to announce the news, but was at a loss for words (probably the first time in his life) until he said: "Comrades Delegates of the Workers and Soldiers Soviet, we have this day begun an experiment that has not its like in history." What do such as these remember of that moment which could give even the sorry Col. Bykov [an *apparat* associate of Chambers] a certain (contemned) eloquence when he described it to me. The time: 1917-18. The place: the Russo-Austrian front. The Russian troops (one rifle to six men) often knee-deep in flooded trenches. The corpses, frozen stiff and piled in the rear like cord wood. The word is flashed by air from the wireless at Tsarskoe Tselo, addressed: "To All! To All! To All!" Or was it whispered from man to man, regiment to regiment, along the 1,000-mile line: "No more war! They are dividing the farm lands!" The trench lines began to crumble. "*Und mit Einmal,*" said Bykov, "*brachte das Alles zusammen und strompte ruckwarts auf das Land los.*" "And, in an instant, that all broke together and flooded backwards upon the land."

And now that that is all over, drowning in a later flood of filth and blood, what do the Petrovs and their reviewer know of the meaning of my friend, a military Communist, a woman of my age, who got out a message to the West from Vorkuta [a Gulag camp which Henry Wallace, under instruction from Owen Lattimore, thought was an outpost of Russian pioneers and so addressed its prisoners] where, when last heard from (1953), she was serving a 20 year term? Her message: "At last I feel free since I no longer fear anything because there is nothing left that life can do to me." Her husband was serving 20 years at Karaganda; her daughter 20 years in the Urals. There had been a subnormal son. When the Germans neared Moscow, the NKVD rounded up those unfortunates from the State institutions

and sent them out to do whatever the gibbering line of flesh could do
to slow the German advance. The boy was never heard of again.

The Petrovs and their reviewer know nothing of this eloquence of
the tormented organism. The reviewer is wrong, too, [in] his chief
point: that the Petrovs have something exceptional to tell us about
the Empire of Fear. Krivitsky, Orlov, a dozen others told us more. It
could not be otherwise since they knew more. I do not mean to be
hard on the Petrovs for whom I have the kindliest feelings and to
whom I wish every success. But I think it unfortunate that they
should be made use of to further confusion....

Whittaker

This letter, as you can see from the date, has been lying around for
most of the week. That often happens here; in the end, I re-read,
say: "What bosh!" and burn. I'd burn this too, if it did not seem
made for a footnote. For I seem to have been fired on again. In the
current *New Leader* occurs a column by W.E. Bohn, long my nomination for the silliest editor alive. Mr. Bohn indulges certain hopes
that Howard Fast [a best-selling pop writer of historical novels and a
Communist, who was making sounds of disaffection following a
decline in his royalties] may become the North Star of U.S. writing.
But he is restrained by a memory: "Our experience with reformed
Communists is not too encouraging. Some of the most gifted writers
who have left their ranks have gone over to the anti-Marxian, anti-
liberal, anti-progressive, and anti-intelligence, pro-reactionary side."
No doubt, it's immodest of me to hog this thrust. But it seems to lie
between Louis Budenz and me. I don't think Mr. B meant Louis B.
Not long ago, a vicious pro-Hiss assault referred to "the brilliant former editor of *Time*." It's the "knock-him-down-McCloskey-on-the-
costly rug" school. Scintillation by murder. I never knew what a
fellow I was until they began to ply their knives. Still, I think it's
funny enough to make a footnote to the time. "Eloquent, gifted,

brilliant"—what a dog! In fact, I am tired; everything is included in
that one word.

[undated]
Dear Whittaker:

When after I publish our epistles to each other and to the heathen
and the liberals—as you have promised that I may do—I may rip out
your letter of the 14 or 15 or whenever. For that letter says far more
than I believe you have confided to the dossiers of the FBI, to Bob
Morris and the Senate Internal Security subcommittee. I have felt
this ever since you wrote of "hearing screams"—screams which however loud and blood-curdling, would not carry across the Atlantic.
You were there, and not merely as a spear-carrier. And there are the
people you have known, who surface briefly in your letters and conversation. They tell another story, though I do not ask what it is.
There are things you have never asked me about hiatuses in my life.
It is wrong of me even to mention this.

As to Bill Bohn—he is a case. He has been editor of the *New
Leader* in name only—an old socialist put out to pasture and allowed
to write his labored nothings, which are taken more or less good-
naturedly. When I was on the *New Leader*, his major contribution to
the culture was his assertion that he always shaved before going to
bed, rather than in the morning, out of deference to the sensitivity of
his wife's skin. And he would hold forth to Daniel Bell and others
that they were too committed to the Jewishness of the socialist movement and should understand America as it was, in cornfields he had
never visited, and not as seen from Second Avenue. It was a strange
crew down at the old Rand School where the *New Leader* was then
quartered. There were the old, *old* socialists who hung on because
there was nowhere else to go after Norman Thomas had deserted
them. Among them was Algernon Lee who marched in the ranks for

decades. Right after the Hiss trial, I was asked to participate in a discussion of the case on WEVD—commercials by Eliot Roosevelt on "matza balls, like mother used to make"—and after the program I invited Lee to have a drink with us young fogies. He contributed little, but at one point he turned to me and said, "What's happened to Gene Debs? I haven't heard from him in a long time."

The amusing thing about all of this is that, during the time I worked for the *New Leader*, I found precious few real socialists, or even social democrats, in the Social Democratic Federation or among the contributors to the paper. Most of the financing came from David Dubinsky and the ILGWU [the International Ladies Garment Workers Union] and Alex Rose, and their major influence was to keep us battling the left-wing unions in New York. Melvin Lasky, who went from the *New Leader* to fame and fortune as editor of *Der Monat* in Germany and later of *Encounter* in London—both financed by the CIA—talked a left-socialist *cum* Dwight Macdonald game ("it's a lost war unless we make it a peepul's war") changed his views when he put on the uniform. Only Dan Bell has persisted in his left socialism. When he went upward and onward to a professorship at your alma mater and mine, students chalked up on campus walls, "Daniel Bell drinks malteds in the Lion's Den" [the basement eatery of John Jay Hall, where undergraduates who had the wherewithal drank beer]. Now Danny condescends to me because he has a Ph.D, while I clutch only two Philolexian Poetry Awards.

Ralph

July 3, 1957
Dear Ralph,

I suppose you knew what you were doing when you dropped [Federico Garcia] Lorca on me, like a Bomb of, as they say now, "smaller or Hiroshima caliber." Familiarity may breed (as first reading notes) an itch to scratch at his *palomas* and *palomitas* and *desnudos*. But this is a very great poet, the greatest (one is tempted to mutter in the blurring after-effect of the first fall-out) since the German—Oh, what's his name?—the *Duino Elegies* [Rilke]. To think that you, First Poet of the Language of the Angels (Spanish), and he, and I, are all Columbia alumni! Not to be left out, I enclose what I contrived a day or so before I last saw you. For I, too, share the secret and incorrigible vice. But this will be the first time in 30 years that I have disclosed to anyone evidence of its ravages. I will never make a poet, though like the comedian craving to play Hamlet, I am unlikely to stop trying; whispering to myself (hypocritically) that rhyme is an aid to prose.

...Our bedroom catches the morning sun. Day after day, I find myself opening my eyes in the morning with, as first thought: "I have lived into another day. How beautiful it is. But why?" That *why* includes all the inconsequence. It is to break violently that inconsequence, which I recognize to be a one-way path, however meandering, that I talk about going abroad.... I should prefer not to move an inch. But not to move, just that, is the setting in of rigor mortis....

I should like to get on with the Third Rome, which I have not tried to explain to anyone. It is a twofold book; and that is perhaps its weakness. It is an attempt to restore what David [McDowell] scratched out from *Witness*, which is the yawning hole in that book, unbalancing all the rest. For to become a revolutionist is the first and last of a historical experience, to which personal factors are only incidentally contributory. You, of course, know this. Now, I am afraid we are reaping a sorry harvest for that gap in *Witness*, to which, for reasons of pressing expediency (and, on the whole, rightly, I think) I agreed. Here are the closing lines of that Chapter II against which David wrote the words: "Too strong."

"Now, in the light of its late sundown, you tell me that you took one look at Communism and knew at once that it was a fraud. My

friend, you are mistaken. In the terrible decade, 1915-1925, you
scarcely knew the word Communism. You did not know that, for
multitudes, Communism hung, like a star-shell, lurid, but casting the
only steady light into that bleeding, dark and ruined world. It is only
now that you know that Communism is a fraud. You only know now
that, of the way of saving the world, Communism is not one. I know
that too—now. I learned it in another school. I learned by trying, in
the day of disaster, to do something, and doing the wrong thing,
because I did not see what else to do. Life has been more gracious to
you—or perhaps your judgment is better. For you did nothing at all."

So you see, editorially David was right, for the year 1952 and its
publishing problems. Now it is later; I am older. I should like to complete my work. So the Third Rome says, "Two journeys we must have
taken in this time: the Rhine Journey and the Steppe Journey"—that
is, Germany from 1923 (when I first saw it) to the end of the 1000-
year Reich; Russia from 1917 to date. In the course of those journeys
we must wear out, like the peasant girl in the Russian folk tale that I
cite: "Three pairs of iron shoes, three iron staffs, and eat three iron
wafers." At the end of that iron course, it brings you to the little rise
from which it is given some to see....

But perhaps I should tell you that the first part of the Third Rome
is called: Slon and the Vision of the Third Rome. Slon (elephant, in
Russian) is my name for a self-taught, Marxist shopkeeper whom I
once knew, and who first told me about the Third Rome. A long
quote, I fear:

"Slon and the Anarchist (his partner) kept a little shop.... The
shop was a grudging pretense, necessary since one must pretend to
live somehow, of earning a living. But, for those with eyes to see, it
was something else. It was the mouth of that stairhead, which, when
the unexpected slab is pried up (in the *Arabian Nights*), leads the
nervous down cobwebby steps, through a dark room with walls and
ceiling of precious stone, where have lain for buried ages, the Singing

Bird and the Fountain of Living Water. These are the imaginary treasures, of course. They existed, for those who could read such minds, only in the minds of Slon and the Anarchist (of whom, perhaps, I shall have more to say later on—he presently went insane). These treasures never exist at all except for those who can tell them from heaps of old tin pots or boots, or the drip of a leaky tap.

"Coming out of one of his long silences, Slon glanced at me one day with one of his shy smiles. Where had his thoughts been? One can only guess that they had been back in his boyhood; far from the ugly street outside the window (N.Y. slum), though in streets no less ugly, perhaps, in their own style, but which memory had touched for a moment with conniving light, and with the pathos of what has once been known, and will, we know, too, after a certain age, never be known again.

"Slon began to tell me how a peasant of the Moscow countryside prepares to go to that big, wicked, baffling, swallowing city (this would have been before the Russian Revolution, of course). He needs money and must sell something; some wretched keepsake that will yield him, in his need, a few kopeks; or, it may be, some vegetables slung in an old soiled cloth. The peasant wakes, if he has slept at all before so great an enterprise, in his hut, in the middle of the night. He walks till dawn. Then, in the breaking day, he glimpses, perhaps from the Sparrow Hills, the outlines of the City, detaching themselves from the darkness. He sees the first sunlight touch, far off, the gilded domes and turrets of the Kremlin, with the two-and-three-armed crosses (the slanted arm symbolic of Christ's broken bones); and the neighboring domes of St. Basil's. (These are the bulbous domes that Henry Adams called: 'the turnip with its root in the air,' when he visited Moscow with the late Senator Henry Cabot Lodge (the father of our UN ambassador). What he saw did not much impress Henry Adams, the grandson and great-grandson of

American presidents. He noted that the turnip with its root in the air
is no real improvement on the turnip with its root in the ground.

"Slon, to judge from his eyes and voice, felt differently; and so did
his peasant. Slon claimed that, on seeing Moscow, all peasant behave
always in exactly the same way. At first sight of those gilded domes,
shimmering in the morning air, the peasant stops short. He snatches
from his verminous head his dirty cap, and repeats, as a man might
whisper when, looking in at night, he sees the hair of a sleeping child
spread on a pillow:

> *Moskva, Moskva,*
> *Zolotaya golova!*
> *Moscow, Moscow,*
> *Golden head!*

"Thus, I learned that Slon, the godless, knew what reverence is."

What the peasant sees, of course, is the vision of the Third Rome,
at once immanently pagan and transcendently Christian; and a center
of power, of which Filofei the Monk wrote: "And take heed, O religious and gracious Tsar, that all Christian kingdoms are merged into
thine alone; that two Romes have fallen"—Rome and Byzantium—
"but the Third Rome stands; and there will be no fourth." Much later
on, it is said: "To a non-Russian, there seems to be, even about those
Russians whom he knows extremely well, something that is never
quite get-at-able; something elusive and enigmatic that the Russian
himself seems to be furtively screening from us (perhaps from himself, too), so that we catch only chance glimpses of it. At that shad-
owy depth, the Third Rome has its springhead, as if it welled up
concealed under the slanting birch, firs and springing mushrooms of
the Russian woods. There The Third Rome is not a vision of con-
quering the world. It is only the world's necessity, a form such as we
know reality often regrettably takes in life. But at the cool depth
where the springhead takes its rise, the promise of the Third Rome is

a redemptive promise. It is the dream of the Russian people redeem-
ing mankind."

This, I maintain, is an energy unique in the world. I seek to show
how I came to know its spell. I claim to know that it is still in play,
though how fallen and transformed. But what has the West to
advance against that energy? This is too much about the Third
Rome, but I think you must know something about the book.

...I am sorry the boys had so poor a time here. But come again the
first warm day and they... will hear the bells of the Lake City of
Ktesh, tolling underwater. Besieged by the Tatars, the inhabitants
prayed to God to save them. The city was translated in the night to
the bottom of the lake. "The Orthodox people" (for in Russia faith
and nationality are one) sometimes hear the bell, far below the water,
when the wind sets right.

Whittaker

Since this was written, news has arrived by passenger pigeon that
Mol, Mal, and Kag have been removed.... Serves them right, too.
Posing as Communists for 30 years, they were really the running
dogs of Methodism and the agents of Billy Graham and Lavrenti
Beria.

EXERCISES

[Handwritten] This is great nonsense but your poem about Lorca
is beautiful and generous

> *First Light*
> *The fox pounces,*
> *The leveret screams;*
> *The sun rises,*
> *And it beams.*
> *"Light! Light!"*
> *The bird sings,*
> *Releasing, as it flies,*
> *The umbel of the flower that swings,*
> *Unimplicated, over stones*

Where the blood already dries
In fluff of fur
And clotted bones;
While expeditious emmets stir,
Triggered mystically to feed,
Before flies breed
Maggots to compete.
Against the morning's heat,
Ovening the air,
The fox bespeaks his lair;
Sleeping, like an angel, where
Earth and torpor soothe all sound;
And does not hear the closing hound.

Spring Rain

All things work together for good,
As every field
Of springing grain
Is dunged with filth and death,
And rots the falling rain;
Which double duty does,
Multiplying yield,
And simulating peace;
Which always for the ear
That cannot hear;
For the eye that is blind,
Or set behind;
Is always for the ending;
Never for the beginning, breath.
Is the web where hangs
The suavely packaged fly
That for only meaning had
A little sizzling cry,
Whereby,
It confides, to the capable arachnid,
The monotony of the agony
Of its plea to die
At once; and at the same time not to die,
A dualism that it sums
In the vision that it hums:
"The fangs! The fangs! The fangs!"

[Of the poems, I would only offer technical comment, since it was my opinion that a poet must write the obituary of his own verse. I respected them and was moved by them, but one learns only from self-immolation. The mythology of the Third Rome reached out far more effectively. Chambers and I had an understanding that the mysticism of Russia and the mysticism of Spain were to a considerable extent akin. Repeatedly his and my fingertips had touched—and that was what he meant when he said repeatedly, "You and I, we are Europeans." Both he and I understood what Miguel de Unamuno had said to my aunt, that there is a *pared*, a human *wall*, against which a writer tosses his ideas to clarify them for himself. What Chambers wrote about the Third Rome reflected his failure to come to terms with the Roman church—a failure shared by me for I could never forget what Church and state had done to my ancestor, Daniel de Toledo—the particle of nobility having been granted by Ferdinand and Isabela—and to his family....

As a result of my close friendship with Whittaker Chambers, I had gone through what we call a "religious experience"—during the dark days of the Hiss case—but I had never set it down on paper until Leonard Robinson of the *Reader's Digest* had asked me to—but had never published the result. It became a part of my novel, *Devil Take Him*, slaughtered by its publisher—written long after the death of Chambers—but I had discussed part of it with Chambers after the Third Rome letter, particularly the stripping away of the flesh and the sense of being naked before God. The Third Rome? It is a fact of political life in Russia, but few Americans or Western Europeans understand it.]

23 October 1957
Dear Whittaker:

I've just finished reading your *National Review* piece... and its
relaxed yet incisive prose and sound argument. "The Old Master," I
said to me, "he's really got it." But such a setting for the sparkle!... In
Revolt of the Masses or wherever Ortega y Gasset notes that when
the mob riots for bread, the first thing it does is burn the bakeries.
Sometimes I think that *NR* seems to be applying the same methodol-
ogy to the propagation of conservatism. And what is that, dear sir,
what is conservatism? I have entered into the fourth or fifth attempt
at answering the question for [*Lament for a Generation*], and the
chapter still remains unaccomplished. I am tempted to tear up the
book and the contract and write about sexually frustrated sputniks.
How sad then that I had saddled you [after our last visit] with an
uncorrected and unscanned—as well as unseasoned—first draft of
much of the manuscript. It was a brutal thing to do—and the
moment we had begun to move down your road (we saw three deer)
I wanted to turn back and snatch it away....

It was with a kind of secret relief that we received the news of the
postponement of the trip to Europe. You should go, you should go—
but we hated to think of you so far away.

Ralph

[Howard Rushmore, a staffer on the Communist *Daily Worker*, had
broken with the Party and for years had written about Communist subversion for the New York *Journal American*. When, after the submer-
sion of Senator Joe McCarthy, anti-Communism became suspect in
the media, Rushmore was dropped and moved on to the uncertain
world of general exposés with *Confidential*, a magazine begun by two
Hearstlings, Lee Mortimer and Jack Lait. But the attacks on
Rushmore increased, his wife left him, and eventually he committed
suicide. He was an able journalist, but he never knew how to com-

bine this with playing the "anti-anti-Communist game" which became
de rigueur in the late 1950s.]

Jan. 8, 1958
Dear Ralph,

I don't see how jurisdictionally, you would have written the Rushmore
story. But I don't see how anybody else could have, or would have
known enough to write it that way, or would have wanted to. Those
"crossed stars" don't sound like you. But the whole pitch is too true to
be anybody else. About the facts, it puts heart into you to see a good
end. No more needs saying.

I've got to plead with you to have patience with me about your
book.... The reasons for my slowness... aren't you; they are me. My
daily battle with my own inadequacies. Fourteen days to write seven
or so paragraphs; every day a reformed version piling up on my desk.
But today, I got it as well as I ever will, and that's why you're getting
this letter. It's always that way. It will never be any other way. How
can the result possibly justify such pawing? It can't. That's why I feel
something close to physical revulsion at the sight of something I have
written.... In a week, I shall be ready to report to you....

Jan. 1 with you was the perfect way to begin the new year. But I
thought, as we drove home: How dull I must have seemed, fumbling
for words, blunting the edges of situations.... I eased myself off the
hook a little by thinking: I set out tired.... I don't like the habit of
superstition; there is something spidery about it. But I have developed
one about the "8" years: 1938 (the break); 1948 (the case). 1958?...

Whittaker

Next AM. Besides, there were only three paragraphs, I see by the
dawn's early light. Two weeks to write three rather long paragraphs.
This morning, they seem to me clearer than anything I have written

for a long time to what I want to say. I think that there is a chance
that a few of those who read them will understand that they are written in ice, a difficult medium. A week from now I shall know that this
is not true, that they are just a certain total of words on paper, in
which, besides, there is still left too much warmth. I would not expel
all heat; but I want to let slip the secret that this is the Ice Age, but
without saying it to any but a few initiates like you. One day, the ice
will melt again with a great roar; and that will be a Renaissance.
Since time, as we chart it by its correlatives, now moves much more
swiftly than in the past, that Renaissance may follow much more
quickly than the older one. But it is not for us, as individuals, or for
the masses of this age whose great need, if I understand it at all, is to
learn that Hope springs from ice and rack, as edelweiss grows at the
edge of glaciers. This does not keep me from shivering at the thought
of taking this, through the frozen morning, to the mail-box.

Mar. 17, 1958
Dear Ralph,

...A day or so ago, Dr. Wernher von Braun testified before somebody
that the Government was deprived of the brains of Dr. R.
Oppenheimer. It struck me at once that since von Braun has spoken,
the Man [Nixon] should take the play. I think he should promote it
where that is necessary, and so manage that the press knows what he
is doing. Too small a matter to be worth certain adverse publicity?
Perhaps. Perhaps not. In any case, it's just an idea. I shoot arrows into
the air; where they land isn't my business. But I suspect that, in this
case, time is of the essence. I also suspect that much weight might be
lifted with this little lever. If the Man doesn't lift it, somebody else
will. But it will be lifted. You will notice a trend; my ideas are all
pitched in one direction. That is because everything since 1948 is
being rescinded piecemeal and will soon be reversed faster and

faster. He alone is in a position to profit by the reverse by joining
in....

We have passed the point of decision; history's verdict is in. It
comes, of course, in the form of two choices, one rather terminal.
But I can be a bit aloof about that since, whatever the choice, it isn't
going to be the one I adumbrated. So I wish every housewife from
Texas and the deep enema addicts from California, would stop writing me about the wonders of *Witness*. And that other horde, towards
whom my noticeable antipathy drew a question from you, the other
day, and a remark about anti-clericalism—they are poised, as usual,
to clean up whichever way the game goes. They may, life being as
wearing as it is, and ignorance a function of the masses. Yet I suspect
that the pickings are going to be slimmer; even little children now
play with atomic cannon toys, and, what is more, soon learn what
makes them work. When every little boy is a physicist, blessed are
the meek will not be any less true; only irrelevant. I tried to make my
son a scientist. Twenty years hence, he will see why. It is not a
prospect that I can get really caught up in—the next hundred years.
But I should like to see what forms the fun will take when the human
spirit stages its next great revolt. All I ask is that there be someone to
"turn down an empty glass."

Whittaker

Perhaps I should add for clarity: it seems to me that Oppenheimer's
head might be very useful, and that, as a risk of any kind, he rates
about minus zero.

[undated]
Dear Whittaker:

The point about Oppenheimer is a good one—but The Man is hardly
in a position to move. For one thing, to blow Opje [Oppenheimer]

out of the water would leave some of Nixon's political allies drenched. I have been gathering material on Oppenheimer, the Manhattan Project, and the whole sordid story of atomic espionage. What put the idea in my head were a few remarks made by Igor Gouzenko on my second Intelligence-gathering meeting with him. If the full story were ever told, it would rock the Canadian government, cause a few heads to roll in Britain, and expose the idiocy of responsible people in the U.S.

In the case of Oppenheimer, his membership—or at least a contribution of $150 a month to the comrades—in the Communist Party was known to [General Leslie] Groves [who headed the atomic project] yet he insisted on having Oppenheimer head the project and hire the scientists. That Opje was approached by Soviet agents and asked to turn over scientific data also became known to the security people at Los Alamos—though this came later. That Oppenheimer and his wife—she had been an open Party member—were in touch with Steve Nelson, a high-ranking *apparatchik*, was known to the FBI, which was conducting a surveillance on Nelson and a West Coast spy ring. But the Bureau could do nothing because it had been expressly ordered by Groves to keep out of Manhattan Project security. The security boys in Los Alamos were inexperienced and clumsy, and they were under orders from Groves to handle Oppenheimer with kid gloves, even though it was known that his friends were leaking like a sieve to the NKVD.

The story is no secret, and some of it is in unpublished executive session testimony before congressional committees and in FBI files. But any attempts to snag Dr. Oppenheimer have either failed or led to tragedy for the would-be snagger—*vide* Lewis Strauss. Of course, Strauss had the misfortune of having, with only what he calls a "common school" education, risen to considerable heights—and the even greater misfortune of being a good friend of Herbert Hoover, with whom he got his start. I will probably do the book on atomic espionage since my material, stashed away in a filing cabinet, is encyclopedic. But it is not a book I can write while I am a *Newsweek* editor. Perhaps I should write it all down in letters to you, *à la* Richardson, to see the light of day when our noble correspondence is published.

Ralph

[I did write the first and so far fullest account of atomic espionage, *The Greatest Plot in History*, published in the early 1960s, after I had left *Newsweek* and after the death of Whittaker Chambers. The chapter on Oppenheimer simply stated verified facts, with no conclusions as to his motivations and allegiance drawn, and no statement that he had himself delivered scientific data to the Soviets. For this, I was virulently attacked. In 1994, KGB spymaster Pavel Sudoplatov, in his book, *Special Tasks*, disclosed that Oppenheimer not only allowed his colleagues to supply information to the Soviets on the nuclear bomb— saving the Kremlin years and billions of rubles—but also was a source himself. Had Vice President Nixon, who knew the facts, taken up the cudgels against Oppenheimer, as Chambers suggested, almost everyone, from President Eisenhower down, would have denounced him, Nixon, and it would have been the end of his political career.]

Oct. 10 [?], 1958
Dear Ralph,

Proposition (a familiar one, I expect): *"Pour atteindre la verité, il faut, une fois dans la vie, se faire de toutes les croyances que l'on a reçus; et reconstruire de nouveau, et dès le fondement, tous les systèmes de ses connaissances"* ["To arrive at truth, at least once in your life, you must rid yourself of all the beliefs you have acquired; and to reconstruct anew, and completely, all the systems you have known"]. Comment: Not just *une fois de la vie*, but probably two, or even three, times. In addition to a process that is pretty much continuous.

Proposition: Many years ago, a soldier said to me: "There is only one truth. If you push a man hard enough, he will die. That is all." Comment: I can factor my time with this man's "one truth." I cannot factor with Camus's "invincible summer." I suspect that this is not a season of the world for summers.

In the past week, I have written you several letters, which I then destroyed. This one might be called: small points of departure for a letter that may, one day, be written. Proposition: You are essentially a poet. Comment: So, *con permiso*, am I. Hence, I suspect that, like me, your grasp of pretty damned near all is intuitive. Often, this makes for height, depth, and intensity. But it also makes for (in part from lack of interest, in part from lack of feeling) a thinness about character as it commonly is, as it commonly works and works out. So, in fiction, I, at least, tend to substitute a drama of action (which may give force) for a drama of character (which gives depth). This is very usual for Americans.

It is, for example, the great weakness of Hemingway. And it is almost always true of poets. Shakespeare is the marvelous exception; how marvelous and how exceptional we see by a glance at the distance between him and those who follow next in this mode: Landor, Browning and his spawn (let E.A. Robinson stand as the best of the rest). Without mordant (even wicked, i.e., Dostoevski) grasp of character, no true drama, mood, comment. But, short of that, something very good? Oh, yes. But we were cursed at birth: the demon said, grinning in the direction of the pit: "Let this little soul be a perfectionist." Please put that bowie knife away. Besides, I shot my second fox this year, the other evening, and I'm getting very hubrisious. Come and see us soon, thou fearful Castillian *y muy querido amigo*.

Look, mom, I've done it, I've written a letter.

Whittaker

[In mid-October, I sent Chambers a number of religious and metaphysical poems, some of which were not published until 1995 as *The*

Apocrypha of Limbo. Appended was a note suggesting that they might need an *explication de texte*—a phrase with which my Paris-educated *normalien* father frequently admonished his son after reading some of the earlier and sometimes deliberately obscure verse.]

Oct. 24, 1958
Dear Ralph,

The poems need no *explication de texte* for me. At least, I do not feel that they do, though this may be presumptuous of me. I find their meaning explicit. I think I know exactly what they mean. I think they mean what someone we know [Chambers] wrote many years ago about a Brooklyn Street and its wayfarers: "The river is at this street's end. / And are they marching there to drown?" The answer is, probably not; and yet the river, still, is there. And that is also the pathos. I am speaking figuratively about what is not figurative, but real. I cannot speak otherwise unless you yourself choose to speak first. Nor can I, rightfully, counsel you to do this. I can only say (at the risk of whatever presumption) that I feel myself to be an old, old, old man to whom there is no experience left that is unknown because I will have known one or another of its variants. I have risked presumption; I might as well incur arrogance, and say: There is nothing that you can tell me, that I will not already have largely divined. At that point, there is nothing left but understanding. *Tierra seca / Tierra quieta de noches inmensas* [Dry earth / Earth quiet of immense nights].

But if you have it in mind to publish these poems, then I think, something else is true. I think that they are part of a poetic autobiography; and that they cannot be wrenched from that context. Something comes before them; something will stand after them. For others, their meaning will arise from those somethings; and the meaning will be quite clear without *explication*, which I doubt would otherwise help much. It would be pretty mechanical. If you have not already considered it, I urge you to consider such a poetic autobiography. It would be inclusive, and cumulative, week by week; and has much to commend it just in the terms of the doing. Otherwise, I urge you not to publish—and I may be wrong.

It seems as if, of late, I have spent a good deal of time urging you not to publish. This may offend you. You seem to be, like some of the rest of us, in a state of swift flux. What else could we be (unless we chose deliberately to roost like turtles on a dead log in a stagnant pond) when all around us is swaying to its roots, and is tearing us this way and that, so that all energy is spent in keeping a footing; and all the logic there is lies in that passing posture of position? But it is passing merely; the next gust will enjoin another posture simply to keep upright, to hold ground. Only when the effort no longer consumes us wholly; when we have got beyond the storm, at least to the degree of finding firm footing—only then can we speak for meaning; or its meaning cannot often be spoken out of convulsion.

That is why I urge you not to publish hastily, but to wait for a certain settlement to set in; to get beyond the tossing present moment to a stage where there is space and height to see quietly, and to measure. I know it is all words and blurs. No one can tell anyone anything, I least of all. I might try putting it this way: Do not subscribe to positions since all positions now taken will be taken only to be abandoned. It is not just Soviet man who is in the tightening coil; all are. The revolt is no longer political; it is human. It is also immensely complex; and there is no chart. Whatever is easy and orthodox, above all, will crumble; or simply be by-passed as pointless. The great (and natural) temptation is for some props, supports. My great fear is that you will commit yourself to some from which time will tear you with bleeding fingers. For you are too good to stand pat. You are a poet and will never make a turtle, try how you will.

Of course, the poems are very good.

Whittaker

[In that letter, Chambers was almost writing to himself. He was struggling to write a book which subscribed to positions, at a time when he was in a state of "swift flux." For what had begun as a re-evocation of history and an *éxplication* of the time's plague was running away from him. He could not write about the Third Rome when what was on his mind was the evisceration of mankind by forces that men did not understand or even see. He had said that, when breaking with communism, he had left the winning side for the losing side. What he saw now, in that beautiful autumn of 1958, was that there were neither losing or winning sides but only a roller coaster to damnation—and the vision of Apocalypse escaped him. He saw much to admire in the Catholics, but after intense scrutiny, he did not find the answer in a Catholicism which, as he put it wryly, seemed to exist "in the City of Man, not the City of God." I answered him in Spanish verse, written during my army service.]

30 October 1958
Dear Whittaker:

Ojo de murcielago soy,	Bat's eye am I
ciego y encerrado	—blind and locked in,
palabra sin sentido,	word without feeling,
rio llorando por el agua.	river crying for water.
Eso lo digo yo	This I say
en la vejez	in the old age
de mi juventud,	of my youth,
soldado sin arma,	soldier without weapon
en la batalla fria.	in the cold battle.
Eso lo digo yo	This I say
no como niño	not as a boy
hierviendo de vida	boiling with life
pero como hombre	but as a man
que llora el tigre	who mourns the tiger
y corre del leon.	and runs from the lion.
Ay de mi, hijito,	Ay de mi, my son,

la sangre manda,	blood demands,
las manos piden	hands beg
pero son los pies	but nightmare grips our
de pesadilla.	feet.
En las horas de la mañana	In the morning hours,
oigo el ruido duro	I hear the noises
del tiempo que huye,	of fleeing time,
soltando la maldita,	shouting damnation,
y se sin duda	and I know with certainty
que seco y ciego	that sere and blind
no vivo mas en mi,	I am no longer myself
hijito mio, hijito mio	my son, my son.
En las horas de la noche,	In the hours of the night,
perdido y trasperdido,	lost and re-lost,
oigo riendosen de mi	I hear the streets
los callejones.	mocking me.
En el bosque de los suenos	In the forest of dreams,
la luna loca se rie de mi,	the crazed moon laughs at me,
los arboles de plata	ensilvered trees
gritan, doblandosen	shout, contorted
de risa bruja.	in bewitched laughter.
Ay de mi, hijito,	Ay de mi, my son,
duermo y no vivo,	I sleep but do not live,
sueño y no duermo,	I dream but do not sleep
ojo de murcielago,	a bat's eye,
en la luz agonizante	in the agonized light
a ciegas me voy.	I blindly go.

Dear Whittaker, this is perhaps the best answer to your letter—a letter which moved me both for what it said and for what it must have meant to you to write it. Let me put it this way: During my last emotion-racked visit to New York—terrible and drowned in whiskey—I was walking with Cap Pearce and I said to him, "It's a lonely, lonely world." And there *en plein Lexington Avenue* he burst into tears.

So it is—a lonely world, and we find our solace and our strength in striking out savagely, in taking self-destructive positions, in strange beds, and in putting together small poems. Sex and liquor and the little poems are the Miltown which permit us to face the skeleton which lurks in every doorway, reminding us that die we will, but live we must. This is all I can ever tell you. The rest is detail—sordid or dull or amusing, as the case may be.

I fight, you fight, he fights…. Who can contend with the seas as they sweep over a submerging Atlantis? But if we must arrive at positions, it can only be now. My dialectic is Aristotelian, so I have always believed that tomorrow's position is always forged in the destruction of today's. Each poem is a position and an autobiography and should be published when it is written. This, of course, is an academic argument in my case; since few will publish me. But I must make the effort, for what I write but do not publish becomes a festering sore. Paraphrasing the old joke, I've got a drawerful of festering sores. This is my desk literature, my *samizdat*, even as every Soviet writer has his own—pieces and poems he creates because he must, but which he cannot publish.

The poems I have saved over the years, the small collection from which juvenalia has been lost or destroyed, do not add up to an autobiography. They are the interior voices of an unwritten concerto. They could never add up to the project you so generously suggest. And if I did—*à quoi bon?*… The market for self-pity is very small.

Ralph

10 November 1958
Dear Whittaker:

Going through some old papers, I came across this effort, one of my more prophetic verses, on what Gagarin [the Soviet cosmonaut and first man to go into space] heard. Should I maybe send a copy to Dr. Kilian [head of the space program]?

Sin embargo, dijo la luna,	Nevertheless, said the moon,
gozo la vida.	I enjoy life.

Ya se que tengo la cara	I know that my face
quemada del sol	is burned by the sun
y el trasero siempre frío.	and my behind is always cold.
Pero figurate, amigo,	But consider, my friend,
si tuviera la cara	if I had a face
en el oscuro bolsillo eterno	in the pocket of eternal darkness
y el culo en el aire,	and my arse exposed
en vista de todo el mundo?	to the sight of all the world.

Ralph

[In the spring of 1959, Chambers discussed with me what was always on his mind: his fear that should he die suddenly, there would be no one to take care of whatever obligations there were to continue his son John's education and to launch him on a career. I promised Chambers to stand *in loco parentis*, so that John could continue his education at whatever the cost to Nora and me, as if he were our son, and to start John off in journalism. The need for making myself responsible for John's education never arose. But when I became Washington Bureau chief for the Taft Broadcasting network, I brought John in as my assistant, paying John's salary out of my own pocket and giving him the experience and contacts in radio-TV journalism so that when my connection with Taft Broadcasting ended, he could move on to a position with a major radio news organization.]

May 12, 1959
Dear Ralph,

If I had been you, I think I might have felt my yesterday's response to what you have in mind for John somewhat tepid. In many ways I am a backward reactor. Before the high hills, if they come unexpectedly into view, I often have to stand and gawk and let them grow on me. It is a slow process. Perhaps a difference between me and some others in life, is that, if those really are high hills, in most cases they do grow on me presently; and I set off across whatever country to meet and know them. I am not talking, of course (in this matter of you and John) of a reality that may, or may not, come to pass, but of a generosity on your part that is here, now, and very real. If the reality does not come to pass, your intention is still what counts. If it does come to pass, it will lift from me one of my great remaining concerns—my son's step-off into life. In these matters, the opportunity is usually decisive. The rest is up to him. My gratitude for your intention is beyond my power to express, except by noting that it is beyond me.

My anger at something you told me yesterday is still burning slowly. I have nothing in principle against expediency. Sometimes it is good and necessary, and may best serve particularly the short turn. But I have only contempt for an expediency which is merely self-limited, empty, brittle, and not fed and tempered by a true human understanding where friends are concerned. This incident seems too patly to bear out soundings I took years ago, and which seemed to me to be confirmed (though the intended impression was just the opposite) more recently. This explains my vigorous hands-off attitude in that quarter.

The world is rather sensibly ordered, I think, among lions and mice, and many indeterminate species down to doodlebugs and blind-worms. But I have little respect, I question the wisdom of, the Lion who seems not to grasp the workings of that order—its necessary compensating interactions. Or who forgets what mice meant to him in the inglorious days, and may mean again. A Lion may also look at a mouse, in that rather astigmatically majestic way lions have of surveying the universe. He may indifferently watch the little creatures spin about, all of a summer's day, and many such days on end—and never change expression. But if a day comes when mousie nibbles at his great paw, then the majestic beast would do well to know that there are times when cats must be growled back, and even a particle of cheese let fall (if that is wanted), and a roar roared that will clear the way for the Lion's more modest ally to have in peace what he wants and needs. For, in sum, that will also be the best for the Lion. If he doesn't know this, I think the Lion has forgotten that even summer days are interspersed with, and sometimes terminated by, the night of the hunter. Then the Lion may roar: "Mouse! Mouse!" but finds he is lord only of the closing jungle, or a veldt whose false peace dissembles the nets no mouse will gnaw him free of, while the treacherous forms circle softly in.

I count myself a mouse, by preference and out of a life-experience that teaches not to aspire beyond the defining logic of one's species. So do not take amiss the humble image. And do not be surprised that my anger at the Lion burns on a wick of disrespect for what I consider his failure truly to grasp the larger workings even of expediency.

Whittaker

[The Lion in this case was Richard Nixon, who had betrayed a friendship with me, whose job he had frequently put at risk. *Newsweek* had asked Nixon, whose election to the presidency seemed set, if he would mind if I were fired. Nixon's answer was: "I'm not the editor of *Newsweek*." At the time, I did not see it in the way Chambers did— though I changed his mind when I saw how Nixon turned on old friends and those who had labored and fought for him. But clearly the letter indicates that Chambers, who had defended Nixon against the criticisms of many influential conservatives, had long felt some doubt as to Nixon's sense of loyalty to those who had given him theirs.]

14 May 1959
Dear Whittaker:

I will answer your letter only to this extent. Whatever I can do for John I will always do because he is your son and because he is himself.

As to the second point you raised, there is no cause for anger.
That's the way of the world. I dreamt last night that we had two cats
and three mice for pets—and one of the mice put the cats to flight by
filling an eye-dropper with water and squirting them. What I need, I
suspect, is a good eye-dropper.

Ralph

Dec. 2, 1959
Dear Ralph,

I think I must get this on to you. The enclosure and Bill's note
explains why. I suppose it should be brought to the proper attention.
[The enclosure was an anonymous letter, threatening Chambers, and
I passed it on to Nixon and to friends at the FBI.] I have been so
filled with myself of late that I have almost forgotten certain of the
side effects of 1960 [the presidential election year]. It occurs to me
that it might be well for me to spend the gamier latter months of that
year outside this land. If I thought the enclosure was just the
Communist Party, I shouldn't worry. It may be the Democratic
National Committee and that I find more terrifying than the CP;
much more ruthless in this kind of thing.

There is a line which you might, with my compliments, offer to
the same quarter [Vice President Nixon] as this enclosure. The line
is: Generals usually prepare for the wrong war; i.e., they prepare the
next one in terms of the past one, terms already outdated. But not
only generals make this mistake. There is a widespread tendency to
fight the wrong war against Communism now. When Communism
had an ideological and other appeal, subversion was the main danger.
In the recent past, war was the main danger. Today, the underdevel-
oped nations are the main danger. There the war for the world will
be fought and decided. Etc. etc.

...And how is Frank The Meyer, that "brooding metaphysical omnipresence"?

Whittaker

Jan. 15, 1960
Dear Ralph,

A quick one to let you know that you are much in our minds though we are silent. On the morning of my Russian final, I was up at 3, to get some extra hours of cramming. The plan was to stop by with you on our way home.... It was about 6 when we went out to the car; still dark, cold, muddy underfoot. We backed out of the shed and set off with a loud thumping—a flat.... At the moment, I could think only that I had worked hard for a year only to be defeated at the very end by a flat. While I was brooding on fate.... Esther took off for the house and telephoned Mr. Pennington [who] drove us to Washington.... But we had wrecked Mr. P's schedule and he had to wait around all morning for me. It was simply impossible to ask him to stop by your house and wait some more.... In a way, this, too, was probably for the best: I had a Greek test the following Monday, and a great deal to catch up on in a few hours. I had rolled with the Greek in order to go full on the Russian....

By now I am tired with a deep fatigue. A complaint? Not for a moment. I have discovered (for myself at least) two great values that the century has deprived us of. 1. Retirement from the world without losing touch with it or entering a monastery. 2. Satisfaction in handiwork (scholarship). That loud din outside there is the world, and I gladly forego it, if only I can. My solution did not keep Cicero's dripping head from being spiked up in the Forum. He could scarcely have hoped that it would. But he had had his fun, too, and left the remainder of it that I am having to memorize in Latin for my final:

"For the rest (the world's affairs) are neither for all times nor places. But *these* studies nourish youth; delight old age; adorn daily life; in adversity are a refuge and a solace; edify the home; are no bar to business; spend the nights with us; accompany us on our journeys; live with us in the country." Nice, isn't it? From the *Pro Archia*....

Whittaker

Mar. 26, 1960
Dear Ralph,

Yesterday, I had my last class of Term I, Semester II; so you see I have come three-quarters of the way. Winter has made it much harder.... Once, at the blind curve near Ellen's house [Medfield], a gas truck came barrelling up the one-lane frozen country road. In trying to stop, both of us went into skids; no collision, but he rammed a tree.... [E]very day there was the rather desperate struggle with the deep snow... and always the killing cold. It was almost as if the Divine Wisdom had especially devised everything possible to test my purpose, as I said to Bill [Buckley] on the telephone; but he rather cut me off. Can it be that he distrusts the Divine Wisdom? Of course it's just that he distrusts what I may say next; and I'm quite wrong to tease this way. Anyway, it's been a trying Term.... And this is the long way of saying that I am on Day I of the Spring Vacation; and that I shall number each day, for I need them all.

For lack of time and strength (these are almost interchangeable terms with me), I have only snatched at a page or a paragraph, here and there, in [*Lament for a Generation*]; nothing consecutive. I get an impression, though, that now, it is efficient and streamlined. But here I want to touch only on something personal. Nobody else, I think, has written about me with such generous intention, or is likely to. The image you found for me (what weight water will bear) seems to me absolutely truly seen. It startled me when I first read it in ms.

because this is exactly how I had put it myself. And it is a little eerie to have something so intimate, which you have not put in words, but only felt, said out loud by someone else. I do not know what strength you can have drawn from my friendship; and, of course, I incline to wonder that there can have been any. But I am grateful that you feel that there was; and grateful that you should say so. I want to be worthy of your appreciation; and perhaps that is all that matters, or can.

You and I seem to me to have reached, travelling quite different roads, with different evaluations of the landscape, roughly similar way-stations (at least, as of this momont). But there is a particular difference, which I tend to magnify. In a few days, I shall be 59; from there to 60 is only months away. Let no one tell you that this is not old age in any land or clime or congeries of experience. It is so because the body knows (beyond all the mind's diddlings) that the rest of the way is not merely shorter; it is measurably brief.

A transposition of all relationships follows of itself, regardless of conscious evaluations. Vista is reached, whatever it is worth, whatever one makes of it. You cannot help looking off; and there is a large tract to be looked at; and, if you are me, you cannot help but smile. It is neither a bitter nor an absolving smile—absolving of life, that is.

At this point, I can only say: I know nothing. In the past, too, one has sometimes said this by way of compensatory caution. Now one *knows* it. This is the point at which Faust says: *Deshalb hab' ich mich der Magie ergeben—Therefore, I have given myself to Magic.* I am no Faust; I say: "Therefore I wish to give myself to nothing—nothing but the observance of reality as it unfolds; and in full knowledge that reality cannot be known. I wish only to be an observer, bystander."

This, I think, is the prime difference between us. You wish still to be implicated in experience, an *engagé* in Sartre's sense. I wish not to be, and should refuse the opportunity if it were offered (it won't be, but that doesn't change the fact). I cannot say that you are right or wrong because I don't know; nobody knows. But it troubles me for your sake because... But you can fulfill the sentence. This is not an

age where one can give one's self to anything, because there is nothing to give to; or to anybody because there isn't anybody. All energy,
as you know, is waste, a falling from higher to lower. About that fall of
energy which the waste of any life is, I think (think, only) that I can
entertain one tentative, and instantly revokable generalization: nobility of mind is all that distinguishes the brute from the man, all that, in
the end, matters; your only meter, subject to different readings at different altitudes, phases of light, temperature, digestion. Stepan
Trofinevich's dying words are their own ironic enigma: "If men cannot have something greater than themselves to worship, they will die
of despair."

    That is why this age is dying of despair (not of Communism or
hydrogen bombs); it has withered or absolutely abolished, East and
West, that "something greater" that men can give themselves to. But
nobility of mind is inborn and impredictable; it will re-emerge. I do
not know how, why or when. Until it does, in response to something,
or as that which elicits the response, there is nothing. That is why
implication, *engagement*, in a time like this is so perilous. And that is
why I worry so much about you, who are prone to the temptation to
respond, the generous temptation, whose generosity bears in it in
this time the seed of disillusion, if no worse.

Whittaker

5 April 1960
Dear Whittaker:

There was so much of the valedictory in your letter—and much of
the wave of a man stepping purposefully into the sea. Or not that
really, but the vision of someone who sees landfall disappearing into
the waters as he watches from the deck of a ship which will make no
return. What you write touches the spirit and leaves its pain because
we cannot know what lies beyond infinity. Irwin Edman, who

instructed me in philosophy at Columbia, would tell his classes of the little old lady who insisted that the earth rested on a rock. "But what does that rock rest on?" "On another rock." And another and another. "It's rocks all the way down," she said. The finite mind can say that it is meaninglessness all the way down. But if the finite mind ruled, where would we be?

Perhaps what we both need is a beautiful and uninhabited island in the South Pacific with a good library and a limitless supply of paper and pencils. You write as you write, and there is no gainsaying the validity of your thoughts. And yet you plow through ice and snow to study Russian—and Greek, as well, perhaps to learn husbandry from Hesiod. My father, a brilliant and tragic man who was forced by circumstance to relinquish career and ambition and dreams, still re-reads the 17 (or was it 19) volumes which Thiers wrote on the French *Révolution*, *Consulat*, and *Empire*—and he will continue to roam among the bookshelves—amusing himself by correcting, in public library copies, mistranslations from the French or the Spanish. What a shock it will be to Alger Hiss and the *New York Times* when they learn that you are not at work manufacturing evidence and forging typewriters, but learning Russian. I cannot disagree with your argument, but I cannot see Whittaker Chambers slipping sword into scabbard—no matter what.

Busy, busy covering, with John, the campaign, which does not look so good for the Man. He has made mistakes, but the major one is internal. He has never been able to get over his born-on-the-wrong-side-of-the-track inhibitions or the feelings about his "social" and emotional "betters."... In matters of the spirit or of comportment, he has never had what the Spanish call *la mano ancha* [an open hand]. And he has shown weakness and compromise—even pandering to the Nelson Rockefellers and the Eastern Republican Establishment—where a show of strength, even of ruthlessness, would have won him support.

Ralph

Oct. 18, 1960
Dear Ralph,

The Montero is marvelous. [I had sent him a recording of Germaine Montero reading Garciá Lorca's *Lament on the Death of a Bullfighter*, his greatest poem.] I scarcely expected at my time of life to have the kind of experience that occurs at my son's age: something new and wonderful, since what the young woman is saying in the tone (more than any words) is what has always been there. I thank you for bringing this young *creto-iberienne* to our house.

On a wholly different level, my thanks, too, for the book about conspirators. But one is never much the wiser for reading such books.... The text is plainly drawn from a dozen books by other people, books which it just happens, I have already read.... There can't be anything new, since any newness must lie in the line of historical meaning and setting; and our author has no conceptual grasp for history whatever.... I trouble to say this, because you spoke of working on similar lines. Why should anybody who grasps Montero and F. Garciá Lorca waste his talents on those soiled bandages? Police work is really only for those not suited for anything else.

I enclose an item that turned up in yesterday's mail.... The most instantly striking fact about this piece of mail seems to be the address. Accurate. I assume that they have my telephone number, too. But there are heavier implication. At this late hour, I suppose Mr. Nixon to have lost the election for himself. He will have lost it for me. I think that is what this enclosure is saying. Sad? One is bound to feel so, always. But the years teach ways, never good enough, of course, of getting above the instantly subjective. What one cannot get above is the historical formation one is trapped in. I always knew this. I acted quite deliberately to defy the facts. Hence the implicitly elegiac tone of my voice, which I dislike quite as much as others do. By my actions I meant, not to save this unhappy country (and more importantly the West as a whole), but to give it a better chance. Of

course, I failed, and must, like Rubashov [in *Darkness at Noon*], pay
the price.

But there is one feeling that I cannot help, rather meanly, sensing:
no other will arise to try to save it, or give it a chance. Of that I am
the last. Hereafter there will be casualty lists, of one or another
order. The sole health of this sticky situation is to be able to look, as
objectively as possible, and try to understand why and how it is so.
The steady glance is the only merit allowed one. The others have
thrown it all away, as, in my opinion, Mr. Nixon has done. It isn't
their fault or his; they are what they are; the historical juncture is
what it is. Were it otherwise, none of us would have played out our
parts; would never have had to. So back to my conjugation of the
"M I" verbs; time's running out, and I'd like to complete something
that matters. Please say nothing of this to my son, who has his own
griefs to measure.

Thanks again for the Montero *et al.* We, the other Mediterraneans,
we hear what she is saying.

Whittaker

29 *October 1960*
Dear Whittaker:

I'm glad you liked the Montero. She is a hand reaching out in the
darkness—and the Lorca poem is a fitting answer to *Death in the
Afternoon.* I have been looking, with no success, for her record of
Parisian existentialist songs which I think you will like. There is
much sadness in them: *"Les enfants qui s'aiment, s'embrassent
debout contre les portes de la nuit... Dans l'éblouissante clarté"*
["Children who love each other embrace in night's doorway... in the
dazzling clearness"].

...The book about the conspirators—I have forgotten its title—is as you say a compendium of facts which the author failed to understand. What I had in mind was a treatment of the Sidney Reilly story in the Rebecca West manner. When a man moves down a littered alley, that is simply a fact; how he does it has more to commend it; why he does is the real story since it involves both his motivation and what we used to call in CC-1 [Columbia freshman course, Contemporary Civilization 1] the *zeitgeist*. But I will not write the book if only because it will butter no parsnips.... I have come to suspect that I am no more than a writing machine. Put a piece of paper in the typewriter, sit me down, and the keys begin to clatter. Vanity and compulsiveness were probably responsible for my books... and the vanity was shattered when I tried to write a "good" book like *Lament for a Generation.*

There is a time to sing and a time to shut up. Unlike the man with the wooden tongue in the Stephen Crane poem, I know that the singing is of itself not enough. It must reach others and make them believe that they are also singing. Another poem of Crane: the man eating his own heart. "'It is bitter,' he said, 'bitter. But I like it because it is bitter and because it is my heart.'" Crane died at 28— and at that age I would have said the same thing, though not as well. At 44, I prefer sweetbreads.... Meanwhile, the "good" book sits on the shelf like a clothbound Koheleth. Or Job.

The item you enclosed did not stir me up as much as it did you.... There are people and there is the *canaille*. Beyond that, there is nothing. God must love slobs because there are so many of them. Slobs of the Right and slobs of the Left.... A pox on both of them. What concerns me are the inner voices of your letter which seem to say what is heart-rending and impossible to think of or believe. I will say no more because I can say no more.

Ralph

Afterword

THAT WAS THE last letter in the Chambers-Toledano correspondence. The Nixon defeat left Chambers dispirited and convinced that a Democratic administration would lead the way to reopening the Hiss case or bringing some other form of retribution. This would be required, Chambers felt, to put the finishing touches to Nixon's political career, and rob him of the support and acclaim which had made him a major political figure. With daughter Ellen married and his son John embarked on a career, Chambers felt that he had fulfilled his obligation to his children. "Time's running out, and I'd like to complete something that matters," he had written in his last letter. "Please say nothing of this to my son." But say nothing of what? Of the inner voices that I heard? Did those inner voices say that Whittaker Chambers had come to the end, had lost his will to live, and that he intended to take his life? Or was it that his intuitive mind and heart told him that his time had come? We will never know. He died in the summer of 1961.

Many years after his death, I would say at a memorial meeting: "Not a day has gone by that I have not thought of Whittaker Chambers"— and not a day in which a sense of loss had not engulfed me. Ten years after his death, I wrote in *National Review*:

"It is not true that Whittaker Chambers died ten years ago. He died before his great heart stopped beating, and he still lives today for those of us who loved him…. Time has slipped by, but it could have been yesterday that I sat on the porch of the 'back farm' in Westminster, watching the kingfishers circle, looking down the long vista of trees and hills fading in the sloping light, listening to that quiet voice parse the agony of our era, looking into those blue and prescient eyes which minimized the pain of living even as they saw life plain…. By birth, Whittaker Chambers was a white Anglo-Saxon Protestant—but he was the only American I have ever known who was of heart and mind a Spaniard ('We Mediterraneans,' he would say) with that combination of Caliphate Arab, Jew, and Visigoth which makes up the Spanish character, that pride grown of humility, that understanding of the human condition which found itself in a line from John of the Cross: *'Pues si más vivo mas muero'* ['The more I live, the more I die']."

When the Berlin Wall came down and the Soviet Union, the "evil empire," collapsed, the question was asked: Would Whittaker Chambers still believe that he had left the winning side for the losing side? Long before that day, he had seen that the struggle was no longer between Communism and Western civilization, but one in which Western civilization was destroying itself by betraying its heritage. Were he living today, he would see in the flood and tempest, the fire and the havoc of nature, a sign that perhaps God was telling us something. He would have seen as symptoms of the Twilight of Man the dissolution of moral and human values and the obscenity of what had replaced them. He was no deutero-Isaiah, but he felt that the spirit of man would some day revolt against the self-debasement which had seized it through most of the twentieth century.

Communism had triumphed, not in its Marxist tenet but in its concept of man—a concept which the West has accepted. The battle between what he rightly saw to be Communism and Western civilization could continue only as long as those on both sides sustained a real faith, but this had disappeared in the fog and smoke of our times. As the world moved into the next century, both sides were bereft of the values that had moved them in the past, and history was in a condition of stasis. Would men and their institutions recover? Whittaker Chambers believed they would—a faith he took with him yet left with us.

But there were other sides to Whittaker Chambers, and they are vibrantly apparent in his letters and in his effect on those who, like me, loved and understood him. For it is not only his vision and understanding that must remain with us. He knew life and laughter, art and music, the enchantment of knowledge and the touch of hands. This is what made him the man he was. I will remember him as on one of those breathing spring days in Westminster, when he heard our car approach, opened his door, waved, and smiled. Perhaps on the End Day, if my sins are forgiven, I will once more see that opening door, and the smile.

Index